A Taste of Maryland History

Also by Debbie Nunley and Karen Jane Elliott

A Taste of Pennsylvania History
A Taste of Ohio History
A Taste of Virginia History

John F. Blair, Publisher
Winston-Salem
North Carolina

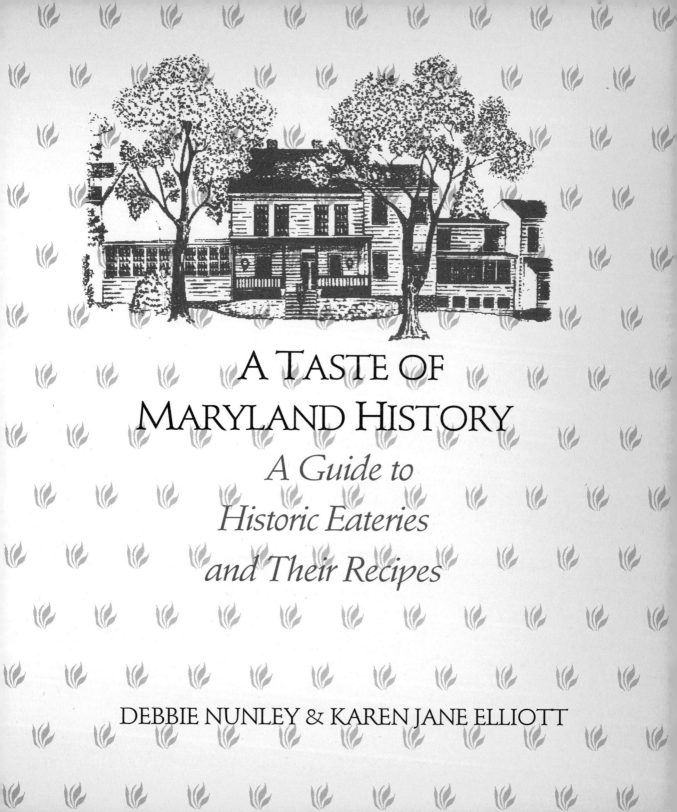

A TASTE OF
MARYLAND HISTORY

A Guide to

Historic Eateries

and Their Recipes

DEBBIE NUNLEY & KAREN JANE ELLIOTT

Copyright © 2005 by Debbie Nunley and Karen Jane Elliott
All rights reserved under International and Pan American Copyright Conventions
Published by John F. Blair, Publisher

The paper in this book meets the guidelines for
permanence and durability of the
Committee on Production Guidelines for
Book Longevity of the Council on Library Resources.

ON THE FRONT COVER, CLOCKWISE FROM THE TOP—
McGarvey's Saloon & Oyster Bar in Annapolis;
Robert Morris Inn in Oxford; Mrs. K's Toll House Restaurant in Silver Spring

Library of Congress Cataloging-in-Publication Data
Nunley, Debbie.
A taste of Maryland history : a guide to historic eateries and their recipes / by Debbie
Nunley and Karen Jane Elliott.
p.   cm.
Includes index.
ISBN-13: 978-0-89587-313-2 (alk. paper)
ISBN-10: 0-89587-313-3
1. Cookery. 2. Restaurants—Maryland—Guidebooks. 3. Historic buildings—Maryland. I.
Elliott, Karen Jane, 1958– II. Title.
TX714.N83 2005
647.59752—dc22   2005023991

Design by Debra Long Hampton

To my parents, Royce and Suzanne Scott,
who nurtured my love of reading,
my sense of adventure,
and my willingness to try new things!

Debbie

To my children, Singen and Cherith,
who exercise great tolerance with my never-ending trips out of town
and who patiently wait for me to return and give them a litte of my time.
I love you both more than you will ever know!

Karen

Contents

Preface xi
Acknowledgments xiii
Map 1

Chapter 1
A Sip of History

White Swan Tavern 4
Gypsy's Tearoom 6
Reynolds Tavern and Tea Room 8
The Little Teapot at Montpelier Mansion 10
Kettledrum Restaurant & Tea Room 12
Strathmore Tea Room 14
Petticoat Tea Room 16
Historic Oakland 18
Lisa Anne's Decadent Gifts & Tea Room 20
The Victorian Tea Cup 22
Aunt Fairie's Tea 24
Thir-Tea-First Street Café! & Tea Room 26

Chapter 2
The Water's Edge

Robert Morris Inn 30
Sherwood's Landing at
    The Inn at Perry Cabin 32
The Bayard House Restaurant 34

Chart House Restaurant 36
The Brome-Howard Inn 38
The Elkridge Furnace Inn 40
McGarvey's Saloon & Oyster Bar 42
The Union Hotel 44
St. Michaels Crab & Steak House 46
Inn of Silent Music 48

Chapter 3
In the Public Eye

Middleton Tavern 52
Old Angler's Inn 54
The Milton Inn 56
Carriage House Inn 58
Fair Hill Inn 60
The Owl Bar 62
Globe Theater & Bistro 64
Sabatino's Italian Restaurant 66
Harrison's Chesapeake House 68
Historic Cozy Restaurant 70

Chapter 4
Out and About

Mrs. K's Toll House Restaurant 74
Brick Ridge 76

Kendall's Steak & Seafood 78
Baldwin's Station 80
Firestone's Restaurant 82
Johanssons Dining House 84
The Plum 86
Gardel's Supper Club 88
Maggie's 90
Isabella's Taverna & Tapas Bar 92

The Inn at Easton 184
Bistro St. Michaels 136
The Brass Elephant 138
The Kings Contrivance 140
Blair Mansion Inn 142

Chapter 5
Gone but Not Forgotten

True at The Admiral Fell Inn 96
Gabriel's Inn 98
Rams Head Tavern at Savage Mill 100
Old Field Inn 102
Kent Manor Inn & Restaurant 104
Rams Head Tavern 106
The Kitty Knight House 108
Venuti's Ristorante 110
The Wharf Rat Fells Point 112
Tiber River Tavern 114

Chapter 7
The National Road

The Casselman Inn 146
Penn Alps Restaurant 148
Tombstone Café 150
JB's Steakhouse 152
Town Hill Hotel Bed and Breakfast 154
Old South Mountain Inn 156
John Hagan's Tavern 158

Chapter 8
Here's to History

Washington Street Pub 162
John Steven, Ltd. 164
Griffins City Dock Tavern 166
The Wharf Rat Camden Yards 168
The Valley Inn 170
Brewer's Alley Restaurant & Brewery 172
Summit Station Restaurant & Brewery 174
Murphey's Pub 176
Riordan's Saloon 178

Chapter 6
Hearth and Home

Quills at the Catoctin 118
Tersiguel's 120
Restaurant Columbia 122
Abacrombie Fine Food & Accommodations 124
The Vandiver Inn 126
The Inn at Buckeystown 128
208 Talbot 130
The Comus Inn at Sugarloaf Mountain 132

Chapter 9
Getting Away from It All

Atlantic Hotel	182
The Imperial Hotel and Restaurant	184
Antrim 1844	186
The Westlawn Inn	188
Cornish Manor Restaurant	190
The General Braddock Inn	192
The Deer Park Inn	194
George's on Mt. Vernon Square	196
Treaty of Paris Restaurant	198
Restaurant Index	200
Recipe Index	203

Preface

Way back in the summer of 1993, we both moved to Pittsburgh and got to know one another at the elementary school our children attended. We quickly found that we shared not only similar interests in volunteer activities but also a love of unique dining experiences. Gradually, lunches out became a monthly occurrence, and the size of our party grew from just the two of us to as many as fifteen people. Our first book, *A Taste of Pennsylvania History*, evolved from those luncheons. Now, four books later, our love for historic eateries continues, and the search for those unique spots extends to any destination that welcomes us. What started out as a hobby has actually become a quest. The focus changed after a chance comment by a restaurateur who told us he didn't see himself as a restaurant owner but as more of a "keeper of the history." In his hands, he felt that his bit of community history was safe. As long as he owned the structure, the history it represented would be saved and conveyed for future generations. We certainly wish more folks were of the same ilk. We're always amazed by what has managed to survive but at the same time saddened by what has been destroyed.

Maryland, although a much smaller state than the others we've researched, has more than its share of history, much of it still intact. The state is refreshing in its diversity—from its shoreline to its mountains, from its big cities to its small towns. Although we got a fair number of seafood dishes, as we expected, the cuisine is varied, making for both interesting eating and creative writing.

When people find out what we do, they're inevitably curious about how we go about researching the restaurants we include. We typically begin on the Internet, then gather as much additional information as possible through word of mouth, local chambers of commerce, and visitor and convention bureaus. Initially, our main concern is of the history of the building.

Typically, we look for establishments that are at least a hundred years old, although we do make some exceptions. The locales might be of national significance but might just as easily be important only in the immediate area, having served the local citizens in some capacity. Once we've accumulated enough information to assure ourselves that a particular site is historic in some way, we schedule an appointment to visit. We don't sneak in or go unannounced because we're not there to critique the restaurant, but merely to gather facts and experience what our readers will enjoy when they go to dine. Sometimes, we talk to owners, managers, and chefs. On other occasions, we do not. It's completely up to each establishment. Since we're there during working hours, we understand that they're busy and try not to intrude on the normal functioning of their eatery. Sometimes we eat a full meal, and sometimes we sample a variety of dishes. Again, each restaurant is different, but that's what makes the traveling and the writing fun. No prepackaged experience for us!

We always research and visit more restaurants than we include. Unfortunately, it's inevitable that we cannot include everything we find. Some folks think there's a catch to being featured that will ultimately cost them the proverbial arm and a leg. Others we eliminate because, although the building is historic, all vestiges of that history have been covered up so that no trace of the building's original ambiance or purpose is actually visible. Still others sincerely want to be part of the project but never quite get around to turning in the few pieces of information we need to create a two-page entry.

The real key to being included is the recipes. No restaurant can be featured without them. We typically allow the chefs to choose, so that they're represented in a manner that suits them—side dish, dessert, entrée. We take all comers, then select among their contributions to avoid duplications. All recipes are indicative of a restaurant's cuisine, but each one printed in the book is not necessarily on the menu all the time. Many restaurants alter their menus seasonally, and some even change their selections daily!

Because people see us as risktakers who reduce their discomfort in trying something new, we are regularly asked which restaurant is our favorite. But that's an impossible question to answer. No one feels like eating the same thing in the same environment day in and day out, and we're no exception. Sometimes we feel like ostrich or antelope (which we discovered during our research for this book), and sometimes we feel like a burger or a BLT. For a wide variety of reasons, these restaurants are our favorites—all ninety of them.

Acknowledgments

We would like to acknowledge the restaurant owners, managers, chefs, and staffs. Without their cooperation, this book would not have been possible.

We'd also like to express appreciation to our families, who managed to survive during our research yet again.

Thanks go out to all of our friends and acquaintances who are always ready with a suggestion or recommendation. Your advice is invaluable to our ongoing efforts.

Finally, we'd like to give kudos to the staff at John F. Blair, Publisher, who in 1998 first gave us an opportunity to pursue our passion and have continued to support our two-person crusade to maintain historic buildings and support local, independent business owners.

RESTAURANTS FEATURED IN *A TASTE OF MARYLAND HISTORY*

1. White Swan Tavern
2. Gypsy's Tearoom
3. Reynolds Tavern and Tea Room
4. The Little Teapot at Montpelier Mansion
5. Kettledrum Restaurant & Tea Room
6. Strathmore Tea Room
7. Petticoat Tea Room
8. Historic Oakland
9. Lisa Anne's Decadent Gifts & Tea Room
10. The Victorian Tea Cup
11. Aunt Fairie's Tea
12. Thir-Tea-First Street Café! & Tea Room
13. Robert Morris Inn
14. Sherwood's Landing at The Inn at Perry Cabin
15. The Bayard House Restaurant
16. Chart House Restaurant
17. The Brome-Howard Inn
18. The Elkridge Furnace Inn
19. McGarvey's Saloon & Oyster Bar
20. The Union Hotel
21. St. Michaels Crab & Steak House
22. Inn of Silent Music
23. Middleton Tavern
24. Old Angler's Inn
25. The Milton Inn
26. Carriage House Inn
27. Fair Hill Inn
28. The Owl Bar

29. Globe Theater & Bistro
30. Sabatino's Italian Restaurant
31. Harrison's Chesapeake House
32. Historic Cozy Restaurant
33. Mrs. K's Toll House Restaurant
34. Brick Ridge
35. Kendall's Steak & Seafood
36. Baldwin's Station
37. Firestone's Restaurant
38. Johanssons Dining House
39. The Plum
40. Gardel's Supper Club
41. Maggie's
42. Isabella's Taverna & Tapas Bar
43. True at The Admiral Fell Inn
44. Gabriel's Inn
45. Rams Head Tavern at Savage Mill
46. Old Field Inn
47. Kent Manor Inn & Restaurant
48. Rams Head Tavern
49. The Kitty Knight House
50. Venuti's Ristorante
51. The Wharf Rat Fells Point
52. Tiber River Tavern
53. Quills at the Catoctin
54. Tersiguel's
55. Restaurant Columbia
56. Abacrombie Fine Food & Accommodations
57. The Vandiver Inn
58. The Inn at Buckeystown
59. 208 Talbot

60. The Comus Inn at Sugarloaf Mountain
61. The Inn at Easton
62. Bistro St. Michaels
63. The Brass Elephant
64. The Kings Contrivance
65. Blair Mansion Inn
66. The Casselman Inn
67. Penn Alps Restaurant
68. Tombstone Café
69. JB's Steakhouse
70. Town Hill Hotel Bed and Breakfast
71. Old South Mountain Inn
72. John Hagan's Tavern
73. Washington Street Pub
74. John Steven, Ltd.
75. Griffins City Dock Tavern
76. The Wharf Rat Camden Yards
77. The Valley Inn
78. Brewer's Alley Restaurant & Brewery
79. Summit Station Restaurant & Brewery
80. Murphey's Pub
81. Riordan's Saloon
82. Atlantic Hotel
83. The Imperial Hotel and Restaurant
84. Antrim 1844
85. The Westlawn Inn
86. Cornish Manor Restaurant
87. The General Braddock Inn
88. The Deer Park Inn
89. George's on Mt. Vernon Square
90. Treaty of Paris Restaurant

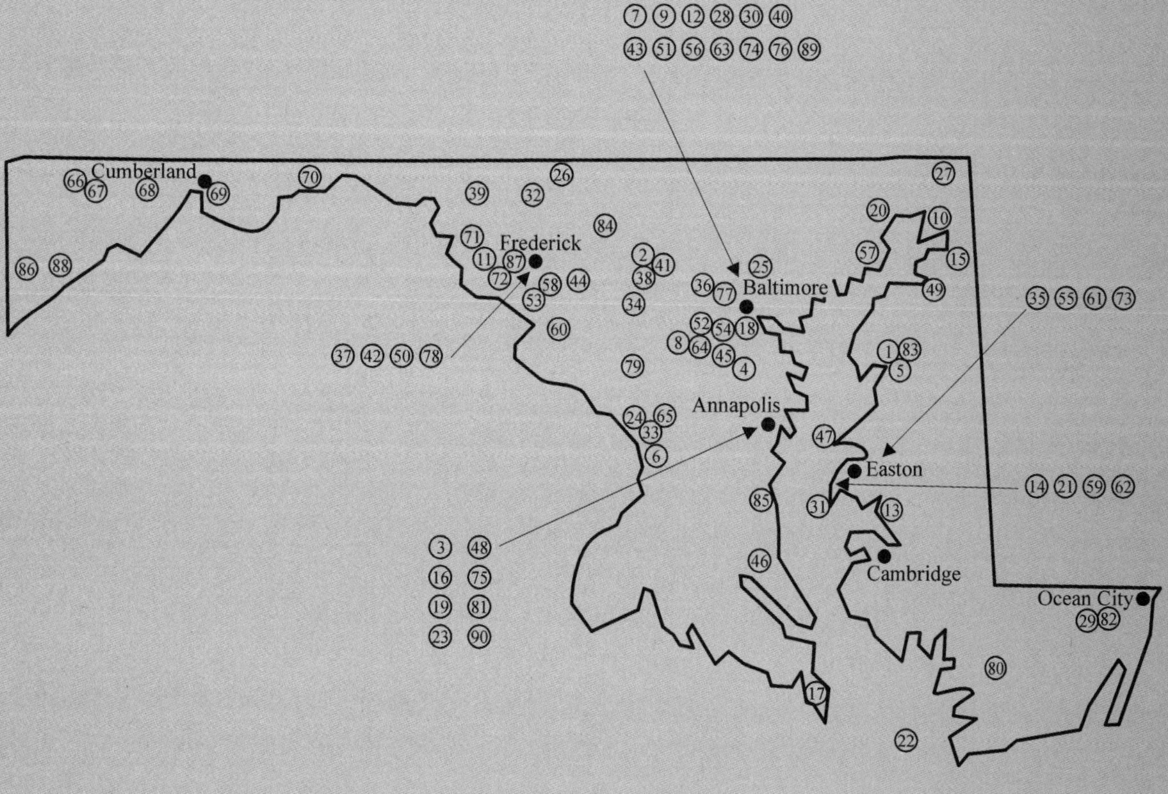
Cumberland
Frederick
Baltimore
Annapolis
Easton
Cambridge
Ocean City
7 9 12 28 30 40
43 51 56 63 74 76 89
37 42 50 78
35 55 61 73
14 21 59 62
3 48
16 75
19 81
23 90
66 67 68 69 70 26 27 39 32 20 10 84 71 15 57 2 41 25 11 87 72 58 44 38 36 77 49 53 34 60 52 54 18 8 64 45 4 1 83 5 79 24 65 33 6 47 85 31 13 46 29 82 80 17 22 86 88

CHAPTER 1
A Sip of History

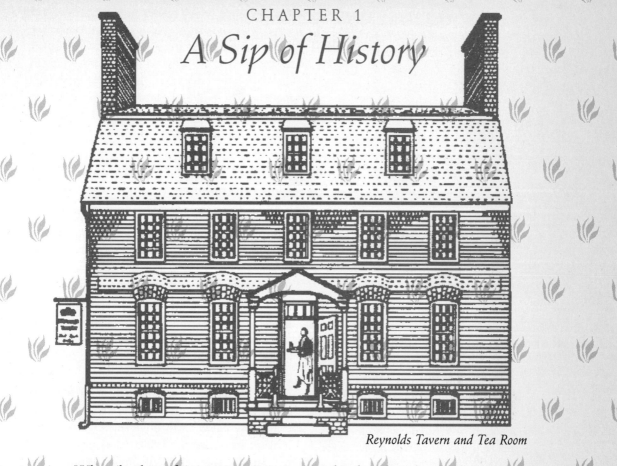

Reynolds Tavern and Tea Room

When looking for inspiration to write this heading, we did an Internet search on quotations related to tea. Imagine our surprise when we found a site with six full pages of quotes! Perhaps William Gladstone summed it up best in 1865 when he said, "If you are cold, tea will warm you. If you are too heated, it will cool you. If you are depressed, it will cheer you. If you are excited, it will calm you." May you find enjoyment in the following pages. We think these locales will be "just your cup of tea."

White Swan Tavern

231 High Street
Chestertown, MD 21620
www.whiteswantavern.com
410-778-2300

In researching establishments in the Chestertown area, we came across several blurbs for the White Swan Tavern. Comments like "Most authentic in the area" and "Exquisitely decorated with antiques" were certainly enough to grab our attention and make us eagerly anticipate our appointment for afternoon tea. A bed-and-breakfast, the White Swan provides afternoon tea to its guests from three to five every afternoon. In addition, the general public is invited to come and enjoy this delightful property. Reservations aren't necessary, so it's common for tourists to wander in and locals to drop by for the buffet-style goodies. Some come and go quickly, while others stay to play checkers, peruse the many books around the room, or sit and chat in the cozy environs.

One of the favorite items is the Raspberry Almond Bars. Also available on the day of our visit were Checkerboard Cookies, Almond Thumbprint Cookies, Chocolate Caramel Brownies, and divine Coconut Key Lime Bars. One was definitely not enough!

Much of what is known about the tavern's early history was uncovered in an archaeological dig that accompanied the 1978 restoration of the structure. Prior to 1733, the site was a tannery operated by Chestertown's shoemaker of the day, John Lovegrove. His one-room dwelling, the first building constructed on the property, is used today as Lovegrove's Kitchen, one of the six period guest rooms at the White Swan Tavern.

In 1733, the property was conveyed from Lovegrove to Joseph Nicholson, who built his home where the front part of the current structure stands. Nicholson was a member of the Committee of Correspondence and thus had an important role in the evolution of our new nation. He also valued education and was influential in the founding of Chestertown's Washington College, the tenth-oldest liberal-arts college in the United States.

In 1793, the property came under the ownership of John Bordley, who enlarged the residence for use as a tavern. Write-ups credit much of the charm of today's structure to the alterations made by Bordley. Considered the best tavern in town, it went through several owners and innkeepers during the 1800s. Most interesting to us was the Reverend William H. Wilmer, who was pastor of St. Paul's Church in Alexandria, Virginia, at the time he owned the tavern. Wilmer also served as president of the College of William and Mary and as rector of Bruton Parish Church in Williamsburg. Obviously, the importance of taverns in nineteenth-century community life rendered ownership by a man of the cloth much different than it would be perceived in today's society.

Today, one room of the structure is entirely devoted to the artifacts found during renovation. The two front rooms are furnished according to two historic inventories. Even the stoneware dishes have links to previous days, having been modeled after a set of early chargers recovered during the dig. When visiting the White Swan Tavern, you're not just experiencing history, you're totally immersed in it! And that's just fine with us.

RASPBERRY ALMOND BARS

1¼ cups sliced almonds, divided
1 cup butter
1¼ cups sugar
2 egg yolks
1 cup flour
1 teaspoon almond extract
1 cup raspberry jam

Preheat oven to 325 degrees. Toast and chop 1 cup sliced almonds and set aside. Line a 9-by-12-inch pan with foil and spray with nonstick cooking spray. Beat butter and sugar in a mixing bowl until fluffy. Add yolks. Add flour, almond extract, and chopped almonds. Spread batter in pan and bake until golden brown. If edges have risen, gently press down with a metal spatula. Let cool. Spread with jam and sprinkle with remaining sliced almonds. Bake 5 additional minutes. Cut into 6-inch-by-4-inch sections, then cut diagonally. Yields 4 dozen bars.

LEMON POPPY SEED CAKE

½ cup poppy seeds
½ cup milk
1½ cups butter
1½ cups sugar, divided
grated rind of 2 large lemons
8 large eggs, separated
2 cups cake flour
½ teaspoon salt

Soak poppy seeds in milk for 2 hours. Drain and rinse in a very fine sieve under cold water. Preheat oven to 350 degrees. Grease and flour a 10-inch tube pan. In a medium bowl, cream butter with a wooden spoon. Slowly add 1 cup sugar to butter. Beat well. Add poppy seeds and beat well. Add lemon rind, again beating well. Add egg yolks 1 at a time, beating well after each addition. Beat egg whites with clean beaters in a separate large bowl until peaks form. Add remaining sugar to egg whites and beat until stiff peaks form. Stir flour and salt together and add slowly to egg-yolk mixture. Fold in beaten whites slowly. Pour batter into prepared pan and bake for 1 hour. Cook, slice, and serve. Serves 12 to 16.

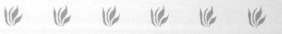

Gypsy's Tearoom

111 Stoner Avenue
Westminster, MD 21157
www.gypsystearoom.com
410-857-0058

The Winchester Country Inn, which houses Gypsy's Tearoom, is the oldest home in Carroll County. William Winchester, who hailed from Winchester, England, and founded the town of Westminster, Maryland, built the structure in 1760. It was originally known as White's Level. Its style is uniquely English, down to the original central chimney. The back-to-back fireplaces are a rare find; there are very few examples extant in the United States. Even rarer is the fact that they're still in working condition, although rarely used. Winchester and his wife, the former Lydia Richards, raised ten children here. A portrait of their eldest son, William, hangs in the front hallway.

Through the years, the home had many owners. In 1976, the property was deeded to the citizens of Carroll County. Under county-government stewardship, the land was rented to area farmers. Nine years later, the lease went to Target Community and Educational Services, operating under the auspices of McDaniel College. After significant renovation, the complex became a bed-and-breakfast facility providing vocational training to socially dependent individuals. Considering that a family of twelve was nurtured here, this undertaking seems fitting. The bed-and-breakfast continued until 2002, when a gift shop called Inspirations, the Westminster Gift Basket Company, and Gypsy's Tearoom came on board. They continue to provide ongoing training to Target clients in a unique and caring environment.

We read several reviews prior to visiting Gypsy's. They all said something like "I definitely recommend it" or "You will not be disappointed." The queen mother of a local Red Hat Society chapter wrote, "We will definitely return." Our experience echoed all of these sentiments. We were seated in a glassed-in porch called The Atrium. It was charming and cozy, twigs and birds decorating nooks and crannies. There was a cart of hats for guests to don, and we had a few moments of fun playing dress-up.

The Winter Vegetable Soup with White Beans that began our tea had an aroma that reminded Debbie of her grandmother's kitchen. It was a perfect start to a very snowy day. The Orange-Cranberry Scone that was delivered with the soup passed Karen's English muster. The tossed salads and accompanying Basil Ranch Dressing and Orange-Cranberry Vinaigrette were good as well. When our tower of sweets and savories arrived, we could tell we were in for a treat. We thoroughly enjoyed the Cucumber Sandwiches with Lemon Butter, the Blue Cheese on Crostinis, the Roast Beef Sandwich with Raspberry Mayonnaise, and the Rye Circle with Tomato Aspic and Cream Cheese. Honey Madeleines, Peach Mango Crisp, Fudge Brownies, and Cranberry Raspberry Sorbet completed our plethora of treats. And of course, you have plentiful choices of hot teas here, each arriving in its own teapot carefully snuggled into a padded tea cozy.

If offerings such as these aren't reason enough to visit, Gypsy's offers themed teas as well—Murder Mystery Teas, Civil War Teas, and Friendship Teas. In addition, the proprietors are very involved in local charity events, frequently donating proceeds from special teas to wonderful causes. What better reasons could you find for a spot of afternoon tea?

 ORANGE-CRANBERRY SCONES

2 cups flour
1/3 cup sugar
1 tablespoon baking powder
1 teaspoon salt
1/4 teaspoon nutmeg
1 teaspoon orange extract
1/2 cup orange juice
1 egg
5 tablespoons shortening

Preheat oven to 400 degrees. Sift together flour, sugar, baking powder, salt, and nutmeg. Add orange extract, orange juice, egg, and shortening. Knead until ingredients are well combined. Turn dough onto a floured surface and flatten to a 1-inch thickness. Use a 2-inch round cookie cutter to cut 12 scones. Place scones on a greased baking sheet. Brush top of each scone with additional orange juice and sprinkle with sugar. Bake about 20 minutes until tops are firm to the touch. Yields 12 scones.

LEMON BUTTER COOKIES

1 cup butter
2 cups sugar
2 eggs, beaten
1/4 cup milk
2 teaspoons lemon extract
4 1/2 cups flour
2 teaspoons baking powder
1/2 teaspoon salt
1/4 teaspoon baking soda

Preheat oven to 350 degrees. Using a mixer, cream butter and sugar together in a medium mixing bowl. Add eggs, milk, and lemon extract. Combine remaining ingredients in a separate bowl and add to butter mixture. Chill at least 2 hours, then roll dough out on a floured surface to 1/8-inch thickness. Cut dough with a round cookie cutter and place cookies on an ungreased baking sheet. Bake 8 to 9 minutes until bottoms are very lightly browned. Yields 2 dozen cookies.

Reynolds Tavern
and Tea Room
7 Church Circle
Annapolis, MD 21404
www.reynoldstavern.org
410-295-9555

At one point in its history, this structure was known as The Beaver and Lac'd Hat. Under that moniker, it served as the storefront where William Reynolds, a hatter and dry-goods salesman, ran his business while also renting rooms and operating an ordinary. This was a place to eat, drink, sleep, play cards, leave important messages, buy theater tickets, and even stable horses. After Reynolds died in 1777, his third wife, Mary, continued operating the tavern until she, too, passed away. The inn was then taken over by William Reynolds's daughter, who maintained possession until 1796.

When the structure was sold to John Davidson, it fetched fifteen hundred dollars, quite a handsome sum in the late eighteenth century! After the Davidson years, the building came under the ownership of Farmers National Bank for more than a century. In 1935, the Standard Oil Company tried to buy the structure with the intent of tearing it down to build a modern filling station. Fortunately, a group of local residents had the foresight to save the property, using leftover funds from the Female Orphan Society to convert it for use as the Annapolis Public Library. When the library outgrew that space in 1974, the title was transferred to the National Trust for Historic Preservation.

In 2002, Jill and Andrew Petit purchased the property, revived it as a tavern, and named it in honor of its original owner. Guests can experience Reynolds Tavern in a variety of ways. The Sly Fox Pub, located in the cellar of the building, showcases the original stone foundation. Guests also enjoy the walk-in fireplace and the eighteenth-century Rumford boiler. The second floor contains overnight guest accommodations. A trip to the third story is well worth the climb to see a fireplace decorated with images drawn prior to the Revolutionary War.

We spent our visit on the first floor, used for lunch and tea during the day, then transformed into an elegant casual restaurant for evening dining. After being seated at a cozy table with a view of Church Circle, we perused the tea menu. Guests can choose a light Cream Tea, consisting of a pot of tea and two scones; Colonial High Tea, which includes both sweet and savory treats, along with quiche, salad, or soup; or several other versions of tea. Debbie opted for the Savory Tea, consisting of tarts and sandwiches, while Karen ordered the Sweet Tea, which includes a variety of pastries and goodies. We enjoyed every bite of treats such as Cucumber Sandwiches, Shrimp Tartlets, Lemon Bars, Truffles, Lavender Shortbread Cookies, and Raisin Scones with jam and cream. Had we arrived slightly earlier, we may have chosen from the luncheon menu, which features options such as a Wild Mushroom Tart; Chicken, Gorgonzola, and Walnut Salad; a Toasted Chicken, Mozzarella, and Basil Sandwich; and Thai Steak Salad. We'll be sure to stop by again because one visit to Reynolds Tavern is not enough.

 BAKEWELL TART

2 cups flour
4 tablespoons plus 2 teaspoons sugar, divided
1 teaspoon salt
1 cup butter, divided
2 eggs, divided
1 tablespoon milk
½ cup raspberry jam
²/₃ cup ground almonds
1 cup pound-cake crumbs
½ teaspoon almond extract
2 tablespoons unsalted butter
1 cup powdered sugar
2 tablespoons heavy cream
1 teaspoon vanilla extract

Combine flour, 2 teaspoons sugar, salt, and ¾ cup butter in a food processor until it resembles fine breadcrumbs. Combine 1 egg with milk and add to dry mixture until dough holds together. Wrap in plastic wrap and refrigerate at least 30 minutes. Roll thin and line a 7-inch tart pan. Preheat oven to 350 degrees. Spread jam in bottom of pastry shell. In a separate bowl, cream remaining butter and sugar until pale. Beat in remaining egg, ground almonds, cake crumbs, and almond extract. Spread over jam. Bake for 30 to 40 minutes. While tart is baking, melt unsalted butter in a small saucepan. Remove from heat. Stir in powdered sugar, cream, and vanilla. Spread glaze over tart while still hot. Cool on a wire rack. Serves 8.

 LEMON BARS

¾ cup butter
1½ cups flour
1½ cups plus ¹/₃ cup sugar, divided
³/₈ teaspoon salt, divided
3 eggs
1 tablespoon grated lemon peel
¼ cup fresh lemon juice
2 tablespoons powdered sugar

In a medium bowl, combine butter, flour, ¹/₃ cup sugar, and ¼ teaspoon salt until smooth and spreadable. Spread into bottom of a greased 9-by-13-inch pan. Preheat oven to 350 degrees. Combine remaining ingredients except powdered sugar until smooth. Pour over crust. Bake for 20 to 30 minutes until set. Cool on a wire rack. Dust with powdered sugar. Yields 30 bars.

THE LITTLE TEAPOT

at Montpelier Mansion
MD 197 and Muirkirk Road
Laurel, MD 20708
301-953-1376

Upon our arrival, we wondered about the sand timers on each table. When we received our tea, our server turned the timer over to start the flow. Once the sand completely drained to the other end, the tea was brewed and ready to be enjoyed.

The assortment of goodies that accompanied our tea was as attractive as it was tasty. The sandwiches of Cucumber, Ham, and Dill Mustard; Tomato and Bacon; Chicken Tarragon; Chicken and Sprouts; and Apple and Cinnamon Cream Cheese were delicious. And the sweet treats including a Bakewell Tart, Gingerbread, a Lemon Pastry, an Apple Cinnamon Scone, and Chocolates were equally enjoyable. The food was enhanced by the lovely Montpelier Mansion, built in 1783 by Major Thomas Snowden.

The Snowden clan first came to this land in the 1600s, although the exact date of Richard Snowden's arrival is unknown. Records do exist of a payment by Snowden and partner Thomas Linthicombe of eleven thousand pounds of tobacco for five hundred acres of land described as "the Iron Mine." Although the Snowden family farmed, a portion of its income was derived from mining and smelting iron ore. Records indicate that on at least two occasions, George Washington ordered iron implements for his Mount Vernon estate.

The 1700s saw the Snowden landholdings grow. In 1770, Major Thomas Snowden, the great-great-grandson of Richard Snowden, inherited four hundred acres of the family property from his father. Although the Snowden family was wealthy, when Thomas married Anne Ridgely in 1774, he was described as "having got a larger fortune by his wife who was an heiress to a large estate." It's believed that this may have provided the means to finance the construction of Montpelier.

Through the years, the Snowdens hosted many distinguished guests at their home. Abigail Adams once wrote that Montpelier was a "large, handsome, elegant home, where I was received with my family, and with what we might term true English hospitality." On his way to the Constitutional Convention, George Washington, feeling indisposed, decided to stop here and recover before proceeding. His wife and her traveling companions were guests in 1789 as they made their way to New York for the presidential inauguration.

The house is operated as a museum. Extensive research has been completed on many of the rooms, which are furnished to represent the period between 1800 and 1830. The décor and furnishings used today are based on an inventory taken in 1831 after the death of Nicholas Snowden, son of Thomas and Anne. The staff of this National Historic Landmark, together with the Friends of Montpelier, offer tours, concerts, festivals, exhibits, lectures, reenactments, weddings, luncheons, and receptions.

Teas like the one we enjoyed are usually served at least two Fridays a month in conjunction with The Little Teapot, the mansion's gift shop, located in the estate's carriage house. During the Christmas season, a four-course Afternoon Tea complete with Christmas crackers is served. Lovely in any season, Montpelier is a destination not to be missed.

 SHREWSBURY CAKES

1 cup butter
1½ cups sugar
3 cups flour
½ teaspoon grated nutmeg
⅓ cup dried currants
2 eggs
1 to 2 tablespoons brandy

Preheat oven to 350 degrees. In a medium bowl, beat butter and sugar together until light and smooth. Add flour, nutmeg, and currants, stirring well to combine. Beat eggs in a small bowl. Pour eggs and brandy over dry mixture and stir to moisten. Knead mixture well to form dough. If mixture is still too dry, add either another egg or another tablespoon of brandy. Roll dough out to ¼-inch thickness. Cut into rounds with a scalloped-edged cutter. Place rounds fairly close together on a cookie sheet and bake for 15 minutes until golden brown. Yields 3 or 4 dozen cookies.

 POTTED RED CABBAGE

1 medium red cabbage
2 tablespoons oil
1 medium onion, chopped fine
2 green apples, pared and diced fine
1 tablespoon fresh lemon juice
1 tablespoon sugar
salt and pepper to taste

Cut cabbage into very thin slivers and set aside. In a large sauté pan, heat oil and sauté onions until translucent. Add cabbage and cook over low heat for 30 minutes, stirring occasionally; do not add any water. Add apples, lemon juice, and sugar and cook for 30 minutes. Season to taste. Serves 4. Note: This recipe is very good served with roast pork.

117 Cross Street
Chestertown, MD 21620
www.kettledrumtea.com
410-810-1497

Although the Kettledrum Tea Room also serves lunch and dinner, I opted to enjoy Afternoon Tea. Debbie had stopped just down the road to do a little research of her own, so it was up to me to enjoy all that this little eatery had to offer. There are several versions of tea to choose from, the proper Afternoon Tea being the most sumptuous. A three-tiered server was brought to my table with a large assortment of delicious goodies—Tomato and Cucumber Sandwiches, Shrimp and Cream Cheese Open Sandwiches, Baked Brie and Beef Wellington Puffs, Crab Pie, Dill Sticks, Zucchini Bread, Strawberry Nut Bread sandwiched together with Cream Cheese, Strawberries and Mint, Chocolate Torte, and Sugar-Glazed Grapes. Every item was simply divine, including the Cranberry and Cinnamon Scones, served with Strawberry Jam and Cream. I had a wide variety of loose teas to choose from. Patrons can select a white tea such as Darjeeling or a green tea like the Mandarin Orange Sencha I enjoyed. Oolongs, black teas, herbal selections, and even Rooibos, which are red teas, are offered.

The dinner menu features items such as Prime Rib, Roasted Chicken, and Crab Pie, which is Kettledrum's version of a crustless quiche absolutely filled with crab. The lunch selections range from a hearty Ham and Cheese Sandwich to Pulled Pork to the Kettledrum Salad, which sounds absolutely scrumptious. Made from field greens topped with sliced pears, goat cheese, Cinnamon Pecans, and Raspberry Vinaigrette, it's a selection Debbie certainly would have chosen.

The cute green building trimmed in cream with burgundy shutters was constructed in 1890. Once a doctor's office, it was converted to a butcher shop about forty years later. Over the years, other businesses have come and gone. The sun shone brightly as the double front doors welcomed Sunday visitors. Inside, comfortable Windsor chairs and walls in hunter green and burgundy provided a restful atmosphere. Thanks to the quiet, attentive service, any mealtime here is one of enjoyment and relaxation.

Although most people think of the timpani in a symphonic orchestra when they hear the word *kettledrum*, it actually has relevance to the tea tradition. The word was popular in nineteenth-century England, when it meant a tea party. *Kettle* referred to the tea kettle, while *drum* was a colloquialism for tea. During that time, a true kettledrum was Afternoon Tea, rather than High Tea. Finger sandwiches, cakes, pastries, and possibly some fruit were served. All this, of course, was accompanied by well-brewed pots of tea. There is always something lost in the translation of terms and traditions from England to America. When the word *kettledrum* came into common use in America in the late 1800s, society women took it literally, sometimes serving tea on a drum head or even going so far as to beat a tiny drum during the occasion. That being the case, it's not surprising that the ritual of Afternoon Tea never quite caught on in the States!

🌿 HIBISCUS TEA SORBET 🌿

2 cups water
1 cup dried hibiscus flowers
1 cup sugar
1 tablespoon lemon juice
1 tablespoon lime juice

In a small saucepan, bring water to a boil. Remove from heat and add hibiscus flowers. Allow to steep for 15 minutes. Strain liquid and return to saucepan. Add sugar and bring to a boil, stirring continuously until all sugar is dissolved. Remove from heat and chill for at least 2 hours. Add lemon juice and lime juice, stirring well to combine. Place in an ice-cream maker and freeze according to machine directions. Yields 12 scoops.

🌿 SKIPJACK OYSTER BISQUE 🌿

2 tablespoons bacon grease
1 pint oysters
2 potatoes, peeled and cubed
4 cups half-and-half
6 strips bacon, cooked and chopped
Old Bay seasoning to taste
chives to taste

In a medium sauté pan, heat bacon grease and sauté oysters about 5 minutes until edges curl. Remove oysters from pan and set aside. Add potatoes and half-and-half to pan. Bring to a boil, then reduce to a simmer for about 10 minutes until potatoes are cooked. Add oysters and bacon to potatoes, season with Old Bay, and garnish with chives. Serves 4.

STRATHMORE®

Tea Room

The Mansion at Strathmore
10701 Rockville Pike
North Bethesda, MD 20852
www.strathmore.org
301-581-5168

The setting was just perfect. It was a sunny day, and we were seated in the Music Room, listening to a delightful concert of Bach sonatas for four hands. It would be hard to equal the elegance of the extravagant appointments at Strathmore. The Music Room is wrapped in oak, the twelve-foot-high panels featuring ornate wooden carvings. The huge white marble fireplace would dwarf a smaller room but instead adds visual interest here, as do the organ pipes high in the walls above.

Afternoon Tea at Strathmore is understandably very popular. It's best to make a reservation, since tea is not served every day. We loved the pink floral tablecloths, the fresh flowers, and the beautiful assortment of bone china. Karen was impressed that the teapots arrived at the table nestled in their own tea cozies. Strathmore's signature blend of tea was soothing and a perfect foil for the treats yet to come. Executive chef Bruce Barnes is responsible for the delectable goodies served here. Currently working for Restaurant Associates, the exclusive caterer for Strathmore, he built a heralded career as ex-

ecutive chef for many of New York's hottest eateries.

Our tea began with sandwiches. We duly savored bite-sized morsels of Peekytoe Crab Salad, Smoked Salmon, Ham and Cheese, Mushroom, Deviled Egg, Mini-Quiche, and fresh fruit. The Lemon-Poppy Seed Scone with Marmalade and Cream was an unusual combination. We paused for a while to enjoy the music and the conversation. The wait staff seemed to adapt to the pace of each table. The guests at some tables raced through their tea, while others, like us, preferred a more leisurely pace in the gracious surroundings. When the desserts arrived, we pronounced them delicious.

The first land patents for this tract were recorded as early as 1694. Not much is known about the use of the land for quite some time after that. A pike road passed the property in 1823. It is likely that a tollgate was located on the property, which became a stagecoach station operated by Frank Ball during the mid- to late 1800s. In 1899, a prominent Washingtonian, Captain James Frederick Oyster, and his wife, Emma, purchased the tract. Almost immediately, work began on excavating white quartzite rocks for the foundation of the mansion. The nine-bedroom summer home, constructed in the Colonial Revival style, was immediately pronounced "a conspicuous ornament to the landscape."

The Oysters and their children continued to visit until 1908, when the property was sold to Charles I. Corby, and his wife, Hattie. Charles and his brother, William, patented machinery and techniques that revolutionized the baking industry. The Continental Baking Company, makers of Wonder Bread, eventually purchased the

Corby Bakery. The mansion remained within the Corby family until Hattie's death in October 1941. Two years later, it was conveyed to St. Mary's Academy. The academy's sisters purchased the mansion fully furnished right down to the china and used it as a convent and school for the next thirty years.

Today, the mansion and grounds are owned by Montgomery County and operated by the Strathmore Hall Foundation as a center for the arts. There is so much here to see and do. Strathmore shouldn't be missed!

CURRIED CHICKEN SALAD WITH DRIED APRICOTS

1 pound boneless chicken breasts or thighs
3 cups chicken stock
salt and pepper to taste
3 stalks celery, diced fine
2 tablespoons minced red onions
¼ cup chopped dried apricots
2 tablespoons chopped parsley
½ cup mayonnaise
zest of 1 orange
juice of 1 orange
1 tablespoon Dijon mustard
2 tablespoons curry powder
1 teaspoon ground cumin

Place chicken, stock, and salt and pepper in a medium saucepan. Bring to a gentle simmer for about 10 minutes or until chicken is cooked. Remove from heat. Drain chicken and set aside to cool. When chicken is cool, pull apart and place into a medium bowl with celery, onions, apricots, and parsley. Stir to mix. In a separate bowl, combine mayonnaise, zest, juice, mustard, curry, and cumin. Season to taste. Add mayonnaise mixture to chicken and stir well to combine. Serves 4.

PEEKYTOE CRAB SALAD ON RED ENDIVE

1 pound crabmeat, picked
3 tablespoons lemon juice
2 tablespoons Old Bay seasoning
2 tablespoons chopped chives
¼ cup mayonnaise
4 red endives

In a medium bowl, combine crabmeat, lemon juice, Old Bay, chives, and mayonnaise. Set aside in refrigerator for 2 to 3 hours to allow flavors to blend. When ready to serve, cut tips of endives and fill with crabmeat. Serves 4. Note: Strathmore uses Peekytoe crabmeat for this recipe.

PETTICOAT TEAROOM

814 South Broadway
Baltimore, MD 21231
www.petticoattearoom.com
410-342-7884

In 1726, an English Quaker by the name of William Fell bought land and named it Fells Prospect. At that time, the area was also known as Long Island Point and Copus Harbor. It wasn't until 1763 that the town of Fells Point was officially founded.

With the harbor lapping up to the very edges of its cobblestone streets, water played an important role in the development of Fells Point. The very first frigate of the young Continental Navy, christened the *Virginia*, was produced here in 1775. Another well-known ship, the USS *Constellation*, also came out of the local shipyard. The relationship between Fells Point and the adjacent waterways has continued through today. The piers, docks, and wharves are as busy and bustling as they were way back then.

There is so much history here that it's not surprising to learn that Fells Point was Maryland's first National Historic District. One of the items I found most interesting relates to Frederick Douglass. It seems that he came to Fells Point in 1826 and stayed until 1838, when he escaped to the North and his freedom.

Douglass had long since fled when The Anchorage, a seamen's hostel, was established. As many as fifty thousand seamen a year were lodged in that boardinghouse. Today, Petticoat Tea Room and the Southern Accent Gift Shop occupy a portion of the old hostel. The businesses are run by Kitty Knoedler, who came to Baltimore in 1997. At that time, Fells Point was well beyond its glory years and was mostly a home to bars and souvenir shops. So Kitty decided to add a feminine influence by opening Southern Accent, an upscale shop. A few years later, she moved the shop to its present location and acquired the space to open the tearoom as a complement to her store. Kitty figured it would be the only "girly" place in Fells Point and that she'd have a corner on the market. Her business acumen proved right on target.

Karen had other commitments, so I had a girl's day out with my daughter, Dori, to enjoy all that this establishment provides. We sampled many items, including the Butternut Squash Soup and the Chicken Noodle Soup. The Shrimp Salad was wonderful and the Corn Salad quite unique. The Fruit Cup, drizzled with Poppy Seed Dressing, was refreshing. The tea sandwiches that day were Egg Salad, Cucumber, Tomato, and Spinach Spread, all of which were tasty. Dori also sampled one of the specialties of the day, a Turkey Sandwich with Cranberry Chutney. It was accompanied by Southern Potato Salad, a Cheese Straw, and Brownie Rosette. In addition to High Tea, for which reservations are requested, the tearoom also serves Table Tea, which includes scones, cream, and jam; Dessert Tea; and Afternoon Tea, which includes finger sandwiches and fresh fruit. Those wanting a heartier midday meal can order sandwiches and salads from the menu. The tearoom's brochure says that it offers "southern charm with its own flavor." We agree that Kitty Knoedler has successfully brought her native Mississippi farther north.

KITTY'S CORN SALAD

3 11-ounce cans shoepeg corn
1 bunch green onions
1 or 2 large tomatoes
1 tablespoon minced jalapeño peppers, or to taste
1 or 2 tablespoons mayonnaise
lettuce leaves, if desired
corn-chip scoops or crackers, if desired

Drain corn in a colander. Chop onions, stems and all, then chop tomatoes and drain them in a separate colander. Combine corn, onions, tomatoes, and jalapeños. Mix in 1 tablespoon mayonnaise at a time. Use just enough to hold mixture together; too much mayonnaise will make the salad runny. Serve on a bed of lettuce as a side dish, or serve with scoops or crackers as a party dip. You can also add cooked shrimp and serve in a blossomed tomato as an entrée. Yields about 4 cups.

EASY AS PIE BREAD PUDDING

4 cups bread pieces (white bread, French bread, or croissants)
1 cup sugar
3 cups milk
2 tablespoons cinnamon
1 tablespoon nutmeg (use fresh if available)
1 teaspoon vanilla
6 tablespoons butter
1½ cups confectioners' sugar
3 tablespoons rum

Preheat oven to 350 degrees. Combine first 6 ingredients, making sure all bread is soaked. Pour into a 9-by-13-inch baking dish and cook until firm. To make sauce, melt butter and add confectioners' sugar. Stir until a white paste forms. Add rum and stir to incorporate. Dish out individual portions of bread pudding and pour sauce over top. Serves 4.

HISTORIC OAKLAND

ESTABLISHED 1811

5430 Vantage Point Road
Columbia, MD 21044
www.historic-oakland.com
410-730-4801

Columbia is a planned community. During the planning, Jim Rouse took care to preserve some of the area's historic buildings. Oakland Manor was one of the oldest in Howard County. The Columbia Association undertook the renovation of Oakland in 1986 under the leadership of Michael Trostel, an expert with the American Institute of Architecture. This exquisite home is used for a variety of functions, but one day a month, visitors to Historic Oakland can enjoy Afternoon Tea while stepping back in time.

The area was surveyed in 1688, prior to the formation of Howard County. At that time, an eleven-hundred-acre tract of land known as Felicity contained two homes. Mrs. John Sterrett inherited the land from her father's family, the Ridgelys. When Deborah Sterrett died, Felicity went to her son, Charles. Charles changed his surname in 1790, adding the Ridgely name in order to inherit from his uncle. By 1811, Charles Sterrett Ridgely was the speaker of the Maryland House of Delegates. He built Oakland as his country home. It was constructed by

Abraham Lerew in the Federal style but today is a blend of Federal, Greek Revival, and Colonial Revival architecture.

Oakland was sold for the sum of forty-seven thousand dollars to Robert Oliver, a wealthy merchant. The estate then passed to Oliver's son, Thomas, for use as a summer home. At that time, the property encompassed about 567 acres. However, the Olivers were able to purchase nearby tracts, increasing their holdings to 775 acres. They continued their ownership for the next thirteen years, until the property was purchased by George Riggs Gaither. Gaither, who held the rank of major in the Maryland militia, raised and trained a cavalry squadron here.

The property passed to the Tabb family in 1864. The Tabbs constructed a half-mile racetrack and bred quite a few racehorses that earned notoriety during the latter part of the nineteenth century.

The property was acquired by the Rouse Company in 1965. Following that, Oakland served as the first headquarters for the Columbia Project, as Dag Hammerskjold College, as Antioch College, and as the county American Red Cross office.

Self-guided tours are available. I took advantage of the opportunity to marvel at the home's gracious interior. Stepping into the foyer, guests pass under one of the oldest and largest leaded-glass fan lights in Maryland. Another few steps brought me into the sunny yellow ballroom overlooking the back veranda. I was seated for tea with Angie Pitzer and Rachael Cox, who own The Tea Trolley, a fabulous catering company responsible for the sumptuous teas at Oakland. It was a real pleasure to relax and chat with such interesting women. I knew that Debbie would be sorry she missed this. The offerings for tea were as delicious as the surroundings. They included savories such as Cucumber and Cream Cheese Sandwiches, a Spinach and Cheese Stack, and Curried Chicken Apple Puffs. I particularly enjoyed the Cherry Almond Rounds, although the Baby Cheesecake and the Caramel Tortle were also extremely good. Surroundings and tasty treats like these make me want to step back in time and stay there!

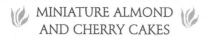

MINIATURE ALMOND AND CHERRY CAKES

4 egg yolks
¾ cup plus 1 teaspoon sugar, divided
2 tablespoons milk
½ teaspoon almond extract
½ cup all-purpose flour
¼ teaspoon salt
2 egg whites
4 teaspoons powdered egg whites
¼ cup warm water
¾ cup superfine sugar
20 sweet cherries, stems attached
½ cup heavy cream

Preheat oven to 350 degrees. Grease a 9-inch-square cake pan and line it with parchment paper. Butter parchment and dust with flour. Beat egg yolks, ½ cup sugar, milk, and almond extract in a large bowl until well combined. Mix in flour and salt. In a separate bowl, beat egg whites with an electric mixer (using clean beaters) until they just hold soft peaks. Gradually add ¼ cup sugar and mix at low speed until egg whites form stiff peaks. Stir about ⅓ of egg whites into flour mix-

ture, then gently fold in remaining whites until combined. Pour mixture into cake pan, spreading evenly. Bake for 14 to 16 minutes. Cool cake in pan.

To make sugared cherries, combine powdered egg whites and water in a small bowl. Place superfine sugar in another small bowl. Taking 1 cherry at a time, cover it with egg whites, then coat with sugar. Place on a rack to dry.

Beat heavy cream and remaining 1 teaspoon sugar until stiff. Set aside.

When cake is cool, cut into small circles using a 1½-inch round cutter. Top each circle with a teaspoon of cream and place a cherry on top. Yields 3 dozen miniature cakes.

CURRIED CHICKEN APPLE PUFFS

12 ounces boneless chicken breast, baked or poached
½ cup finely chopped apple
¼ cup finely chopped green onions
¼ cup sour cream
¼ cup mayonnaise
1 teaspoon curry
½ teaspoon salt
pinch of pepper
12 puff pastry shells
additional green onions for garnish

Chop chicken and combine with next 7 ingredients. Cover and chill at least 1 hour. Fill pastry shells with mixture and garnish with green onions. Yields 1 dozen puffs.

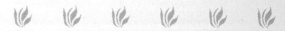

Lisa Anne's
DECENT GIFTS & TEA ROOM

2121 North Charles Street
Baltimore, MD 21218
www.theapplelady.com
410-752-4111

The iron gate and grape-colored front door certainly give this old row house a Victorian flair. Upon climbing the steps, guests are asked to ring the bell. It's charming, allowing visitors to be welcomed in for tea. We were greeted by a delightful woman who turned out to be Lisa Anne's mother. She was wearing a very perky hat, a perfect touch. Inside, the fuchsia walls radiate the warmth and enthusiasm of Lisa Portera, owner of Lisa Anne's Decadent Gifts. The decadence manifests itself in delicious chocolates and hand-dipped apples in a variety of flavors, including Toffee Original, Pecan Chocolate Truffle, Peanut Butter Cup, and S'mores Crunch.

A wedge of one of the apple varieties always finds its way onto the tray for tea, which Lisa serves on Saturdays by reservation. Some references to the experience refer to it as High Tea, while others call it a Victorian luncheon. Regardless, it's quite an experience. We had read reviews of Lisa's English Shepherd's Pie and were delighted to find that our meal started with her version of this perennial English fare. It certainly lived up to its reputation, and we quickly found ourselves at the bottom of the bowl. The service here is very leisurely, so we sat quietly enjoying the dining room's eclectic ambiance, created by high ceilings, wide moldings, a large chandelier, an original marble fireplace, tables covered in white linen, bright, geometric-patterned area rugs, and an interesting collection of botanical prints, Oriental art, and paintings of Victorian ladies hung on walls of fuchsia and pink.

The pale pink hue of Karen's Raspberry Hibiscus Iced Tea matched the walls perfectly. Served in a cut-glass tumbler with a colored straw and a mint-leaf garnish, it was as attractive as it was refreshing. The flavor of Debbie's Lemon Ginger Tea, served in a petite teacup, matched the sunny spring day outside. A traditional English Trifle arrived for our second course. The fresh strawberries amid the custard, pound cake, jam, and cream reinforced the fact that winter had finally been left behind. It was wonderful to enjoy an old favorite. Classical music flowed and conversation bubbled as we anticipated the third course. Slices of one of Lisa's special hand-dipped apples, swan-shaped Cream Puffs, Fruit Tarts, and freshly baked Scones put the finishing touches on an afternoon of lunch and leisure.

Many of Lisa Anne's scrumptious creations are for sale in the tearoom and in her retail stores in the Baltimore area. They can be found on the Internet as well. The apples come in three sizes and several different varieties. The chocolate-covered pretzels, known as Yummy Sundae Stix, are as attractive as they are tasty. Her truffles come in several varieties, including Macadamia, White Russian, Champagne Sparkler, and Triple Chocolate. The Turkish Apricot Truffles are large enough to be dessert for a formal dinner party.

They're wrapped to look like apricots, so they're pleasing to both the eye and the palate. Lisa Anne obviously is very good at indulgence, so go and allow yourself the pleasure.

ENGLISH SHEPHERD'S PIE

10 Yukon Gold potatoes
1 cup butter, divided
½ cup sour cream
½ cup whole milk
salt and pepper to taste
2 pounds lean ground beef
1 medium onion, chopped
½ cup corn
½ cup peas
½ cup pearl onions
6 mushrooms, sliced
dash of Worcestershire sauce
thyme to taste
2 tablespoons chopped parsley, divided
1 cup beef stock
paprika for garnish

Preheat oven to 400 degrees. Cook potatoes in a large pot of salted water until tender. Drain, let cool, and peel. In a large bowl, combine ½ cup butter, sour cream, milk, and potatoes. Mash until mostly smooth. Season with salt and pepper and set aside. In a large skillet, sauté beef until browned. Drain fat and set meat aside. Melt remaining butter in the same pan. Add chopped onions and sauté until tender. Add meat, corn, peas, pearl onions, and mushrooms and season with salt and pepper, Worcestershire, thyme, and 1 tablespoon parsley. Pour in beef stock and let simmer for 15 to 20 minutes. Line 10 individual casserole dishes or 1 large casserole with a thin layer of mashed potatoes. Spoon in beef-and-vegetable mixture, making sure to include only a moderate amount of juice. Spread remaining potatoes over top. Bake for 20 to 30 minutes until top is crisp and golden. Garnish with remaining parsley and paprika. Serves 8.

 CHOCOLATE-DIPPED STRAWBERRIES

8 large strawberries with stems
1 cup chopped high-quality bittersweet chocolate

Wash and gently dry strawberries. Place chocolate in a small, heavy saucepan and melt on low heat or over a double boiler. Dip strawberries in chocolate and place on waxed paper until chocolate hardens. Serves 8. Note: Pineapple rings work well, too.

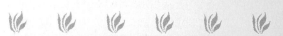

The Victorian Tea Cup Tea Room

7 Wallace Avenue
North East, MD 21901
410-287-9500

Guests can have tea just about any way they want it at The Victorian Tea Cup. Victoria's Tea is served with salad and sandwiches. The smaller Cream Tea includes scones and jam. Half-Tea comes with just sandwiches. Of course, we wanted to sample everything that owner Donna Hinkle's kitchen had to offer, so we sat down to a Full Tea, which featured scones with cream and jam, tea sandwiches, and bite-sized sweets. We began with a Blueberry Scone and an Apple Cinnamon Scone. The jam of the day was Lemon Curd, which brought a taste of springtime inside on a rainy April day. The sandwiches were arranged on the bottom of a tiered tray. We continued with the Raisin Bread with Cream Cheese and Walnuts, followed by a traditional Cucumber Sandwich, Egg Salad, Spinach on Marbled Rye, Salmon Spread, and a Mango Chicken Salad that was absolutely unique. The top tier held the pastries and sweets, which included Cream Puffs, Raspberry Triangles, Brown Sugar Chocolate Roll-Ups, Ladyfingers, and Chocolate Hazelnut Bites. All too soon, our tray was empty.

The choice of teas is ample but not so lengthy that it's overwhelming. Traditional selections such as Earl Grey, Darjeeling, and English Breakfast are available, as are popular fruit varieties such as Peach and Apple Cinnamon. Karen had the Lady Grey, which was scented with orange, lemon, and oil of bergamot to create a light, refreshing blend. To take off the chill from the inclement weather, Debbie opted for the heartier London Cuppa, which combined Kenya and Assam teas to create a deep, rich flavor. We sipped and chatted as we listened to the rain patter away.

The atmosphere here is quite cozy. The two dainty dining rooms seat a total of twenty-two guests. The walls are painted a buttery yellow and trimmed in crisp white, creating a charming cottage feel. Battenburg-style lace tablecloths adorn some of the tables, while others are dressed with crocheted linens. Although the china that Donna uses is an eclectic variety of pieces, it coordinates well thanks to the predominance of pink floral motifs. The rose-themed décor is seen in an arrangement of roses over the mirror, in the teacup centerpieces, and in the painted vine along the back wall. In the front room, a trunk of hats and gloves suggests dress-up time, and a child's tea service and tiny table add to the whimsy.

The Victorian Tea Cup is located in the end unit of a multiuse Victorian-era frame structure painted a fresh cream and trimmed in blue-gray and burgundy. A framed article just inside the front door talks about the Simcoes, the original owners, who once had a lumberyard at this location. Later, the Sadowsky family took ownership. During his tenure, Mr. Sadowsky had a street cut through the property. He named it for his youngest son, Wallace. The street is still so named today, as evidenced by The Victorian Tea Cup's address.

Not only is tea available six days a week, but Donna does specialty teas as well. The Mother and Daughter Teas are quite popular, as are the Candlelight Christmas Teas. After all, there are many ways to enjoy the longstanding tea tradition.

DEVONSHIRE CREAM

8-ounce package cream cheese, softened
3 tablespoons sugar
1 teaspoon vanilla
¼ cup sour cream
¼ cup whipping cream

Using an electric mixer, cream the cream cheese with sugar and vanilla until fluffy. Add sour cream and combine again. Add whipping cream and whip on high until well combined. Serve with scones. Yields about 2 cups.

 MANGO CHICKEN SALAD

¼ cup mayonnaise
¼ cup mango chutney
2 teaspoons curry powder
1 to 1½ pounds boneless chicken, cooked

In a medium bowl, combine mayonnaise, chutney, and curry powder, adjusting amounts to taste. Cover bowl and chill for 1 hour to combine flavors. Finely dice chicken and combine with mayonnaise mixture. Served on lettuce leaves or with crackers, or spread on bread of your choice for tea sandwiches. Yields about 2½ cups.

Aunt Fairie's Tea

200 West Main Street
Middletown, MD 21769
301-639-5518

Tired of highway driving on a gorgeous Saturday afternoon, we opted to take a route less traveled and discovered this charming tearoom not far off Interstate 70. Situated in downtown Middletown, this creamy brick building etched in white has a soft, welcoming appearance. On Saturday and Sunday, guests can enjoy a sandwich or tea in the original parlor and library of what was once a twenty-one-room sanitarium for patients suffering from tuberculosis. In those days, the building also contained a doctor's office, a surgery, and a recovery room.

Sometimes called The Tea Room at the Lamar Center, Aunt Fairie's Tea is owned and operated by Bonita Currey. She generously gave us a few recipes. In fact, she frequently bestows a list of ingredients for a salad dressing or a soup on her guests. However, the Marmalade is a carefully guarded secret. Bonita's main focus is providing her customers with tasty foods and a few fine teas, served in the style of English Midday Tea. For lunch in the winter, Earl Grey and English Breakfast Tea are popular choices to accompany the sweets and savories. However, when warm weather rolls around, guests appreciate the freshly squeezed Lemonade and the Southern-Style Sweetened Mint Iced Tea.

Luncheon Tea is a full five courses, including soup, salad, scones, tea sandwiches, dessert, and a beverage. Dessert Tea includes two scones with clotted cream and jam, along with a selection of sweets. Even though its title excluded us, we'd be quite happy with the Gentleman's Sandwich at just about any lunchtime meal. It consists of three deli meats and cheese, accompanied by Red Onion Remoulade. The soups, prepared daily, range from traditional offerings such as Cream of Broccoli and Brunswick Stew to unusual selections such as Smokey Lentil, Cream of Cauliflower, and Mediterranean Vegetable. The salads are generous concoctions of fresh fruit or marinated vegetables tossed with mixed greens, perhaps some roasted chicken, and a delectable salad dressing. They are as interesting to the eye as they are to the palate.

Almost every weekend the tearoom is open, a special event is advertised. In mid-April, Aunt Fairie's celebrates spring. In May, Mother's Day and Memorial Day celebrations and other festivities are on the schedule. Even Father's Day makes an appearance on Aunt Fairie's calendar. On all of these occasions, and just on regular days, too, refreshments are served against a Victorian backdrop. The pale peach walls are lighted by period chandeliers. Mantels with scrolls and mirrors add to the ambiance, as do the antique cake pedestals, eclectic place settings, and china table service. On our first trip past Aunt Fairie's, we arrived just after service had ceased for the afternoon. Nonplused, we put our noses to the floor-to-ceiling windows and peered in at the collection of teapots and bric-a-brac displayed throughout. There's only one word to describe what we saw—charming.

🌿 ROSE POACHED PEARS 🌿

4 cups water
1 cup sugar
1 teaspoon vanilla
4 to 6 whole cloves
1 stick cinnamon, broken into a few pieces
4 drops red food coloring
2 drops blue food coloring
6 firm, fresh pears (red pears hold up well)

Prepare syrup for poaching pears by placing first 7 ingredients into a 4-quart pot. Bring to a gentle boil. Peel pears. To serve whole pears as a dessert, remove cores from bottom of pears. Place pears in syrup. Cover and cook until pears can be pierced with a fork. Leave pears in syrup. Cool to serve. Serves 6.

An alternate method is to cut the pears in half, scoop out the cores, fan the slices, and continue with the poaching instructions above. Serve atop a salad of your choice.

🌿 STRAWBERRY SALAD 🌿

4 cups fresh, ripe strawberries
¾ cup sugar
¼ cup red wine vinegar
2 teaspoons Worcestershire sauce
¼ cup water
¼ cup chopped fresh basil
4 cups fresh mixed greens

Clean and slice strawberries and place them in a small bowl. Add sugar and stir gently to blend. Allow strawberries to sit about 20 minutes until a syrup forms in bottom of bowl. Drain syrup into a container and reserve. Add vinegar, Worcestershire, water, and basil to syrup. Mix. To serve, place greens on salad plates and spoon sweetened berries onto greens. Pour dressing over salad. Serves 4 to 6.

Thir-Tea-First Street Cafe!
& Tea Room

414 East Thirty-first Street
Baltimore, MD 21218
410-889-7112

The dozens of teapots lining the shelves in the main dining room of Thir-Tea-First Street Café! let visitors know at first glance that this place is serious about tea. Downstairs, lace-covered tables sit amid an Art Deco atmosphere created by the wonderful copper-and-gold-patterned wallpaper. In addition to tea, guests can enjoy breakfast, lunch, and dinner. Breakfast options include eggs, Texas Toast, Pancakes, and other traditional selections. For dinner, the selections include Roasted Chicken, Stewed Chicken over Rice, Salmon, Shrimp, and Crab Cakes.

Upstairs are the two rooms where tea is served. The front room is the tearoom. It is bright and sunny, decorated in lavender and lace. Hats, boas, and costume jewelry festoon one corner, allowing little girls to play dress-up while having tea, or allowing the "little girl" in grown-up women to express itself. We've tried it from time to time as we've had tea—it's fun!

The parlor, the larger room upstairs, is decorated with Victorian flair, including an authentic settee and side chairs. From time to time, it has been used as a sitting room where men wait after having driven their wives to tea. An interesting chess set and a cleverly disguised television set have been incorporated into the room for this purpose. For large parties and on particularly busy days, the room can quickly and easily be converted for serving tea.

Cream Tea, High Tea, and Afternoon Tea are all served. Since we arrived early in the day, owner Denise Washington was kind enough to provide Cream Tea for us. We oohed and aahed our way through Lemon Zest Scones and Very Berry Scones, served with Lemon Curd, Devon Cream, and six different kinds of preserves, including a delicious Cranberry and Karen's favorite, Ginger Pear. We both saved the Apple Strudel Scone for last. Filled with an apple-cinnamon concoction and dusted with cinnamon sugar, it was the most delicious scone either of us had ever sampled. And considering Karen's English heritage, you can bet that's a fair few scones!

For Afternoon Tea and High Tea, the expanded list of items sometimes includes Pear Butter or Crème Fraiche, in addition to the items we sampled. The sandwiches might include Tomato, Turkey Triangles, Vegetable Spread, and Cucumber. Karen was ecstatic to find out that Denise uses English cucumbers, which they both agreed are superior. One of the favorite items served here is the Sweet Potato Biscuits, a recipe handed down from Denise's grandmother.

Thir-Tea-First Street Café! & Tea Room was created out of what was once a summer home built in 1887 by a family that lived in the Mount Vernon Square area of Baltimore. At that time, the city limit was North Avenue, and folks came out this way to enjoy the cool breezes and green grass. Although the city has expanded, this locale still offers a means of escape—through the ritual of serving tea.

 TURKEY TRIANGLES

6 slices 12-grain bread
¼ cup cranberry sauce
2 large leaves romaine lettuce
2 slices turkey bacon
2 slices roasted turkey
8 sprigs fresh rosemary

Lightly toast bread. Spread cranberry sauce on 2 slices of bread. Place romaine leaves on top of cranberry sauce, then top with turkey bacon. Place a second slice of bread on top of bacon. Top bread with a roasted turkey slice. Place third slice of bread on top. Cut each sandwich diagonally into quarters. Spear each triangle with a sprig of rosemary. Yields 8 triangle sandwiches. Note: Denise says that these "taste-tea" sandwiches are a hit with the men who take tea.

ROASTED RED POTATO SOUP

15 baby red potatoes
¼ cup chopped fresh herbs (rosemary, sage, thyme, marjoram, basil, or oregano)
1 tablespoon seasoned salt
½ cup butter, divided
½ cup chopped celery
⅔ cup flour, divided
½ cup cream
2 cups hot water, divided
½ cup shredded fresh Parmesan cheese for garnish

Preheat oven to 375 degrees. Wash potatoes and leave skin on. Quarter or halve potatoes. Spray a baking sheet with cooking spray. Place potatoes in a single layer on baking sheet, sprinkle with herbs and seasoned salt, and dot with ¼ cup butter. Bake for about 15 minutes until tender. Melt remaining butter in a Dutch oven. Sauté celery until tender. Sift ⅓ cup flour into pan while stirring with a wooden spoon. Slowly add cream and 1 cup hot water, continuing to stir. Add potatoes. In a small bowl, combine remaining flour and water. Add mixture slowly to potatoes, stirring. Add more water as required to make sufficient broth for soup. Simmer for 10 minutes. Serve hot in tiny bowls or teacups. Garnish with Parmesan. Serves 10.

CHAPTER 2

The Water's Edge

McGarvey's Saloon & Oyster Bar

There is always something soothing, something mesmerizing
about water, whether it's loudly crashing or gently lapping at its boundaries.
There's a constancy in the restaurants featured here as well.
Good food, excellent service, and pleasing ambiance combine
to bring diners back time and again, just like the ebb and flow of the tide.

314 North Morris Street
Oxford, MD 21654
www.robertmorrisinn.com
410-226-5111

Robert Morris, Jr., helped finance the Revolutionary War and signed the Declaration of Independence, the Articles of Confederation, and the Constitution. He counted George Washington among his friends. In fact, he, George Washington, and George Ross were the members of a secret committee that commissioned Betsy Ross to make the first flag. Morris was perhaps best known as "the financier of the American Revolution," a title that referred not only to his position as superintendent of finance but also to his role in raising funds and supplies for the continental government.

The inn is named for his father, an English trading agent of the same name who lived in the house in the 1730s, after the company he worked for purchased the home so Morris could represent its interests in Oxford. The four original rooms predated Morris's arrival by twenty years, having been built by ship's carpenters in 1710. Unfortunately, Robert Morris, Sr., met an untimely death when the wadding from a ship's gun being fired in his honor accidentally struck him. Since this occurred before the American Revolution, the elder Morris never knew of his son's significant contribution to the history of this country.

At one time, the village of Oxford was Maryland's largest port. Today, it is a protected harbor where fishermen harvest delicious delicacies from the Tred Avon River and the Chesapeake Bay. Not surprisingly, seafood is the primary focus of the menu at the Robert Morris Inn. As a matter of fact, author James Michener rated the inn's Crab Cakes the best on the Eastern Shore. We therefore had to try them, although deciding which version proved challenging. Karen sampled Crab Cakes the Oxford Way, meaning lightly breaded and fried. Debbie selected the oven-baked Crab Cakes Morris. Owner Ken Gibson, who dined with us, had the Au Gratin Cakes, which consist of crab and shrimp combined with Monterey Jack and cheddar before being baked. Every bite was as tasty as Michener avowed. We also sampled a variety of side dishes. The Onion Rings were excellent, as were the Coleslaw, the Cucumber and Onion Salad, and the Corn Nibbles. These were similar to hush puppies, although cheesier and slightly sweeter. We finished up by sharing a piece of Strawberry Pie, prepared at the inn using a very old recipe.

We were seated in the tavern, which has a definite rustic flair. The wood and walls are dark. To add to the ambiance, beverages here are served in pewter horn-shaped tankards embellished with the Morris family crest. The main dining room has a casually elegant colonial feel. Crystal chandeliers provide the overhead lighting, shining on the murals, which have a history of their own. The menu here is more upscale, although tavern fare is still available. Seafood Scampi, seafood platters, Prime Rib, and the ever-popular Crab Cakes are among the choices.

The mansion has been used for a variety of purposes through the years. It has served as a town hall, a general store, and a soldiers' convalescent home. Since 1971, the Gibson family has been at the helm of the inn, rightfully earning recognition for their warm, sincere hospitality. Long may they reign.

OYSTER CASSEROLE

½ cup dry breadcrumbs
½ cup coarse cracker crumbs
5 tablespoons butter, melted
1 pint oysters
½ teaspoon salt
$^1/_8$ teaspoon pepper
$^1/_8$ teaspoon grated nutmeg
2 tablespoons chopped parsley
10½-ounce can condensed cream of mushroom
   soup

Preheat oven to 350 degrees. In a large bowl, combine breadcrumbs, cracker crumbs, and butter. Place half of mixture in a greased 1-quart casserole. Arrange oysters in layers, sprinkling each layer with salt, pepper, nutmeg, and parsley. Pour mushroom soup over oysters and top with remaining crumbs. Bake for 1 hour. Serves 4.

SPICY CRAB AND SHRIMP SOUP

3 tablespoons butter
½ cup chopped onions
½ cup chopped celery
6 cups tomato juice
14-ounce can diced tomatoes with juice
2 tablespoons dry sherry
¼ cup pearl barley
1 bay leaf
1 tablespoon Worcestershire sauce
1 teaspoon Old Bay seasoning
1 teaspoon dried oregano
½ teaspoon garlic powder
½ teaspoon Tabasco sauce
¼ teaspoon cayenne pepper
1 pound uncooked medium shrimp, peeled and
   deveined
½ pound crabmeat, picked
salt and pepper to taste

Melt butter in large, heavy saucepan over medium-high heat. Add onions and celery. Sauté about 6 minutes until tender. Add tomato juice, tomatoes, and sherry. Bring to a boil. Add next 8 ingredients. Simmer about 25 minutes until barley is tender, stirring often. Add seafood. Simmer about 3 minutes until shrimp are cooked through. Season to taste. Serves 4.

Sherwood's Landing at The Inn at Perry Cabin
308 Watkins Lane
St. Michaels, MD 21663
www.perrycabin.com
410-745-2200

To quote Samuel Taylor Coleridge, "Water, water, everywhere." The rest of that famous line isn't applicable to The Inn at Perry Cabin, but certainly the beginning fits perfectly with the inn's ambiance, as it sits grandly along the Miles River, a tributary wending its way to the Chesapeake Bay. The Inn at Perry Cabin was built by Purser Samuel Hambleton, a veteran of the Battle of Lake Erie in the War of 1812 and the aide-de-camp to Commodore Oliver Perry. After the war, Hambleton retired, settling in St. Michaels in 1816. Supposedly, his design of the property was inspired by the commodore's cabin aboard the USS *Niagara*.

This home isn't the only link to the War of 1812 in St. Michaels. In fact, the whole community is quite proud of its reputation as "the town that fooled the British." The townspeople hung lanterns in the trees, causing the British to miscalculate the location of the buildings and thus overshoot the town.

During the 1950s, the property was converted from use as a private home and farm to a riding academy. In 1980, the long, low white mansion house became an inn and restaurant. Sir Bernard Ashley, cofounder of the Laura Ashley company, took the helm in 1989, expanding the property and creating the first of his series of inns. After the turn of the new millennium, The Inn at Perry Cabin was acquired by Orient Express Hotels and earned recognition as one of the top hotels in the world.

The Sherwood's Landing dining room at Perry Cabin has a nautical theme. The colorful stripes in the carpet resemble ropes, and a Turkish ottoman in the center of the room resembles a lighthouse. The view of the water is fabulous, the tables for two set so that both parties can enjoy the panorama. Our favorite reference to seamanship was the collection of oars, sextants, nets, an oyster rake, and a capstan. Combined with the American and Maryland flags that created a bit of heraldry above the fireplace.

The fabulous menu was created under the direction of executive chef Mark Salter. His signature dish is Crab Spring Roll with Pink Grapefruit, Avocado, and Almonds, which appears on the list of starters. The Smoked Bluefish Pâté is also a popular choice, as is the French Bean Salad with Golden Beets, Pickled Mushrooms, and Toasted Hazelnuts. The entrée selections lean toward seafood offerings like Truffle-Crusted Halibut and Wild Rockfish on Caramelized Zucchini and Squash.

Although we'll certainly go back to enjoy the dinner creations and the view, we decided to indulge in Afternoon Tea on this trip. Our service began with a Peach Bellini brought to the table promptly by our server. We were treated to petite triangle sandwiches of Smoked Salmon, Cucumber, and Turkey, attractively presented on a silver tray. The sweets that followed included a Chocolate Chip Cookie, a Sugar Cookie, a Chocolate-Covered Strawberry, a Fruit Tart, moist Nut Bread, Pound Cake, and a Raisin Scone. This last we both topped liberally with Raspberry Jam and Clotted Cream. The food unequivocally speaks for itself.

MARINATED SKEWERED PORK TENDERLOIN

1 pound pork tenderloin
2 tablespoons cracked black pepper
2 jalapeño peppers, minced
4 lemon grass skewers
1 cup Salter's Tamari and Orange Dressing or
    similar dressing of your choice
Chinese Vegetable Slaw (see below)

Trim tenderloin and cut into 2-ounce medallions. Season pork with pepper and jalapeños. Skewer medallions onto lemon grass. Marinate in dressing for 1 hour. Heat grill to high. Remove pork from marinade and grill for 1 minute on each side. Turn down flame on grill and continue to cook for 3 to 4 minutes or finish in a preheated 375-degree oven for 4 minutes. Drizzle with more dressing. Serve atop Chinese Vegetable Slaw with a fried soft-shell crab on the side. Serves 4.

CHINESE VEGETABLE SLAW

1½ to 2 cups shredded cabbage
1½ to 2 cups shredded bok choy
1 to 1¼ cups shredded carrots

2 tablespoons lime juice
½ teaspoon chili powder
4 tablespoons chopped scallions
2 tablespoons chopped fresh cilantro
½ cup Salter's Tamari and Orange Dressing or
    similar dressing of your choice
1 cup vegetable oil
1 package won ton skins, cut into ½-inch strips
salt and pepper to taste

In a large bowl, toss cabbage, bok choy, and carrots together until well mixed. Add lime juice, chili powder, scallions, and cilantro. Toss with dressing and refrigerate. Heat oil in a deep pot. Place won ton strips a handful at a time into oil; scoop out and drain almost immediately to keep from overcooking. Season just prior to serving. Sprinkle with won ton crisps to garnish. Serves 4.

CORN RELISH

3 ears white corn
2 tablespoons olive oil
2 tablespoons diced red onions
½ teaspoon ground cumin
½ cup sour cream
1 plum tomato, diced
½ ripe but firm avocado, diced
1 teaspoon chopped cilantro
juice of 1 lime
salt and pepper to taste

Peel corn and remove silk, using a damp cloth. Shuck corn from the ears and sauté in olive oil over medium heat for 3 minutes. Add onions and cumin and stir well. Remove from heat and let cool. Fold mixture into sour cream. Add remaining ingredients and gently toss to mix. Serves 4.

11 Bohemia Avenue
Chesapeake City, MD 21915
www.bayardhouse.com
877-582-4049

Obviously, we're enthralled with *old*. In our book (literally and figuratively), the older the better. So when we read that The Bayard House is considered the oldest building in Chesapeake City, our interest was more than a little piqued. It seems that in the early 1780s, Sam Bayard built the original manor in what was then known as Bohemia Village. Upon the construction of the Chesapeake and Delaware Canal between 1804 and 1829, the town began to grow. Its name was changed to the more fitting Chesapeake City in 1824.

With this expansion, the need for inns and taverns increased. Thus, the Bayard home was converted to that use in 1834. The property passed through a couple of owners before 1858, when it was returned to Richard Bayard, a descendant of the original owner. Under his guidance, it became known as The Bayard House Inn. Offering great views of the marina, it proved so popular a spot that beds were rented in shifts!

A rather infamous event occurred at the inn during the ownership of William Harriott, who took the helm in 1899. Harriott operated the property as an inn and tavern until 1919, when Prohibition changed the rules just a little. The tavern was used as a storefront to sell tobacco, but whiskey continued to be sold illegally to friends and others in the know. Financial distress overwhelmed Harriott during the Great Depression, causing him to take his own life by hanging right in the inn.

Fortunately, our visit was nothing but pleasant. Even though it was fall, the weather was still warm, so we decided to sample a cup of Vichyssoise, a chilled soup created from potatoes and leeks but made unique by the addition of sweet corn, crispy prosciutto, and crab. We also sampled the Maryland Crab Soup, which had just won first place at the Regional Crab Cookoff the day before. As you might expect, the menu offers multiple seafood choices. Some are traditional favorites, such as Crab Cakes and Lobster Tail, while others are unique. The Anaheim Peppers—stuffed with lobster, crab, and shrimp and topped with Green Chili Salsa and cheddar—are quite unusual. The Tournedos Baltimore—twin petite filet mignons, one topped with a crab cake and one with a lobster cake, then finished off with Madeira Cream Sauce and Seafood Champagne Sauce—are absolutely scrumptious. The Orange Hoisin-Glazed Catfish is as tasty as it is creative. Crème Brûlée, Baked Alaska, Key Lime Pie, and Linzer Torte are just a few of the delicacies available to complete your meal.

We decided to walk around the restaurant and peer into some of its nooks and crannies before choosing our dessert. Our favorite discovery was in the bar, known as the Hole-in-the-

Wall Lounge, so named for the wall through which drinks were once served in order to be consumed outside. The eatery takes great pride in its attentive staff, which just goes to prove that even "outsiders" can enjoy all that The Bayard House Restaurant has to offer.

CORNMEAL-CRUSTED ROCKFISH

1-pound rockfish fillet, skin removed
salt and pepper to taste
1 cup yellow cornmeal
2 teaspoons Cajun spice
¼ cup vegetable oil
tomato relish

Cut rockfish into 2 even portions. Lay on plate and sprinkle with salt and pepper. Combine cornmeal and Cajun spice and coat rockfish with mixture. Add oil to a medium sauté pan and heat to about 350 degrees. Add fish and cook on each side for about 3 minutes. Remove fish from oil and place on paper towels to drain. Place fish on plates and top with tomato relish. Serves 2.

SEAFOOD POT PIE

½ cup butter
1 large onion, chopped
2 medium carrots, chopped
1 stalk celery, chopped
1½ cups flour
12 cups shrimp stock
1 bay leaf
1 teaspoon dried thyme
½ pound baby shrimp
½ pound bay scallops
2 cups shucked oysters
1 puff pastry sheet
½ pound crabmeat, picked

Preheat oven to 450 degrees. Heat a large, heavy pan. Add butter and onions and sauté until onions are slightly browned; do not burn. Add carrots and celery and continue to sauté for 5 to 10 minutes. Sprinkle in flour, then whisk. Add shrimp stock, bay leaf, and thyme. Bring to a boil until liquid thickens and begins to reduce. Add shrimp, scallops, and oysters. Boil for an additional 5 minutes, then reduce heat to a simmer. Cut puff pastry to the shape of a 9-by-13-inch baking dish; set aside. Add crabmeat to mixture in pot. Pour into baking dish and remove bay leaf. Cover top of mixture only with puff pastry and press pastry to sides of dish. Bake for 10 to 15 minutes until pastry has risen and browned. Serves 8.

CHART HOUSE
R E S T A U R A N T

300 Second Street
Annapolis, MD 21403
www.chart-house.com
410-268-7166

Take the water taxi from downtown Annapolis across Spa Creek to Eastport to see the Chart House at its very best. The magnificent old Trumpy Boathouse is so enormous that one can take in its breathtaking size only from the water. Once inside, guests are able to look back and appreciate the tremendous waterfront views of not only the City Dock but also the State Capitol and the United States Naval Academy nearby.

Early in the boathouse's history, Chance Marine Construction built wooden sub chasers for World War I. The Vosper PT boats constructed here during World War II saw a significant amount of combat. By the end of World War II, 540 designers and engineers had constructed over 140 boats here for the United States, Russian, and British navies. In 1947, distinguished naval architect John Trumpy moved here and began construction of his world-renowned wooden yachts. Trumpy's yachts, built to the highest levels of craftsmanship, were referred to by the *New York Times* as "the Rolls-Royce of American Motor Yachts." The USS *Sequoia* was one of the most elegant yachts Trumpy ever constructed. The presidential yacht for every president from Herbert Hoover to Jimmy Carter, it was often used to entertain visiting diplomats and royalty.

Inside the building today, guests enjoy the high ceilings with the wooden beams still in evidence. The boathouse is attractive decked in browns and mustards with aqua swirls. The dining areas are light and bright. Large windows overlook the water on three sides of the building.

As expected, the menu focuses on seafood, although the land lubbers among us can choose from a small selection of ribs, steaks, and chicken. I know that if Debbie had been with me, she would have definitely chosen the Coconut Crunchy Shrimp, served with Coconut-Ginger Rice and Sweet Plum Sauce for dipping. I dithered between the Sweet Cajun-Spiced Bronzed Swordfish with Shallot Butter and Crabmeat and the Parmesan- and Garlic-Crusted Rockfish with Angel Hair Pasta and Tomato Basil Sauce. Finally, guided by my excellent server, I opted for the Crab, Avocado, and Mango Stack, an enormous and delicious layered salad in which the jumbo lump crabmeat was gently tossed in remoulade.

The menu is printed anew each morning to reflect the fresh catch. Besides the extensive selection of seafood specials, guests can choose a specific variety of fish and have it grilled, baked, or blackened to their liking. There are many delectable desserts to choose from. A longtime favorite is the Hot Chocolate Lava Cake, which must be ordered with your main course to allow time for preparation. This rich Godiva chocolate liqueur cake with a molten chocolate center is served with Heath Bar Crunch and Vanilla Ice Cream, a scrumptious way to end an unforgettable meal!

VEGETABLE BOWL WITH GRILLED SALMON

2 8-ounce salmon fillets
2 to 4 tablespoons Szechuan oil
½ cup portabello mushrooms, sliced thick
½ red pepper, julienned
¼ cup whole snow peas
½ cup Szechuan vegetables
1½ cups miso broth
1 cup udon noodles, cooked
2 tablespoons chopped basil

Grill salmon for 5 to 6 minutes on each side, depending on thickness of fillets. While salmon is grilling, heat oil in a sauté pan. Sauté mushrooms, red peppers, and snow peas for about 30 seconds. Add Szechuan vegetables and sauté an additional 30 seconds. Add broth and bring to a simmer. Add noodles and simmer an additional 45 seconds, tossing noodles frequently in broth. Place mixture in wide, shallow bowls. Place fillets on top in center of vegetable-noodle mixture. Garnish with basil. Serves 2.

CREAM OF CRAB SOUP

½ cup salted butter
generous ½ cup flour
2 cups water
1 tablespoon chicken base
8 cups half-and-half
1½ teaspoons white pepper
¾ cup sherry
3/8 teaspoon Tabasco sauce
1¼ tablespoons Worcestershire sauce
¾ tablespoon Old Bay seasoning
¼ teaspoon salt
1¼ pounds lump crabmeat, picked

Melt butter in a sauté pan over medium heat. Add flour and mix well. Cook over medium heat for about 15 minutes, stirring occasionally so roux won't brown. In a double boiler, combine water with chicken base. Heat over high heat for 5 minutes. Add half-and-half and mix well. Bring liquid to a rapid simmer and add roux. Stir constantly until mixture thickens. Add remaining ingredients and reduce heat to a gentle simmer. Cook for 10 minutes to blend flavors. Serves 12.

18281 Rosecroft Road
St. Mary's City, MD 20686
www.bromehowardinn.com
301-866-0656

Situated along the St. Mary's River on thirty acres of farmland amidst raised flowerbeds and a garden, this 1840 farmhouse today functions as The Brome-Howard Inn. Built for Dr. John Mackal Brome as a plantation home, it was originally located about a mile down the road on the property where the Historic St. Mary's City living-history museum now stands. During the latter portion of the twentieth century, people began to realize the treasures located in this area, the site of the fourth settlement of British North America, once Lord Baltimore's seventeenth-century capital city. When archaeologists began their work in 1971, they discovered three hundred sites within the limits of the National Historic Landmark, including the site where William Nuthead operated the first printing press south of Massachusetts.

But there was one significant problem. Dr. Brome's old home, then owned by the Howard family, was situated atop a great deal of seventeenth-century information. After significant community uproar, the decision was made to move the house to its current location. Owner Lisa Kelly showed us photographs of the moving process, which astoundingly took only four days from start to finish. The inn certainly fits right in at its present site, taking full advantage of the view. Five miles of walking trails allow guests to explore; they also connect the inn to its previous site, where the original carriage house, smokehouse, dairy house, and slave quarters are visible.

Upon entering the house, which is decorated with a variety of furnishings from the original owners, guests find themselves in the spacious foyer, where ample seating encourages relaxation and the enjoyment of a beverage before dinner. The dining room in which we were seated was cozy, yet elegant, the tables adorned in gold damask and the walls attractively bathed in a shade of rich pumpkin. All the paint colors in the house were carefully researched through color analysis in an effort to duplicate the hues originally used.

Chef Jack Carter and chef-owner Michael Kelly utilize local and regional ingredients to create innovative dining selections. The menu is fairly brief but not limited. In our opinion, such brevity guarantees that each creation is made with the attention guests deserve. The menu changes weekly, further indicating that the kitchen utilizes only the freshest seasonal ingredients. To that end, Karen chose the Pan-Seared Crusted Rockfish with Boursin and Crab Velouté. Debbie considered the Pork Loin Chop with Rosemary and Sweet Mustard Demi-Glace before opting for the Farfalle Pasta with Avocado, Shrimp, and Tomatoes in Basil-Lemon Cream Sauce. Both entrées were absolutely outstanding. We asked about dessert before making our entrée choices, so we'd know exactly how to budget our meal selections. The Chocolate Truffle Torte, the Cheesecake, and the Apple Crumble were all tempting, but we chose the Pecan Tarts, made by Jack every Thursday. Too full to savor them immediately, we had them packed to go and enjoyed them later in our room as we wrote about our delightful evening at The Brome-Howard Inn.

 ## PORK TENDERLOIN À L'ORANGE

3-pound pork tenderloin
½ cup soy sauce
¾ cup orange juice, divided
¼ cup water
½ cup sugar
½ cup red wine vinegar
½ cup beef stock
salt and pepper to taste
fresh orange slices for garnish

Clean membrane and fat from pork. Place pork in a metal or glass container. Combine soy sauce, ¼ cup orange juice, and water and add to pork. Marinate for at least 4 hours or overnight.

Place sugar and vinegar in a heavy pan. Bring to a boil and reduce by half, bringing the total liquid quantity to ½ cup; it should resemble a syrupy sauce when properly reduced. Add remaining orange juice and reduce by half again to the same consistency as before. Add beef stock and reduce again. When finished, sauce should coat the back of a wooden spoon. Season with salt and pepper.

Preheat oven to 400 degrees. Remove pork from marinade and place in a roasting pan. Roast pork about 40 minutes until just pink in the center. Remove from heat and let rest on a cutting board for 3 to 4 minutes. Slice on the bias and place on a plate. Ladle orange sauce over pork and garnish with orange slices. Serves 4.

CHOCOLATE-CRANBERRY SCONES

2½ cups flour
⅓ cup sugar
2 teaspoons baking powder
½ teaspoon baking soda
¼ teaspoon salt
½ cup plus 1 tablespoon butter, cut into ½-inch cubes
1 cup heavy cream
½ cup chocolate morsels
¾ cup dried cranberries
zest of ½ lemon

Preheat oven to 350 degrees. Sift flour, sugar, baking powder, baking soda, and salt into a food processor. Using the bread attachment, mix in butter until it breaks down into small beads. Add remaining ingredients and mix until dough forms and cream is completely incorporated. *Do not overmix*. Place dough ball on a clean work surface. Separate into 2 balls. Pack firmly, then press into two ¾-inch-thick disks (like small deep-dish pizzas). Cut into wedges. Place wedges on a baking sheet sprayed with nonstick spray or lined with parchment paper. Bake for 15 to 20 minutes until golden brown. Edges should be slightly darker. Yields about 20 scones.

The Elkridge Furnace Inn

CIRCA 1744

5745 Furnace Avenue
Elkridge, MD 21075
www.elkridgefurnaceinn.com
410-379-9336

Wandering through the trees along the red-brick path from the parking lot to the front porch of the inn is the perfect beginning to a delicious luncheon at The Elkridge Furnace Inn. The setting is just beautiful. Huge linden, holly, and magnolia trees frame the tall red-brick buildings, and the white columns of the Colonial Revival porch beckon guests to stay awhile. Situated on the bank of the Patapsco River, the inn offers wonderful views from each of its three floors.

We settled into one of the several dining rooms and were immediately at home. All the rooms here have been lovingly restored. Guests love the unique and rich blend of furnishings. Our server was friendly and informative. Before long, a fabulous Lobster Pancetta and Parmesan Soup was before us, swiftly followed by a delicious Marinated Shrimp and Scallop Endive Salad with Bacon Honey Vinaigrette, then the Parmesan-sprinkled Winter Squash Risotto. We would have been extremely happy with any of the offerings on the lunch menu, such as the Tomato Stuffed with Mushroom Duxelle, the Chicken with White Wine-Lemon Butter Sauce, or Shrimp over Dirty Rice with Creole Sauce. The homemade desserts were equally terrific,

from the Wildberry Kuchen to the Chocolate Bourbon Cake.

A quick glance at the dinner menu made our mouths water despite the fact that we were already full. The cuisine here is classic and French provincial, employing ideas from all over the French-speaking world. Executive chef Dan Wecker uses good, flavorful produce, meats, and seafood and prepares his dishes simply to allow the food to speak for itself. Everything is made from scratch as ordered. We would have liked to sample the Roulade Vientiane (Singapore cabbage and julienned vegetables hand-rolled with rice and served with Peanut Dipping Sauce) or the Pan-Roasted Lamb with Oregano and Mint Brioche. The Savory Cheesecake with Bacon, House-Cured Salmon, and Tomato Relish also sounded excellent.

The Elkridge Furnace Inn complex encompasses about sixteen acres in the eastern corner of Howard County, a region originally settled by the Patapsco Indians. In 1608, John Smith of Jamestown was the first white man to explore this area. It wasn't until 1744 that James McCubbin established a tavern here to accommodate the folks working in and around the town of Elk Ridge Landing. Six years later, Caleb Dorsey took over the land and constructed an iron-smelting furnace. The land passed into the hands of James and Andrew Ellicott around 1810. They built an elegant manor house attached to the existing tavern. Both the house and the tavern were constructed in the Federal and Greek Revival styles. In some places, the walls are five bricks thick. The inn has twenty-three rooms and twelve fireplaces. Guests will find a significant amount of history here, from the stairway complete with tiger-maple spindles and a walnut cap rail to the original floors made from longleaf pine. Whether your interest is history, graceful surroundings, or fabulous food, you're sure to find it at The Elkridge Furnace Inn.

 FRESH FRUIT ROMANOFF

3 cups fresh berries
2/3 cup Grand Marnier
2/3 cup sugar
4 cups heavy cream
fresh mint for garnish
candied flowers for garnish

Peel and slice fruit as required. Soft fruit such as peaches, nectarines, ripe apricots, or figs may be used in place of fresh berries. In a stainless-steel bowl, combine fruit with liqueur and sugar. Let mixture soak for at least 1 hour. Fruit may be prepared up to 1 day ahead of time. In a separate bowl, whip cream until it holds stiff peaks. Fold in fruit mixture. Serve in bowls. Garnish with fresh mint or candied flowers. Serves 8.

 MUSHROOM AND BRIE TARTLETS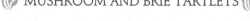

8-ounce package mushrooms or wild mushrooms
2 shallots
1 tablespoon butter
2 tablespoons sherry, brandy, or madeira wine
1 tablespoon breadcrumbs
1 teaspoon chopped fresh thyme
3-ounce wheel Brie cheese
24 prepared tartlet shells

Preheat oven to 400 degrees. Coarsely chop mushrooms and shallots in a food processor. Melt butter in a heavy pan and sauté mushrooms and shallots. When most of the liquid is gone, add sherry, brandy, or madeira and let boil. Remove pan from heat and fold in breadcrumbs and thyme. Set aside to cool. Cut Brie into 24 small squares. When mushroom duxelle is cool, fill tartlet shells with a dab of mushroom mixture and top with a square of Brie. Place on a cookie sheet and bake for about 5 minutes until Brie is melted. Yields 24 tartlets.

 SHORTBREAD SCONES

2 cups flour
1 tablespoon baking powder
½ teaspoon salt
½ teaspoon cinnamon
½ cup sugar
½ cup butter, diced
2/3 cup half-and-half
1 egg

Preheat oven to 375 degrees. Place flour, baking powder, salt, cinnamon, and sugar into a mixer bowl with a paddle attachment. Mix thoroughly on low speed. Add butter slowly until mixture looks like coarse crumbs. In a separate bowl, whisk together half-and-half and egg. Add egg mixture to crumb mixture until just combined. Scoop mixture with a 3-ounce ice-cream scoop onto a greased pan. (Dough may be rolled out and cut into squares, circles, or triangles, if desired.) Bake for about 10 minutes. Yields 8 to 10 scones.

SALOON & OYSTER BAR

8 Market Space
Annapolis, MD 21401
www.mcgarveyssaloon.com
410-263-5772

I had the good fortune of visiting McGarvey's on a Wednesday at lunchtime. As I slid into a booth, I was introduced to John Vorndick, one of McGarvey's regular customers. It seems that in the years he's been a patron, Vorndick has befriended more than three hundred midshipmen from the United States Naval Academy, located here in Annapolis. Part of that alliance includes Sunday brunch at McGarvey's, where a personalized brass plaque identifies Vorndick's table. I took advantage of the opportunity to discuss McGarvey's and the menu, asking for suggestions as to what I should have for lunch. Without hesitation, he said, "Meat Loaf. It's Wednesday." He went on to explain that he'd arranged his whole schedule in order to partake of the day's lunch special. I followed suit and found the generous portion of Meat Loaf, accompanied by Green Beans and creamy Mashed Potatoes, the perfect cure for a raw, rainy fall day.

We were seated in the atrium-like dining room, fashioned out of what was once a warehouse, most likely one that housed tobacco. This frame two-story wing is one of the few remaining eighteenth-century industrial buildings on the Annapolis waterfront. Skylights in the roof allowed sunlight to filter in even on such a gray day. A belt-driven set of ceiling fans, fashioned after those introduced at the St. Louis World's Fair, turned lazily overhead. The large ficus tree growing in the center of the room stretched to the skylights. Melinda, our waitress, joked that the tree survives on water, beer, and nicotine. Evidently, it's hardy. Guests frequently scramble to its topmost branches for a photo op before being shooed down by tolerant staff members.

The staff at McGarvey's deserves a special mention. General manager Jim Fishbuck began at McGarvey's as a busboy and gradually worked his way up. As a token of appreciation for Fishbuck's many years of service and creativity, owner Mike Ashford once presented him with a sports car. Led by Fishbuck, everyone at McGarvey's is warm and personable, clearly enjoying where they work and what they do.

Karen arrived from elsewhere in town just as I was beginning to learn McGarvey's long history. During much of the eighteenth century, the property was owned by Horatio Samuel Middleton and was known as "the Ship Carpenter's Lot." Vessels were built here until the late 1780s. Once the shipyard was cleared, the location became a prime spot for local merchants and shopkeepers to erect stores and warehouses. One operation was run by partners George and John Barber, who stocked goods transported by steam packets running between Baltimore and Annapolis.

Where there is a waterfront, there are sailing men. And where there are sailing men, there is usually a tavern or two. McGarvey's is part of that tradition. It's an all-American restaurant serving all-American food in the ambiance of the 1920s. Aviator Day on Mondays, Locals Day on Thursdays, Mardi Gras, New Year's Eve—from everyday specials to special events, opportunities abound to enjoy McGarvey's.

 BLACK BEANS

1 pound black beans
10 cups water
2 large green peppers, divided
1 smoked ham hock
¾ cup olive oil, divided
1 large onion, chopped
4 cloves garlic, chopped
3 teaspoons salt
½ teaspoon black pepper
¼ teaspoon oregano
1 teaspoon cumin
2 teaspoons sugar
1 bay leaf
2 tablespoons vinegar
2 tablespoons dry sherry

Clean and rinse beans and put them in a large pot with water, 1 whole green pepper, and ham hock. Boil for 2 minutes. Remove from heat, cover, let sit for at least 1 hour, then bring to a boil again. Reduce heat to low and simmer until beans are soft. Remove pepper and ham hock and discard. Chop remaining green pepper. Heat oil, less 2 teaspoons, in a medium skillet and sauté onions, peppers, and garlic until softened. Add sautéed mixture to beans. Add salt, black pepper, oregano, cumin, sugar, bay leaf, vinegar, and sherry. Cook over low heat, stirring often, about 30 minutes until mixture thickens. Just before serving, add remaining 2 teaspoons olive oil. Serves 8.

BURGUNDY BEEF

5 medium onions
2 tablespoons bacon drippings
2 pounds beef tenderloin, cut into 1-inch cubes
1½ tablespoons flour
pinch of marjoram
pinch of thyme
salt and pepper to taste
½ cup beef bouillon
1 to 2 cups hearty red wine
¾ pound sliced fresh mushrooms
crusty French bread or egg noodles

Slice onions and fry in bacon drippings. Remove onions and set aside. Sauté beef in remaining drippings. When beef is browned, sprinkle with flour, marjoram, thyme, and salt and pepper. Add bouillon and wine. Stir mixture well and let simmer slowly for 3 hours, adding more bouillon and wine as needed to keep beef barely covered. Return onions to mixture and add mushrooms. Mix well and continue cooking for 45 to 60 minutes. Sauce should be thick and deep brown. Serve with French bread or over egg noodles. Serves 6 to 8.

The Union Hotel

circa 1790

1282 Susquehanna Road
Port Deposit, MD 21904
www.unionhotel-restaurant.com
410-378-3503

A great deal of Port Deposit's prosperity was tied to the town's role as a port of deposit for items such as flour, potatoes, whiskey, lumber, grain, and coal brought down the Susquehanna on rafts from Wilkes-Barre, Harrisburg, and other Pennsylvania cities. The river wasn't navigable by ships above Port Deposit, so the community served as an exchange point where goods were taken off rafts and loaded on ships for Baltimore and points beyond.

The Union Hotel was built of hemlock logs during the height of the traffic along the Susquehanna Canal. Some of the canal beds can still be seen in front of the building. According to old records, a sawmill was located on the run just north of the hotel. Thanks to the canal and the mill, The Union Hotel was a busy place, providing mill patrons a bite to eat while waiting for their business to be transacted, as well as providing respite and sustenance to folks traveling the river and the canal.

For more than a quarter-century, Janet Dooling has operated The Union Hotel Restau-rant, providing sustenance to those traveling MD 222. For us, it was a cross-country afternoon drive that brought us unexpectedly to The Union Hotel. For others traveling from Baltimore, Philadelphia, and other places, The Union Hotel is a destination. They come for the thirty-two-ounce Prime Rib dinners, the Bear Steaks, the Frog Legs, and the Gator Tails. For less adventurous palates, the restaurant offers dishes like Maple Mustard-Glazed Pork Loin, Sambuca Shrimp and Scallops, Sautéed Veal Liver with Bacon and Onions, and Chicken Country Blue, a boneless chicken breast baked with country ham and Blue Cheese Sauce. The Steak and Cake offers a touch of Chesapeake Bay tradition by pairing a Filet Mignon with a delicious Crab Cake. Debbie thoroughly enjoyed the Spinach Ricotta Pie in flaky phyllo pastry. She would have been equally happy with the Pork Bar-B-Q, the Baltimore Bruschetta, or the Pan-Fried Camembert and Apples. Karen savored the Tenderloin Tips with Mushrooms but also fancied the Broccoli and Portabello Mushroom Pasta and the Country Ham and Tortellini in Lemon Cream Sauce.

We enjoyed the hotel's rustic ambiance and the wait staff in period costumes. The wide plank floors, the punched-tin lighting, and the primitive artwork all added to the feel. The room where we were seated had a large fireplace, a corner cupboard, and whitewashed walls. Accessories such as old tools, well-used decoys, and garlic ropes created the impression that we'd been welcomed into someone's home. Chairs stenciled with a country motif provided the seating at the cozy tables, thirteen of which were fashioned from a felled cherry tree. With such a varied menu and so much history to absorb, The

Union Hotel Restaurant is a place to visit again and again.

WATERCRESS SALAD

4 cups fresh watercress
1 small red onion, sliced thin
8 radishes, sliced thin
½ cup Dijon Vinaigrette (see below)

Carefully remove any large, tough stems from watercress and rinse well. Toss with red onions and radishes in Dijon Vinaigrette. Serve immediately. Serves 2.

DIJON VINAIGRETTE

4 black olives, pitted
1 teaspoon chopped garlic
1 teaspoon chopped parsley
1 teaspoon oregano
1 teaspoon basil
dash of cayenne pepper
½ cup red wine vinegar
¼ cup Dijon mustard
1½ cups olive oil

In a food processor, mix all ingredients except oil until well blended. With the processor running, slowly drizzle in oil. Place in an airtight container and refrigerate. Vinaigrette will keep for about 2 weeks. Yields 2 cups.

BRAISED RABBIT

¾ cup flour
½ teaspoon white pepper
1 teaspoon salt
1 teaspoon garlic powder
1 teaspoon onion powder
1 teaspoon dried tarragon
½ cup olive oil
1 large rabbit, skinned and cut into serving
    pieces
½ cup white wine
1½ cups chicken broth
1 pound baby carrots, peeled
1 large onion, sliced
2 stalks celery, sliced
1 bulb garlic, broken into cloves and peeled
6 cloves
1 tablespoon juniper berries (optional)
$^1/_3$ teaspoon ground mace or nutmeg
salt and freshly ground pepper to taste

Preheat oven to 350 degrees. In a small bowl, combine flour, white pepper, salt, garlic powder, onion powder, and tarragon to make seasoned flour. Heat olive oil in a Dutch oven on stovetop. While oil is heating, dredge rabbit in seasoned flour. Coat evenly and allow to stand for 1 to 2 minutes before shaking off excess flour. Add rabbit to hot oil and brown about 3 minutes on each side. Remove from heat. Add wine, broth, carrots, onions, celery, garlic, cloves, juniper berries, and mace or nutmeg. Season to taste. Cover and bake for about 1½ hours until rabbit is tender. Serves 4.

305 Mulberry Street
St. Michaels, MD 21663
www.stmichaelscrabhouse.com
410-745-3737

Crab Dip, Crab Balls, Seafood Potato Skins, Coconut Shrimp, Oysters on the Half Shell. How is it possible to decide where to begin a meal at St. Michaels Crab & Steak House? Fortunately, we didn't have to, as chef Eric Rosen provided us a sampler plate of many of the items. Guests who find themselves with the same indecisiveness can opt for the Fried Sampler or the 2 + 2 + 2, which includes two Crab Balls, two Clams Annie, and two Mushroom Caps absolutely filled with crab. It's not surprising that seafood figures prominently on this menu. After all, the Chesapeake Bay laps gently at the docks just a few feet away. However, as we chatted with Eric, it became clear that he was equally proud of his steaks and burgers. In fact, even the blue cheese used on the Bacon Blue Burger is made on the premises. Regulars know that if there's something they want that isn't on the menu, Eric will try to make it appear, as long as he has the ingredients. And if you give him advance notice, he'll most definitely be happy to comply with special requests. But we found so many appealing things on the regular menu that it will be many visits before we venture afield.

On the list of salads is a Pasta and Crab duo with Basil Vinaigrette. The Stuffed Tomato filled with Shrimp Salad also sounded perfect for a light meal. Among the list of sandwiches, the Crab Benedict and the Shrimp Melt appear alongside traditional choices such as Crab Cake Sandwiches and a Fisherman's Fillet. Coconut Shrimp, always one of Debbie's favorite dishes, is featured both as an appetizer and an entrée. The seafood platters give guests a wide variety of options, and the tasty chicken choices include Chicken Maryland, topped with Crab Imperial and a delectable Crab Sauce.

This casual, friendly eatery is housed in a building that dates to the 1830s. At that time, it was used as one of St. Michaels' earliest oyster-shucking sheds. Many of the exposed ceiling joists have been around since then. The bricks that form the base of the patio were kilned right in town during the 1800s. The anchors that add to the restaurant's nautical flavor are said to have been used on boats that once trolled the Chesapeake Bay.

After the building's stint as an oyster-shucking shed, it was used as a store dispensing items to boaters who pulled right up to the wharf outside. Later, it became a Gulf gas station, then a Texaco station, whose sign is still visible atop the building. The success of today's venture is directly tied to Eric Rosen. The friendly, outgoing personalities of Eric and his staff combine with his delicious creations to make St. Michaels Crab & Steak House a favorite with locals and a destination for visitors. Go and enjoy—we certainly did!

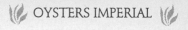

OYSTERS IMPERIAL

30 oysters
1 cup mayonnaise, divided
2 tablespoons mustard
2 tablespoons Parmesan cheese
1 tablespoon plus 1 teaspoon lemon juice,
    divided
½ teaspoon plus a pinch of Old Bay seasoning,
    divided
2 pounds crabmeat, picked
2 eggs

Preheat oven to 350 degrees. Open oysters and set aside. Combine ½ cup mayonnaise, mustard, Parmesan, 1 tablespoon lemon juice, and ½ teaspoon Old Bay. Toss gently with crabmeat to avoid breaking up lumps. Top oysters with this Crab Imperial mixture and bake about 10 minutes. Combine remaining ½ cup mayonnaise, 1 teaspoon lemon juice, eggs, and pinch of Old Bay to make Imperial Sauce. Spoon Imperial Sauce on crabmeat and return to oven for a few minutes until topping is brown. Serves 6 as an appetizer.

CLAMS ANNIE

8 clams
¼ cup finely diced scallions
¼ cup crumbled bacon
1/3 cup shredded Monterey Jack and cheddar
    cheeses

Preheat oven to 400 degrees. In a steamer, steam clams for about 4 minutes until they just begin to open. Dip clams in an ice bath to stop the cooking. Rake shells. Gently open each clam and place each half on a baking sheet. Sprinkle with scallions, then bacon, then cheeses. Bake for about 10 minutes until clams are heated through and cheeses are melted. Serves 4 as an appetizer.

2955 Tylerton Road
Smith Island
Tylerton, MD 21866
www.innofsilentmusic.com
410-425-3541

Although the renowned Captain John Smith of Jamestown Colony fame sailed past this island in June 1608, the island is not named for him. Instead, it takes its name from Henry Smith, who in the late 1600s was granted two thousand acres spreading across what is now the Maryland-Virginia state line. Not bad for someone who, for reasons forgotten, was said to be running from the law!

In 1693, Henry Smith traded two hundred acres of his land patent to John Tyler for nine thousand pounds of Tyler's tobacco. Much of those two hundred acres remained in the Tyler family for over 160 years. It was John Tyler's grandson, Butler Tyler, who was the founder of the community of Tylerton and the man for whom it is named.

In 1855, the Tyler family sold farmland at the southern end of the village. The purchaser was Thomas Bradshaw. Thirty-five years later, the acreage was divided among Bradshaw's five sons and his widow. Andrew Bradshaw was the son who received the lot on which today's inn stands. Local history now brings us to 1896, when Andrew Bradshaw and his wife sold their parcel to Captain John Cooper Marshall, a third-generation islander. He passed the property to his son, Captain Howard Wesley Marshall, in the early 1900s. It was the younger Marshall and his wife, Venie, who constructed the main wing of the current inn. The back wing was added in the 1930s. It seems that at its previous locale, the home of Captain Alonzo and Lola Hoffman was beset with tidal flooding. To alleviate the problem, they moved the house by raft to become the back section of this building. We were fortunate to be given overnight accommodations in the upstairs bedroom of the Hoffmans' old home.

After Miss Venie moved in 1967, the structure sat empty for a while until it was refurbished by Charles and Margaret Morgan as a seasonal home to share with their children and grandchildren. The home ultimately passed into the hands of today's innkeepers, Sharryl Lindberg and Leroy Friesen. We arrived by passenger ferry and were met by Leroy, with whom we enjoyed the three-block walk to the inn.

Dinner is advertised as being served thirty minutes before sunset. Unfortunately, it was a drizzly evening, so we didn't get to see nature paint the skies around Smith Island, but we did enjoy the gentle breeze, the quiet lapping of the water, and the serene surroundings. The other guests at the inn that evening were also from Pennsylvania, so we had plenty to discuss over our delicious meal of Rockfish in Herbed Breadcrumbs, Green Beans, and Rosemary Potatoes. Leroy and Sharryl joined us for coffee while we sampled two traditional island desserts. Both the Fig Cake and the Eight Layer Cake were heavenly, as were the Peach Puff Pancakes we enjoyed for breakfast the following morning.

Heavenly is a word that might be used to describe the atmosphere here. The name Inn of Silent Music was chosen to emphasize the peacefulness of the locale. The inn certainly is a place to rest, relax, reflect, and renew.

ROLLED CILANTRO OMELET

1 cup milk
6 eggs
½ cup flour
¼ cup butter, melted
¼ teaspoon cayenne pepper
¼ cup plus 2 teaspoons chopped fresh cilantro, divided
1 jalapeño pepper, seeded and chopped fine
1 cup shredded cheddar cheese
1 cup seeded and chopped tomato

Preheat oven to 400 degrees. Grease a 10-by-15-inch jelly-roll pan. Line pan with parchment and grease again. In a large mixing bowl, combine milk, eggs, flour, butter, cayenne, 2 teaspoons cilantro, and jalapeños at medium speed until well blended and frothy. Pour into pan and bake 18 to 20 minutes until roll is set and slightly puffed. Remove from oven and sprinkle with cheddar, tomatoes, and remaining cilantro. Beginning with one of the short ends, carefully roll up the omelet. Cut into 1-inch slices. Serves 4 to 6.

GERMAN APPLE PUFF PANCAKES

¼ cup plus 6 tablespoons butter, divided
¼ cup brown sugar
4 apples, peeled and sliced
6 eggs
1 cup milk
1 cup plus 2 tablespoons flour
dash of salt
1 tablespoon powdered sugar
    syrup, if desired

Preheat oven to 400 degrees. Spray 6 gratin dishes with nonstick cooking spray. Place 1 tablespoon butter in each, then place dishes in oven to preheat. Melt remaining butter in a medium skillet. Stir in brown sugar and apples and cook until tender. Whisk together eggs, milk, flour, and salt for batter. Pour batter into hot gratin dishes. Add apple mixture on top of batter. Bake for 20 minutes until puffed and golden brown. Sprinkle with powdered sugar and serve immediately with syrup on the side. Serves 6.

CHAPTER 3
In the Public Eye

The Milton Inn

Why is it that we human beings are so fascinated by the rich and famous? Regardless of what it is that makes us want to rub elbows with such folk, we frequently look for opportunities to walk in their shoes. At each of these establishments, well-known personalities have been regular guests. Go and visit. You never know who you might see!

Middleton Tavern

2 Market Space
Annapolis, MD 21401
www.middletontavern.com
410-263-3323

It is believed that the building that houses Middleton Tavern existed as early as 1740. Records show that in 1750, Elizabeth Bennett sold the property to Horatio Middleton, who subsequently operated the location as an "Inn for Seafaring Men." After Middleton's death, his wife, Anne, continued the business, followed later by their son, Samuel. The tavern was a haven not only for sailors and sea captains but also for political figures. George Washington, Thomas Jefferson, and Benjamin Franklin were among the tavern's most notable patrons. Members of the Continental Congress were regular visitors on such historic occasions as the resignation of George Washington's commission and the ratification of the Treaty of Paris.

The fact that the Middletons also operated a ferry from this location, providing transportation across the Chesapeake Bay, no doubt aided their tavern business and gave rise to the opportunity for such men to visit. Jefferson's personal records note payment to the Middletons for passage on the ferry. More importantly, Tench Tilghman used the service on his way to Philadelphia as he carried the all-important message of Cornwallis's surrender at Yorktown. After James Monroe was elected president, it is believed that he also stopped by. Monroe knew Annapolis mayor John Randall, who by that time owned the tavern.

Considering this longevity, it's not surprising that the tavern has gone through multiple names and owners. When Jerry Hardesty bought the establishment in 1968, he took over from Cleo and Mary Apostol, who had operated the Mandris Restaurant on the premises for more than thirty-five years. Hardesty changed the name to reflect the heritage of the structure. Considerable renovation, remodeling, and expansion in the mid-1980s retooled the tavern and brought about the oyster bar.

With Karen elsewhere in town, I arrived for an early dinner. I loved the location I was given, a cozy little blue-and-white-gingham-covered table nestled in a nook next to one of the structure's longstanding fireplaces. Distressed paneling, fishing nets, mounted fish, and navy walls gave the place a nautical feel. The old weapons and tools were also interesting. Since it was Boat Week in Annapolis, quite a few wind-blown sailors were swapping boating stories over a brew or two.

Monday night is Lobster Night at Middleton Tavern, so I decided to participate in the theme, ordering a bowl of Lobster Bisque, accompanied by an ample House Salad drizzled with Honey Mustard Dressing. The bisque had a delicious flavor and was chock-full of lobster. The Lobster Roll—Lobster Salad tucked in a flaky bun—also sounded tasty. The Filet Mignon Oscar gets a slightly different topping on Monday—you guessed it, lobster rather than the traditional crabmeat. If lobster isn't your favorite, you have plenty of other choices, such as Sesame-Crusted Salmon, Prime Rib, and the intriguing Seafood Tower for Two, consisting of Clams Casino, Oysters Rockefeller, Fried Calamari, and Grilled Shrimp and Scallops over Cucumber Salad. Regardless of which night you visit this rustic red-brick building, you're sure to enjoy the menu, the history, and the eighteenth-century feel.

MACADAMIA NUT-CRUSTED GROUPER

8 ounces macadamia nuts
6 tablespoons olive oil, divided
2 10-ounce grouper fillets
Szechuan Vegetables (next column)
Mango-Lime Butter (next column)

Preheat oven to 350 degrees. Coarsely chop nuts by hand or in a blender and place in a shallow dish. Place ¼ cup oil into another shallow dish. Completely coat fillets in oil, then nuts. Heat remaining oil in a medium ovenproof sauté pan. Sear grouper for 1 minute on each side until nuts are toasted and golden brown. Place pan in oven for 6 to 8 minutes. Serve fillets over Szechuan Vegetables with a large dollop of Mango-Lime Butter. Serves 2.

SZECHUAN VEGETABLES

1 medium yellow squash
1 medium green squash
2 large carrots, peeled
1 small head broccoli
1 tablespoon olive oil
2 tablespoons honey
1 tablespoon soy sauce
dash of red wine vinegar
salt and pepper to taste

Dice yellow and green squash and carrots. Cut broccoli into very small florets. Bring a large pot of water to a boil. Scald vegetables for 1 minute, them remove from water and drain. Heat oil in a large sauté pan and add scalded vegetables. Cook over medium heat for 5 minutes. Add honey, soy sauce, and vinegar and toss well to combine. Season to taste. Serve immediately. Serves 2.

MANGO-LIME BUTTER

½ mango
zest of ½ lime
juice of ½ lime
1 cup butter, softened

Peel mango and remove stone. Cut into several pieces and place in a blender. Place lime zest in blender and add lime juice and butter. Purée until smooth. Butter may be kept in a sealed container in refrigerator for several days. Yields about 1 cup.

10801 MacArthur Boulevard
Potomac, MD 20854
www.oldanglersinn.com
301-299-9097

When President John Quincy Adams shoveled the first scoop of dirt at nearby Little Falls, it marked the beginning of a canal that helped define this valley as an artery of commerce and travel. However, the Algonquin nation had maintained a trading post not far from the site of today's inn many years earlier. The name Potomac is derived from their word for the traveling traders who did business at that post.

The canal has links not only to John Quincy Adams but to George Washington as well. Young Washington, in support of General Edward Braddock, crossed the Potomac River nearby on his way to fight the French at Fort Duquesne during the French and Indian War. A man of many talents, Washington also designed the locks on the canal, which today sit only about two hundred yards from the inn.

The Old Angler's Inn opened in 1860 to serve those traveling the canal in and out of the nation's capital, as well as ladies and gentlemen of social significance living in Washington and the outlying Maryland countryside. Shortly af-

ter its inception, the inn became a place of respite for couriers carrying messages to and from the capital during the Civil War.

After the war, a California soldier returned to his home state and subsequently discovered gold. He operated a mine there until 1880. One of the owners of the gold mine so appreciated the fine food and good company he'd enjoyed at the Old Angler's Inn that he presented the proprietor with a set of solid-gold fishing hooks. From those hooks, the Order of the Golden Hook, headquartered at the inn, was born.

Many have cast their lines in the nearby waters, but perhaps none of the "old anglers" is as famous as Teddy Roosevelt, who fished at a naturally formed link of the canal at the base of the slope where the inn is situated. In his day, the menu probably tended toward the local catch. Today, guests can sample treats such as Crispy Skin Scottish Salmon, Pepper-Charred Hawaiian Ahi Tuna, Pistachio-Crusted Chilean Sea Bass, and Pan-Seared Scallops with Paella-Style Couscous and Saffron Cream. Old Rough and Ready would have been equally impressed with entrées such as Cocoa-Dusted Seared Venison Loin with Black Truffle Sauce and Pan-Roasted Duck Breast with Figs and Port Wine Sauce.

We arrived just as the kitchen opened. Other guests were already relaxing and enjoying a beverage in the comfortable seating areas arranged around the wood-burning fireplace. Having to climb a tiny, twisting spiral staircase piqued our interest as to what we'd find above. The opening expanded into three dining rooms carpeted in rich burgundy. Floral draperies and white linen cloths added to the elegant atmosphere beneath the eaves. On a warmer day, we'd be just as happy to sit outdoors, enjoying this old stone-and-stucco structure, its food, and its lovely wooded environs.

POT PIE OF WILD MUSHROOMS

1 cup wild mushrooms (shiitake, oyster, chanterelle, or black trumpet)
2 to 3 tablespoons unsalted butter
2 tablespoons finely chopped shallots
1 tablespoon finely chopped garlic
¼ cup chopped carrots
¼ cup chopped celery
½ to 1 cup red wine
1 tablespoon flour
sea salt and black pepper to taste
2 to 3 sheets puff pastry
1 egg, beaten
1 tablespoon water

Clean mushrooms, remove stems, and cut into bite-sized pieces. Melt butter in a heavy skillet on medium-high heat and sauté mushrooms, shallots, garlic, carrots, and celery for about 5 minutes. Reduce heat to simmer. Add ½ cup wine and cook for 30 minutes, stirring occasionally. If needed, add more wine. Sprinkle flour over mixture and cook an additional 3 minutes.

Season with sea salt and pepper and place mixture in a 2-cup cassolette or 4 individual ramekins. Cut puff pastry to fit on top of cassolette or ramekins. Combine egg and water and brush on top of pastry. Bake pastry according to package directions. Place cooked pastry atop mushroom mixture and finish in a 450-degree oven for 3 to 5 minutes. Serves 4.

SALMON WITH ORANGE HORSERADISH CRUST

2½-pound salmon fillet
sea salt and freshly ground pepper to taste
zest of 1 orange
juice of 1 orange
1½ tablespoons prepared horseradish
½ cup breadcrumbs
½ cup unsalted butter, cut into pats
2 tablespoon minced fresh dill

Wash salmon and season with sea salt and pepper. Refrigerate. Combine remaining ingredients in an electric mixer and beat until well mixed. Roll into a ball, cover with wax paper, and chill before rolling out. Preheat oven to 450 degrees. When crust mixture is chilled, roll it out between 2 layers of wax paper to size of salmon. Cover salmon, including sides, with crust. Roast salmon for 25 to 35 minutes until done. Serves 4.

14833 York Road
Sparks, MD 21152
www.miltoninn.com
410-771-4366

Appetizers flowed from the kitchen for us to sample. The Seafood Martini was delicious. The Foie Gras was exquisite. The same could be said of the Clams Casino. The Wilted Winter Salad of field greens, mustard greens, Bosc pears, and chèvre appealed to Debbie, and the Micro Greens—combining pea greens, red orach, popcorn shoots, baby celery, and yellow and red teardrop tomatoes—piqued Karen's interest. On our next visit, it will be difficult to know where to begin. Chef Brian Boston sat and chatted with us as we enjoyed each of the dishes presented. Passionate about The Milton Inn, he has a vision that incorporates a sense of the past, represented by the structure, and a look to the future, represented in the menu items he creates.

We were seated in the dining room to the right of the main entry. Its restful blue décor captured the feel of an English country house. Thankfully, the fireplace crackled its welcome, since the temperature had dropped significantly during the day. After contemplating the list of entrées, which included Pan-Seared Red Snapper with Shrimp Risotto and Pepper-Encrusted Black Angus Strip Steak topped with Peach and Bourbon Sauce, Debbie opted for the Wild Mushroom Phyllo, served atop a bed of Sautéed Spinach and Tomato and Red Pepper Coulis. Karen deliberated at length before selecting the Salmon with Curried Marinara. We each enjoyed our choice so much that we shared only a single bite.

Brian graciously offered to give us a tour before we enjoyed our desserts. The Cardinal Room across the hall was one of our favorites, its corner fireplace adding to the charm. Upstairs are two additional dining rooms, each with its own unique décor yet in sync with the overall ambiance. The most-requested dining room is the Hearth Room, to the rear of the restaurant. There, the atmosphere is more rustic, thanks to the oversized fireplace along one wall.

We ordered the Macadamia Torte with Chocolate Ganache Frosting. However, Brian and our server, Edmund, had other ideas. We were served the torte, along with a sampling of the Molten Cake, the Crème Brûlée, the Chocolate Flourless Torte, and Karen's favorite, Tiramisu. That's not a dessert that is normally on Debbie's list of choices, but she would select The Milton Inn's version again and again. The only problem is that the desserts are all outstanding, so selecting just one is almost an impossibility.

The history of The Milton Inn is as interesting as its menu. John Wilkes Booth, assassin of President Lincoln, is perhaps the best known of those educated here in the "classic" school operated by John Emerson Lamb, who catered to the sons of prominent Maryland planters and merchants. This fieldstone structure is the oldest in Baltimore County, dating to around 1740. The house was first used as a coach stop for Quakers who came to worship at the New Gunpowder Meeting House, which stood a few miles away. During that time, the area was called Priceville, after Quaker John Price. His descendants still reside nearby, a testament to the deep historic roots of The Milton Inn.

 MELINI VEAL CHOP
WITH WHITE BEAN RAGOUT

1 cup pinto beans
6 cups chicken stock, divided
½ cup julienned bacon
1 carrot, diced fine
2 stalks celery, diced fine
¼ red onion, diced fine
salt and pepper to taste
4 10-ounce veal chops
1 tablespoon oil
1 shallot, diced
1 cup red wine
1 tablespoon thyme
2 cups veal stock
1 tablespoon chopped chives

Soak beans in 2 cups chicken stock for 4 hours or overnight. Cook beans in remaining 4 cups stock until cooked through. Render bacon in pan until it starts to get color. Add carrots, celery, and red onions and cook for 2 minutes. Remove from heat. Strain beans and add to vegetable mixture. Season with salt and pepper. Preheat grill. Season veal chops with salt and pepper and grill to medium-rare. Add oil and shallots to pot. Deglaze with wine. When 90 percent of wine has evaporated, add thyme and veal stock. Add chives. Spoon vegetable mixture onto plates, top with veal chops, and drizzle with

wine reduction. Serves 4. Note: The Milton Inn uses Melini red wine and serves this dish with Dried Tomatoes and Roasted Baby Squash, Baby Zucchini, and Baby Beets. Serves 4.

SEAFOOD IMPERIAL

1 pound mussels
1 pound scallops
1 teaspoon Worcestershire sauce
1 egg
1 teaspoon dry mustard
1 tablespoon Dijon mustard
white pepper to taste
2 cups mayonnaise
Old Bay seasoning to taste
½ red bell pepper, minced
½ teaspoon celery seed
dash of Tabasco sauce
1 pound crabmeat, picked
1 pound lobster meat

Preheat oven to 400 degrees. Steam mussels and scallops in a medium pot. Continue to cook about 5 minutes until mussels and scallops open, then remove from pot and allow to cool. Remove meat from shells and set aside. In a large bowl, combine Worcestershire, egg, mustards, white pepper, mayonnaise, Old Bay, bell peppers, celery seed, and Tabasco. Set aside ¼ of mixture. Add crabmeat, lobster, mussels, and scallops to remaining ¾ of mayonnaise mixture. Toss. Place mixture in small casserole dishes and bake for 10 to 15 minutes. Top with remaining mayonnaise mixture. Brown. Serves 10.

Carriage House Inn

Circa 1857

200 South Seton Avenue
Emmitsburg, MD 21727
www.carriagehouseinn.info
301-447-2366

Historic Emmitsburg is just minutes away from the Civil War battlefield at Gettysburg, Pennsylvania. However, this community has a history of its own. It is the site of the Grotto of Lourdes, the Saint Elizabeth Ann Seton Shrine, Mount St. Mary's College, the National Fire Academy, and the Carriage House Inn. The inn is located in a building that has been around since 1857. It first served as a warehouse. After the turn of the twentieth century, it was utilized as a broom factory. It later became a bus depot before beginning duty as a restaurant in 1943, when it was aptly named The White House for its expansive white facade, complete with white railings and pillars. More than forty years later, the multiuse structure was purchased by the Hance family, who continued the restaurant operation but renamed it the Carriage House.

The main dining room downstairs is reminiscent of days gone by. The half-paneled walls are enhanced by old photos of the town and its environs. A large stone fireplace sits toward one end of the room, while a wide assortment of antiques and unusual knickknacks is displayed on a high shelf running around the walls. JoAnn's Ballroom, a large room on the second floor with a polished wooden floor and enormous wooden beams, is favored for wedding receptions and holiday parties. Check out the very crooked chimney on the far side of the room, reputed to have been built that way on purpose to prevent witches from climbing down.

Arriving for a late lunch, Karen ordered the tasty Ham and Bean Soup, while Debbie favored the Seafood Chowder, which arrived in a bread bowl. The Turkey Wrap with Cranberry Sauce and Cream Cheese was filling and delicious, as was the Honey Chicken Salad, served over a bed of greens and accompanied by fresh fruit, vegetables, and cheeses. The signature lunch selection, the Jumbo Lump Crab Cake Sandwich, is quite popular, as is the Angus Beef Steak with Sautéed Mushrooms and Caramelized Onions. Other popular items include the platters of fresh flounder and haddock, served with potatoes and fresh vegetables.

For dinner, the range of choices runs from Crab Cakes to Stuffed Lobster, Stuffed Shrimp, and Broiled Scallops. At least three beef selections appear on the menu. Portabello Sauté, Veal Oscar, Pork Marsala, and a chicken-and-crab dish round out the offerings. There is obviously something for everyone here.

We sat with owner Bob Hance. His favorite memory of the Carriage House is the unexpected visit by President and Mrs. Clinton in September 1999. Since Camp David is fairly close by, a presidential visit is always a possibility, although it happens very rarely. The Clintons, who arrived with a number of other guests for a birthday celebration, were gracious enough to spend a significant amount of time chatting with staff members and having their photograph taken. Many fond memories were created that day. Visit the Carriage House Inn and create a special memory of your own!

🌿 PECAN-CRUSTED ROCKFISH 🌿

2 8-ounce rockfish fillets, skinned and boned
2 teaspoons Dijon mustard
2 teaspoons mayonnaise
¾ cup finely chopped pecans
salt and pepper to taste

Preheat oven to 400 degrees. Pat fillets dry with a paper towel. Spread a thin layer of mustard and mayonnaise on top of each fillet. Top with a generous amount of pecans. Season fillets and place them in a lightly greased ovenproof dish. Bake for 8 to 10 minutes until fish flakes easily. Serves 2.

🌿 CRAB AND SHRIMP WHITE PIZZA 🌿

1 lemon wedge
1 9-inch tortilla
2 slices provolone cheese
2 slices muenster cheese
3 ounces fresh jumbo lump crabmeat, picked
4 small shrimp, cooked and diced
1 teaspoon chopped fresh basil
¼ teaspoon garlic powder
1 teaspoon chopped fresh parsley
2 teaspoons grated Parmesan cheese

Preheat oven to 350 degrees. Squeeze lemon over tortilla. Top tortilla with provolone and muenster; cut up slices to cover tortilla evenly. Spread crabmeat and shrimp evenly over cheeses. Lightly dust top of pizza with remaining ingredients. Place tortilla on a baking stone or an oiled baking sheet and bake for 5 to 7 minutes until edges start to become crisp. Serves 1.

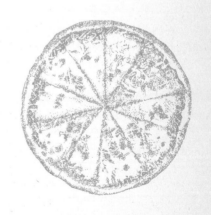

Fair Hill Inn

MD 273 and MD 213
Fair Hill, MD 21921
www.fairhillinn.com
410-398-4187

The Mitchell House sits atop a knoll at the crossroads of MD 273 and MD 213. In the spring, the grounds are awash with color as the immaculate landscaping comes to life. Listed on the National Register of Historic Homes, the stone structure dates to the 1700s. During its long history, the building has been used as a post office, a store, and a hotel, as indicated by an 1838 map.

Dr. Abraham Mitchell, a well-known area physician who used his Elkton home as a hospital for Continental soldiers during the Revolutionary War, bought the house and two hundred acres from John Strawbridge in 1781. Dr. Mitchell retired to this country home, where he spent his final days. After his death, the property was left to his son, Colonel George Mitchell, himself a physician but perhaps better known for his political accomplishments. An officer in the War of 1812, George Mitchell also served his country during three terms as a United States congressman. As such, he had the honor of introducing the Marquis de Lafayette to Congress on his revisit to this country. Lafayette visited George Mitchell at the Fair Hill estate and later sent a gift of cherry trees that were planted on the grounds. The Cecil County Historical Society has copies of correspondence between these two international friends.

The Colonial Room at what is now the Fair Hill Inn is the dining room in the oldest part of the structure. Here, fieldstone walls, exposed beams, and a walk-in fireplace create a truly charming ambiance. The Mitchell Room features a double fireplace that dates to 1764. The Hunt Room utilizes wood paneling, fireplaces, original art, and antiques to create a cozy atmosphere. The fourth dining room, the Victorian Room, is used primarily for private parties.

The inn serves lunch, dinner, and Sunday brunch. Many of the menu items reflect the Italian heritage of the Graziano family, who have operated the restaurant since the late 1970s. Tortellini Stuffed with Veal and Linguine Alla Carbonara are two of the many choices. The Breast of Chicken di Saronno, concocted of chicken sautéed with amaretto, orange, and toasted almonds, is wonderfully innovative. I enjoyed the Veal Saltimbocca, with its combination of prosciutto, mozzarella, brandy, and Sage Sauce. I was sorry Debbie couldn't be there to sample it, too. The lunch menu features a delicious Fillet of Flounder Meuniere and an interesting Tuna Salad with apples and pecans, served on a bed of mesclun greens. Egg offerings such as a quiche du jour, Eggs Benedict, and an omelet du jour make for a unique lunch. The traditional Maryland crab dishes available for lunch and dinner range from Backfin Crabmeat Cocktail to Crab Imperial to Mushrooms Stuffed with Crab.

Mr. and Mrs. Anthony Graziano bought the property in 1978. At that time, it was nothing more than a dilapidated old house, its history shrouded in years of neglect. After authentic restoration, the Fair Hill Inn has proudly recaptured the aura of its early years.

BREAST OF CHICKEN DI SARONNO

2 tablespoons sliced almonds
2 chicken breasts
1/3 cup flour
1 egg, beaten
2 tablespoons vegetable oil
1/4 cup chicken stock
1/2 cup amaretto
1 orange, separated into sections
2 tablespoons whole butter
zest of 1 orange
1 teaspoon chopped parsley

Preheat oven to 375 degrees. Toast almonds and set aside. Dredge chicken in flour, then dip in egg. Heat oil in a sauté pan. Sauté chicken in oil for 3 to 4 minutes on each side. Remove chicken from sauté pan and place in a baking dish. Place chicken in oven for 12 to 15 minutes. Degrease sauté pan, then deglaze it first with chicken stock, then with amaretto. Reduce by half. Finish sauce with orange sections and butter. Plate chicken, top with sauce, and garnish with almonds, orange zest, and parsley. Serves 2. Note: The Fair Hill Inn uses Amaretto di Saronno.

MUSSEL SOUP WITH CURRY

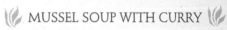

100 black-shelled mussels
4 cups white wine
1 onion, diced fine
8 cups heavy cream
1/2 cup butter, chopped
curry to taste

Steam mussels with white wine and onions in a large stockpot until mussels open. Remove mussels from pot and add cream. Bring to a light simmer. Remove mussels from shells and add back to soup with all the juices. Discard shells. Before serving, stir in butter and season with curry. Serves 12.

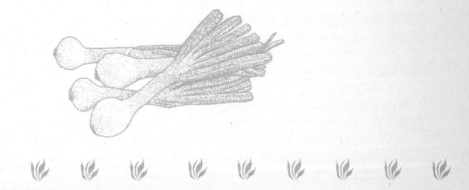

Owl Bar

1 East Chase Street
Baltimore, MD 21202
www.theowlbar.com
410-347-0888

The Owl Bar is located off the lobby of what was once the Belvedere Hotel, built in 1903. The opening of the structure on December 14 of that year was the social event of the season. The hotel was erected on land that was once part of the vast estate of General John Eager Howard, one of the heroes of the American Revolution, and was named after the Howard mansion, Belvedere. The Democratic National Convention that nominated Woodrow Wilson was a ten-day event held at the Belvedere in 1912. Today, the building is well known as a Wednesday-night dance destination. The old hotel also includes Truffles, a lovely dining room used for catered events.

We may have missed The Owl Bar altogether if it hadn't been for a chance comment made by someone sitting nearby at dinner one evening. Fortunately, we heeded the tip, arriving at The Owl Bar for a late-evening bite to eat. The décor in the dining area is more opulent than the eatery's name would suggest, yet the ambiance is comfortable, with an air of centuries past. Some reviewers have described it as having Germanic overtones, noting its leaded-glass windows and dark-stained wood. Our favorite touch was the vaulted ceiling. The tile floors and period murals hinted that Shakespeare just might have been at the next table. Through further research, we discovered that The Owl Bar was at one time known as the Falstaff Room, so we weren't too far off the mark. The feature of The Owl Bar that stands out in most people's minds is the elaborate herringbone brickwork in the pub area.

Karen enjoyed the Wedge Salad but would have been equally happy with the Chicken Stir-Fry Salad, the unusual Almond-Encrusted Brie Salad, or the Blackened Blue Salad, all of which sounded tasty. Chili, Quesadillas, Crab Cakes, and sandwiches such as a Fried Oyster Po-Boy and a Turkey Melt with Cranberry and Pepper Jelly appear on the menu. However, it's not just bar food here. Offerings such as Butternut Squash Risotto, Coconut Peanut Chicken, and Clams Casino are also available.

At one time, the Belvedere was one of the premier hotels in Baltimore. Done in the Beaux-Arts style, it offered four hundred rooms in the city's upscale Mount Vernon Square neighborhood. Lining the lobby today are hotel memorabilia and photographs of folks who have visited. Among the guests were political figures such as members of the Kennedy family, President Taft, Harry Truman, George and Barbara Bush, and Chiang Kai-shek and entertainers like Richard Dreyfuss, Sarah Bernhardt, Tommy Dorsey, Henry Fonda, Clark Gable, Al Pacino, Roy Rogers, and the Smothers brothers. Other notables such as David Brinkley, John Philip Sousa, Kirstie Alley, Mitch Miller, Jack Dempsey, Anna Pavlova, and Tim Allen have also visited. This is a wide range of folks, to be sure. Then again, The Owl Bar is the kind of place that appeals to just about everyone.

POTATO CHIPS WITH BLUE CHEESE FONDUE AND CHIVES

peanut oil
2 baking potatoes, washed
sea salt and freshly ground pepper to taste
1 clove garlic, sliced
2 tablespoons dry white wine
¼ cup heavy cream
8 ounces blue cheese, crumbled
2 tablespoons chopped chives

Heat oil to 325 degrees in a deep, heavy pot. Thinly slice potatoes using an Oriental vegetable slicer. Cook potato slices in hot oil in small batches until golden brown and crispy. Place chips on a paper towel to drain. Season with sea salt and pepper. To make fondue, rub garlic on bottom of a medium saucepan. Add wine and cream. Bring to a boil, then reduce heat. Add blue cheese slowly, stirring to incorporate. Continue to stir until creamy and smooth. Place potato chips in a serving bowl. Pour fondue over chips and garnish with chives. Serves 2.

MARYLAND OLD BAY STEAMED SHRIMP

2 ears sweet white corn, shucked
½ cup unsalted butter
12 16-20 count shrimp, shells on
1 large sweet onion, diced
4 Red Bliss potatoes, quartered
3 tablespoons Old Bay seasoning
1 lemon, cut into wedges
2 tablespoons chopped parsley

Cut corn into 1-inch segments. Slice butter into 8 tablespoons and bring to room temperature. Put shrimp, onions, potatoes, and corn in a steamer or a double boiler and steam for 10 to 15 minutes until shrimp are cooked. Put butter slices in a large mixing bowl. Pour shrimp into mixing bowl with butter and stir to coat. Add Old Bay and stir until coated evenly. Decorate with lemon wedges and garnish with parsley. Serves 2.

12 Broad Street
Berlin, MD 21811
www.globetheater.com
410-641-0784

We were out exploring downtown Berlin, shopping in the few spare minutes before we made a northern trek through the Eastern Shore. Our favorite discovery of the morning was the Globe Theater & Bistro. Initially, this 1907 building was the town's first garage. When the garage closed around 1917, the structure was converted into another local first, becoming Berlin's inaugural movie theater.

Today, the old theater has been adapted to a multitude of uses. In the old balcony area, owner Kate Hastings has created an art gallery. Karen perused the wide range of exhibits, all for sale, while I scribbled a few notes. The lobby has been converted into a gift shop that stocks a wide range of interesting and unusual items. We then meandered to the wine shop, café, and coffee bar. Some locals stop in for a cup of coffee and a quick chat, while others grab a muffin on the go. For dining in, guests are seated on a large section of the theater's old stage, where the walls have been painted a dramatic deep eggplant. This section of the building is further defined by the traditional red velvet stage curtains and the brass stands with red velveteen ropes that once cordoned moviegoers into orderly lines.

The interesting menu changes regularly. It might include items such as a Lobster and Crab Martini and a Wasabi Crab Cake with Mango Tartar Sauce. For those wanting a sandwich, Fresh Fish and Bistro Steak Sandwiches appear on the menu, as does a Boneless Chicken Breast Sandwich with South of the Border Rub. The list of dinner entrées is brief but quite appealing. The seafood selections include Crab Salad and Shrimp Fra Diavlo, which consists of spicy tomatoes, onions, peppers, and shrimp over linguine. The Breast of Chicken Eugene is made of chicken layered with sage dressing, country ham, and sautéed mushroom caps.

We made our selection from the "Sandwiches Made to Order" menu. These choices are all named for movie stars, reflecting the bistro's origins. We considered the Mae West, described as "a big, lean roast beef sandwich served on a Kaiser roll," but opted for the Uncle Miltie, a smoked turkey wrap with Herb Cream Cheese, avocado, tomato, sprouts, and cucumbers. Half of the wrap was an ample lunch portion for each of us, and we both thoroughly enjoyed the freshness of the vegetables tucked inside.

Not only does the Globe function as a gift shop, restaurant, and gallery, but the theater portion is still viable as well. Kate brings in a variety of entertainment ranging from rhythm-and-blues bands to classical performances to comedians. Plays are frequently offered in a dinner-theater format. The movie *Runaway Bride* starring Julia Roberts and Richard Gere was filmed in Berlin. Considering all that the Globe and its community have to offer, it's a place we'd definitely run to!

🌿 CRAB SALAD WITH 🌿 FRIED GREEN TOMATOES

¼ cup mayonnaise
zest of 1 lemon
juice of 1 lemon
1 green onion, chopped
1 teaspoon capers
½ pound crabmeat, picked
salt and white pepper to taste
1 cup breadcrumbs
¾ cup flour
2 medium green tomatoes
½ cup peanut oil

Place mayonnaise, lemon zest, lemon juice, green onions, capers, and crabmeat into a medium bowl and toss gently to combine. Season to taste. Allow mixture to sit in the refrigerator for at least 30 minutes.

Combine breadcrumbs and flour in a shallow dish. Season to taste. Slice each tomato into 3 equal slices and dredge in breadcrumb mixture. Place peanut oil in a heavy skillet and heat on high. Fry tomato slices until golden brown on each side. Be careful not to overcook. Place fried tomato slices on 2 plates and top each slice with ⅙ of crab mixture. Serves 2.

🌿 GREEN TOMATO LOBSTER BISQUE 🌿

10 tablespoons butter, divided
¾ cup flour
4 medium shallots, chopped
3 medium green tomatoes, chopped
1 clove fresh garlic, chopped
2 1¼-pound lobsters
1 teaspoon pickling spice
⅓ cup heavy cream
¼ cup dry sherry
salt and pepper to taste
fresh tarragon, chopped

Melt 6 tablespoons butter in a small saucepan over low heat. Add flour and whisk to make a roux. Continue to cook over low heat until smooth and shiny. Set aside. Place shallots, tomatoes, and garlic in a food processor and purée until smooth. Set aside. Place enough water in a large pot to cover lobsters. Add pickling spice. Bring water to a boil and add lobsters. Simmer for 20 minutes until lobsters are cooked. Remove lobsters from liquid and set aside to cool. Strain liquid through a fine sieve and set aside also. Split lobsters and pick out meat. Dice meat, leaving claws for garnish.

Melt remaining butter in a large sauté pan and sauté puréed vegetables for 3 minutes. Add reserved lobster stock and bring to a simmer. Add roux a little at a time until mixture is desired thickness. Remove from heat and add cream and sherry. Stir to combine. Add lobster meat and stir to combine. Adjust seasonings. Serve garnished with lobster claws and tarragon. Serves 6 to 8.

901 Fawn Street
Baltimore, MD 21202
www.sabatinos.com
410-727-9414

Sabatino's is an experience not to be missed. Rarely have I come across staff more concerned about my comfort and well-being. The whole experience was just like coming home. From the moment I stepped across the threshold to be welcomed by owner Vincent Culotta until I left the building, when careful inquiries were made about my travel arrangements, I felt like family. It was very clear that other guests felt that way about the experience, too.

Located at the corner of Fawn and High Streets, the entrance to the restaurant is housed in what used to be the neighborhood candy store. The single column that holds up the corner of the building is most distinctive. Many of the older residents in Baltimore's Little Italy remember purchasing candy here. As time passed, the store's name changed from Granese's to Lou's to Corky's.

The building was purchased by two Italian immigrants in February 1955. Friends Joseph Canzani and Sabatino Luperini combined their resources and talents to open a small restaurant.

Seating only 50 guests, it was a success almost immediately. Delicious food served in generous portions kept them in business. Now, five decades and three expansions later, Sabatino's encompasses three row houses and seats 450. The exteriors of the row houses have been maintained individually with separate colors, stoops, and chimneys. On the inside, it is still possible to tell in which house you are seated, whether it's the last house purchased or the confectionary where Sabatino's began.

The tradition of preparing family recipes with the freshest and finest ingredients shows in every dish brought to the table. The choices are extensive. After much thought, I chose the Veal Saltimbocca, preceded by a large salad with delicious, creamy Italian Dressing. The veal was done to perfection, pounded extremely thin and nestled in Sherry and White Wine Sauce. Other guests around me were clearly enjoying the Eggplant Parmigiana, the Chicken Vincenzo, and the Baked Rigatoni. The Lasagna—with its homemade pasta ribbons layered in tomato sauce, ricotta, mozzarella, ground veal, salami, and mushrooms—sounded wonderful, as did Sabatino's Special Appetizer, a sampling of the most popular appetizers, including Clams Casino, Shrimp Renato, and Sautéed Sausage and Green Peppers, served with wedges of Garlic Bread. I could not resist sampling the Garlic Bread myself. It was fabulous—crisp on the outside, moist in the center, and very delicately flavored. Debbie would have loved it!

Dessert was another difficult choice. After hearing descriptions of the Spumoni, the Chocolate Cheesecake, the Tiramisu, and many others, I finally decided on a Cannoli, which was definitely the best I've ever had. It's perfectly clear why generations of loyal customers have returned time and again to Sabatino's. Frank Sinatra and Liberace both ate here. Rumor has it that when Anthony Quinn was in town for a two-week theater run of *Zorba the Greek*, he dined here seven times. What a testimony to the delicious food and the dedicated employees!

🌿 VEAL SALTIMBOCCA 🌿

1 to 2 pounds veal scaloppine
salt and pepper to taste
3 tablespoons butter
4 tablespoons oil
2 tablespoons flour
¾ cup sherry
¾ cup white wine
juice of ¼ lemon
¾ cup chicken broth
8 thick slices mozzarella cheese
4 or 5 thin slices prosciutto
fresh parsley, chopped

Turn on broiler and place top oven rack into highest available slot. Pound each slice of veal between layers of wax paper. Season with salt and pepper. In a heavy skillet, heat butter and oil and sauté veal until thoroughly cooked; the time required will vary depending on thickness of veal. Remove veal and set aside on a warm platter. Add flour to pan and whisk until smooth. Add sherry, wine, lemon juice, and chicken broth, stirring constantly until well mixed and smooth. Simmer for 3 minutes. Sauce should achieve a thick consistency. Place veal in a single layer on an ovenproof platter. Pour sauce over veal. Top each piece of veal with a slice of moz-

zarella. Cut prosciutto into 1-inch-square pieces and scatter them over veal. Place platter on top rack under broiler until cheese is melted. Garnish with parsley and serve. Serves 4.

🌿 RIGATONI WITH VEAL SAUCE 🌿

½ cup sliced mushrooms
¼ cup olive oil
½ cup fresh green peas
1 clove garlic, chopped
½ pound ground veal
½ cup dry sherry
¼ cup sweet Marsala
½ cup butter, melted
2 cups tomato sauce
½ to 1 pound rigatoni
Parmesan cheese, grated

In a heavy skillet, sauté mushrooms in oil for 2 to 3 minutes until almost done. Add peas and garlic and sauté an additional 1 to 2 minutes. Mix in veal and cook until browned. Drain grease and set aside. In a small bowl, combine sherry, Marsala, and butter. Add tomato sauce and stir well to combine. Add tomato mixture to sauté pan and bring to a boil. Reduce heat and allow to simmer for 10 to 15 minutes. Cook rigatoni al dente. Drain. Add veal sauce to rigatoni and toss to combine. Serve with Parmesan. Serves 2.

HARRISON'S CHESAPEAKE·HOUSE

21551 Chesapeake House Drive
Tilghman Island, MD 21671
www.chesapeakehouse.com
410-886-2121

There is something about the quiet whir of a ceiling fan overhead. Regardless of how rapidly it's spinning, its quiet hum serves to slow down those things around it. We witnessed this phenomenon as we arrived at this end-of-the-road locale ready for our first meal of the day. The sportfishermen had long since had their six o'clock breakfast and were out enjoying the "Buddy Plan," a program available at the Chesapeake House that offers fishermen an ample breakfast, a hearty box lunch, eight hours of fishing, and a belt-stretching dinner. The fleet is captained by Buddy Harrison, Buddy Jr., and other local fishermen. Through the hundred-plus years that the family has been in business, it has amassed the largest privately owned fishing fleet in the United States.

Although the oldest part of the building dates to 1856, the Harrison family didn't entertain its first guests until ten years after the Civil War. In the Victorian era, paddle-wheelers crossed the bay, bringing ladies with parasols and gentlemen in bowler hats ready to escape the hustle and bustle of Baltimore, Philadelphia, and New York as they summered on Tilghman Island. Captain Levin Harrison's reputation for hospitality, quality sportfishing, and fabulous country cooking quickly became well known. When Senator Barry Goldwater visited, he called Miss Alice (Mrs. Alice Harrison), daughter-in-law of the original Captain Harrison, "the world's greatest hostess." Today, Levin F. Harrison IV, Alice's grandson, represents the fourth generation involved in managing the business. Six grandsons of Captain Buddy (Levin Harrison III) are at the helm and behind the rod, keeping this unique family history alive.

Even if you aren't a fisherman, Harrison's Chesapeake House is not to be missed. The dining room has been changed over the years, but not the menu. Many restaurants try to please all the people all the time, but in making that attempt, they end up not doing anything terribly well. Instead, Harrison's has long understood that its success comes from the fresh seafood and comfort foods traditionally served to guests. Eastern Shore specialties like Chesapeake Surf and Turf, Maryland Fried Chicken, Backfin Crab Cakes, homemade Coleslaw, hot rolls, and vegetables served family-style are but a few of the items available to sate even the hungriest of guests.

Since we were there for breakfast, we enjoyed a different version of home-style cooking. Debbie's plate was crammed with two eggs over easy, Home Fries, bacon, and rye toast. Karen's Western Omelet was absolutely stuffed with ham, mushrooms, peppers, and onions. The serving sizes were ample enough to get us through most of the day.

Family, friends, and guests are all-important

to the Harrisons. Photos of astronauts, presidents, and sports figures hang on the wall. After our experience, we can wholeheartedly agree with the popular description of Harrison's Chesapeake House as a Fourth of July picnic that goes on all year long. Bring on the fireworks!

YEAST ROLLS

½ cup milk
3 tablespoons sugar
3 tablespoons shortening
1 teaspoon salt
½ cup cold water
1 package yeast
¼ cup warm water
3 to 3½ cups all-purpose flour
1 egg, beaten

In a saucepan, combine milk, sugar, shortening, and salt. Heat almost to boiling. Remove from heat, add cold water, and set aside. Dissolve yeast in warm water. Mix in 3 cups flour. Add extra flour as needed to make dough workable. Knead until dough becomes elastic. Put dough in a bowl, cover it with a cloth, and set it in a warm place. Let dough rise about 1½ hours until it doubles in size. Preheat oven to 400 degrees. To form cloverleaf rolls, pinch off small balls of dough, place 3 small balls in each cup of a lightly greased muffin tin, and let rise again. Brush top of each roll with egg. Bake for about 15 minutes until golden brown. Yields 2 dozen rolls.

BROILED STRIPED BASS

⅔ cup butter
2 teaspoons lemon juice
salt and pepper to taste
1 medium onion, cut into 6 slices
2 strips bacon, cut in half
2 striped bass fillets
2 dashes of paprika

Melt butter and simmer with lemon juice and salt and pepper. Place 3 slices onion and 2 half-strips bacon on each fillet. Pour lemon butter over fillets and cook under broiler until lightly browned. Sprinkle with paprika and serve immediately. Serves 2.

BACKFIN CRAB CAKES

1 tablespoon prepared mustard
1 tablespoon mayonnaise
salt and pepper to taste
1 egg, beaten
1 teaspoon chopped fresh parsley
¾ teaspoon Old Bay seasoning
⅓ cup saltine cracker crumbs or fine breadcrumbs
1 pound backfin crabmeat, picked
1 cup shortening

In a large bowl, combine all ingredients except crabmeat and shortening. Add crabmeat, handling carefully so as not to break up lumps. Shape mixture into 8 patties and fry in very hot shortening in a heavy skillet. Serves 4.

103 Frederick Road
Thurmont, MD 21788
www.cozyvillage.com
301-271-4301

If buffet dining is a pastime of yours, then this is a place not to be missed. Offering eleven dining rooms, each with its own personality, and a buffet with even more choices, Historic Cozy Restaurant makes it impossible not to find something to suit your palate. Wilbur R. Freeze began this unique establishment in 1929. It has grown from just 12 stools to a space that will accommodate up to 750. To date, over 20 million people have enjoyed what is called "the Cozy experience," which means different things to different people. Some come for day trips, others for romantic getaways, some to shop, some to be entertained. But almost all come to feast. In the past, guests have enjoyed the company of such notables as Winston Churchill, Babe Ruth, and Tennessee Williams!

We arrived for lunch on a frigid winter day. We couldn't think of a better way to escape the snow and freezing rain than by sating ourselves with the sumptuous buffet offerings. Not surprisingly, we were unable to sample everything we wanted from among the nearly eighty items. The Barbecued Ribs and the Fried Catfish were both yummy, and the Chicken Wings and the Lasagna were equally good. We vowed to not taste the same things, in an attempt to cover the widest range of choices possible, but before we knew it, we were sharing our favorites, including the delicious Seafood Casserole and the Fried Shrimp. Add to that nearly thirty homemade dessert offerings—including Apple Crumb Pie, Lemon Meringue Pie, and Spice Cake—and it would take a small army, or at least many enjoyable visits, to try it all.

The Cozy prides itself on using only the freshest and finest ingredients. To that end, many of the herbs and vegetables are home-grown in the village's gardens. The desserts and breads are baked fresh each day to ensure the most delicious dining experience possible.

Although the location of Camp David is supposed to be secret, it is, in fact, near Cozy Village, situated in the lovely Catoctin Mountains. Because of this, the restaurant has become a kind of unofficial headquarters for the news media when the president happens to be in the area. Back in 1979, the Russian entourage that accompanied Leonid Brezhnev to Camp David set up shop here, installing a telephone line linked straight to Moscow. Several showcases at the restaurant are filled with pictures, autographs, and miscellaneous memorabilia of those who have visited, including not only the media but presidents and other political dignitaries as well. Even the rooms at the Cozy Inn are decorated to celebrate the lives, accomplishments, and personalities of the many politicians who have either visited the Cozy or Camp David. Rather than "Hail to the Chief," we're sure many media members and politicos have left here humming "Hail to the Chef" instead.

4 cups milk
½ cup margarine
2 15-ounce cans fruit cocktail (no cherries)
1 cup raisins
1 loaf stale cinnamon or raisin bread
6 eggs
1½ cups sugar
1½ teaspoons vanilla
1 teaspoon nutmeg
2 teaspoons cinnamon
¾ teaspoon salt
½ cup rum sauce

Preheat oven to 300 degrees. Scald milk in a large saucepan. Add margarine and allow to melt. Remove from heat. Drain syrup from fruit and set fruit aside. Add syrup and raisins to milk mixture. Cut bread into ¼-inch cubes and place in a large bowl. Add milk mixture and stir until bread is soaked. Allow to stand 10 minutes. In a medium bowl, beat eggs until foamy. Beat in sugar, vanilla, nutmeg, cinnamon, and salt. Add to bread mixture. Add fruit and stir gently to combine; avoid mashing bread. Butter an 8-by-12-inch baking dish. Fill with bread mixture. Bake for 2 hours until golden brown. Cool thoroughly. Drizzle with rum sauce. Reheat to serve. Serves 12.

TURKEY CORN SOUP

7 cups turkey broth
1 cup chopped celery
16-ounce can whole-kernel corn
2 tablespoons butter
¼ teaspoon salt
¼ teaspoon pepper
1 tablespoon plus 2 teaspoons sugar
¼ teaspoon dried thyme
1½ teaspoons dried parsley
1½ teaspoons chicken bouillon
6 ounces turkey scraps, chopped
6 tablespoons flour
1 egg yolk

In a large soup pot, combine turkey broth and all remaining ingredients except flour and egg yolk. Bring to a boil, then reduce heat and simmer for 30 minutes, stirring often. Mix flour with egg yolk and crumble on top of soup. Stir and cook an additional 10 minutes. Serves 6.

CHAPTER 4

Out and About

Baldwin's Station

With the advent of the Industrial Revolution, this country changed from a predominantly rural farming economy to one that was much more diversified. This chapter encompasses a wide variety of establishments, from schools to stores, from carriage houses to train stations. What were once functional sites for folks living in these communities are now eateries serving up good food and history side by side.

Mrs K's Toll House

9201 Colesville Road
Silver Spring, MD 20910
www.mrsks.com
301-589-3500

From horse-and-buggy days until World War I, this building was a tollhouse where travelers had to stop and pay a toll for the use and upkeep of the road. The cost to traverse the Washington, Colesville, and Ashton Turnpike was two cents per horse and conveyance—the same price as sending a letter by U.S. Mail. Old receipts and photos of the era hang throughout the restaurant, including a picture of Mr. Allen, the gatekeeper, whose age in the picture is nearly a hundred. After many years as a tollhouse, the structure became a tearoom, then a popular local roadhouse where Kate Smith once sang.

In 1931, Mr. and Mrs. K (Kreuzberg) bought the roadhouse and began serving good American food amongst their antique collection. The Kreuzbergs had a wide collection of pottery and glass, including pressed-glass plates that have been fashioned, quite literally, into a plate-glass window. One of the all-time favorite pieces is the mouse clock in the lobby, created with the nursery rhyme "Hickory, dickory, dock" in mind. The current owners have made great efforts to maintain Blanche Kreuzberg's vision, still displaying her vast collection. Guests can view an extensive array of Lutz glass in a glass case lining the wall of one of the dining rooms. Blanche's Staffordshire china was displayed on a shelf and in cabinets throughout the room where I dined. An interesting assortment of maxims by Benjamin Franklin, many from *Poor Richard's Almanac*, are mounted in the dining room to the left of the lobby, a room reminiscent of *Snow White and the Seven Dwarfs* because of its adorable coziness.

Arriving just a little ahead of our reservation time, we marveled at the profusion of flowers in the window boxes and planting beds. We enjoyed the beautiful, immaculate gardens before Karen headed off to another appointment. I was quite happy to be seated with a view of the grounds so I could enjoy them a little longer. At Mrs. K's, it has long been the tradition for every entrée, whether at lunch or dinner, to be served with an appetizer, salad, and dessert. The restaurant also offers a buffet for lunch and Sunday brunch. I chose to partake of the buffet. The choices were numerous and delicious. I sampled Chicken Marsala, Barbecued Beef over Rice Pilaf, Halibut in Cream Sauce, Grilled Salmon, Fettuccine Alfredo, Roasted Potatoes, Creamed Spinach, and Green Beans. Had I ordered off the menu, I may have chosen the Chilled Spanish Soup or the Stuffed Grape Leaves with Cucumber Dill Sauce to start, followed by the Rainbow Trout or the Roast Turkey and Dressing. The dessert choices were equally appealing. The Bar Cookie, the Cheesecake, and the Bread Pudding with Lemon Sauce were all quite tasty. Whether you dine from the à la carte menu or the buffet, it's great food at a great price, so a stop at Mrs. K's is well worth today's toll!

CHICKEN CHESAPEAKE

½ small onion, diced
½ cup mayonnaise
juice of 1 lemon
2 teaspoons Old Bay seasoning
2 dashes Worcestershire sauce
Tabasco sauce to taste
1 pound jumbo lump crabmeat, picked
4 boneless, skinless chicken breasts, butterflied
¼ cup water
4 ¼-inch-thick slices ham
¼ cup breadcrumbs
¼ cup shredded Parmesan cheese
paprika to taste

Preheat oven to 400 degrees. In a medium bowl, combine onions, mayonnaise, lemon juice, Old Bay, Worcestershire, and Tabasco. Being careful not to break up lumps, gently fold crabmeat into mayonnaise mixture until well mixed. Stuff each chicken breast with ¼ of crab mixture. Pour water into a 9-by-9-inch pan to prevent meat from sticking during baking. Lay ham slices on bottom of pan. Place each stuffed chicken breast atop a ham slice. Sprinkle chicken with breadcrumbs and Parmesan. Sprinkle with paprika. Bake for about 30 minutes until done. Serves 4.

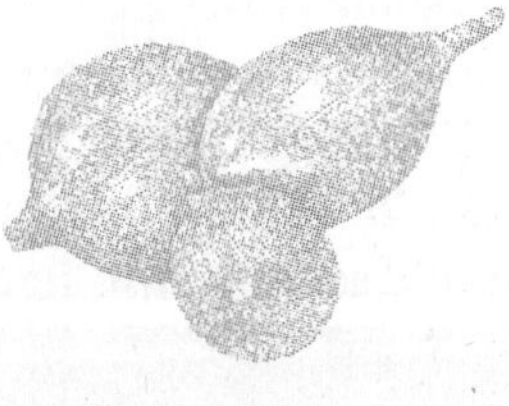

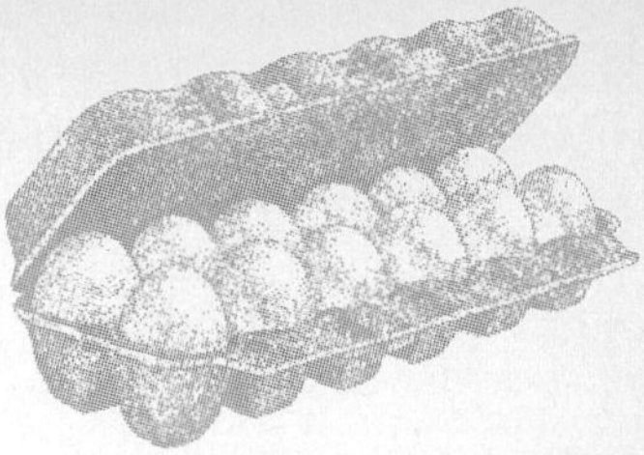

BREAD PUDDING

1 loaf brioche or egg-based bread
½ cup raisins, divided
2 teaspoons cinnamon, divided
½ cup sugar, divided
4 eggs
4 cups milk
1 teaspoon vanilla

Preheat oven to 350 degrees. Crumble half the bread into a lightly greased 10-by-12-inch baking dish. Sprinkle half the raisins evenly over bread. Sprinkle with 1 teaspoon cinnamon and 2 tablespoons sugar. Repeat ingredients to make a second layer. In a separate bowl, beat together eggs, milk, vanilla, and remaining sugar. Pour mixture over bread. Push down with a spoon to help bread absorb liquid. Let sit for 20 minutes. Bake for 35 to 40 minutes until set. Serves 6 to 8.

Brick Ridge

6212 Ridge Road
Mount Airy, MD 21771
www.brickridge.com
301-829-8191

In the mid-1800s, the Cabbage Spring School made its home on what is now the Brick Ridge property. The restaurant is situated in the building known as Ridge Number Four. Patrons can read a plaque above the front entrance that states that the structure served as the Ridge School for more than fifty years, from the time it was built in 1892 until it closed in 1947. Like many schoolhouses of that period, it was built of brick and originally had only one room. A single teacher taught as many as twenty to thirty students ranging from six to twenty years of age.

The building has since been expanded. Bricks brought in from reclaimed sites of the same period and beams from an old farmhouse have been added, so the expansion looks as though it has always been here. I found it absolutely charming. The polished wooden floors and brick walls are enhanced by the white-and-green table linens. The lighting is subdued, and the tiny tea lights on each table add an intimate feel. Even the chairs are reminiscent of school days long ago. The traditional American flag flapping in the wind outside the main entrance completes the atmosphere.

The Brick Ridge culinary team prides itself on its wide variety of classic and contemporary menu items. However, in keeping with the fine tradition of education in this building, the staff is also pleased to offer a little education in regional American cuisine. Each week, the Brick Ridge features traditional items from a selected state in the nation. Todd Bricken, the owner, hopes that diners will enjoy becoming acquainted with the diverse foods and cultures that have shaped American cuisine.

The featured cuisine on the night I visited was from Alabama. All around me, patrons were enjoying Sloe Gin Rickeys, a delicious concoction of sloe gin, Lemon Syrup, and Blackcurrant Syrup over ice. One of the featured entrées was Pan-Fried Catfish with Tarragon Cream and Sweet Gulf Shrimp. Equally appealing from the regular menu were the Pecan-Encrusted Salmon, the Maryland Crab Cakes, and the Porterman's Pie, a casserole of meats and mushrooms topped with whipped potatoes and cheddar, baked golden brown. Debbie would have been as tempted by the Fried Green Tomatoes as I was by the Charleston Cream of Crab Soup. However, I eventually opted for the delicious Sausage Puffs, bite-sized spicy sausage wrapped in puff pastry, served with Creole Mustard Sauce. My catfish was divine but unfortunately left no room for any of the fabulous desserts. Debbie and I will return another day to continue our education with Mascarpone Pie, Chocolate Torte, Applesauce Cake, or Bread Pudding with Bourbon Sauce. This old schoolhouse certainly taught me a few new things!

PECAN-ENCRUSTED SALMON

15-ounce can mandarin oranges, puréed
3 tablespoons brown sugar
¼ cup golden rum
1½ tablespoons cornstarch
2 pounds salmon, skinned
1½ cups chopped pecans
2 tablespoons oil
salt and pepper to taste

Preheat oven to 375 degrees. In a medium saucepan, combine orange purée and brown sugar. Bring to a boil. In a small bowl, combine rum and cornstarch until a slurry is obtained. Add slowly to boiling mandarin mixture and stir until sauce thickens. Remove from heat. Divide salmon into 4 portions. Press chopped nuts into both sides of salmon. Heat oil in a large ovenproof sauté pan over high heat. Add salmon to pan presentation side down. Season with salt and pepper. Cook about 4 minutes until pecans are light brown. Turn salmon over and bake in oven for 5 to 7 minutes. Serve with reserved sauce. Serves 4.

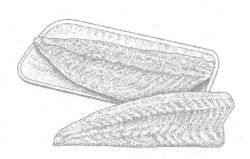

TWIN CITIES CHICKEN

1 cup cooked white and wild rice
1 cup shredded Havarti cheese
½ teaspoon dill
4 boneless chicken breasts
salt and pepper to taste
½ cup flour
1 tablespoon oil
1 tablespoon butter
1 tablespoon chopped shallots
2 tablespoons white wine

Preheat oven to 375 degrees. In a small bowl, combine rice, cheese, and dill. Make a horizontal slice in each chicken breast. Season inside of each breast with salt and pepper and stuff with ¼ of rice mixture. Dust each breast with flour. In a large ovenproof sauté pan, heat oil over high heat. Carefully place chicken topside first in hot oil. Sauté until golden, then carefully turn over. Bake for about 15 minutes until internal temperature reaches 165 degrees. Melt butter in a small sauté pan and sauté shallots until tender. Add wine and season to taste. Bring to a simmer. Continue to simmer until liquid is reduced by half. Plate chicken and cover each breast with ¼ of the sauce. Serves 4.

Kendall's
Steak & Seafood

106 North West Street
Easton, MD 21601
www.kendallsinc.net
410-822-9898

At Kendall's, the Cobb Salad is topped with backfin crab to make it a truly Maryland-inspired concoction. This is just one of several ways that seafood appears on the menu. Yellowfin Tuna, Crab and Corn Chowder, and Oyster Pie are a few of the others. The latter would have been Karen's choice, had she been along. I chose the Maryland Crab Cakes, one of the house specialties. As an early-bird option, it's served with an ample salad. I dressed mine with the Honey Dijon, made on the premises, as are all the salad dressings. All meals are accompanied by warm bread with tasty Orange Blossom Honey Butter. In addition to seafood, the menu features Chicken Piccata, Pasta Alfredo, Lamb Chops, and several steak options for which the restaurant has gained quite a reputation. On another dinner visit, I may try the Stuffed Chicken with Boursin and Wild Mushrooms. At lunch, I might choose the Open-Faced Tarragon Chicken Salad or the Oyster Po-Boy.

Don R. Kendall, Jr., and his mother, Barbara (known around Easton as "Bobi"), opened this eatery in 2004. Don has many years of restaurant experience, including training with Paul Prudhomme, Robert Greaualt, and Walter Scheibe, chef de cuisine for President George W. Bush. As a matter of fact, Scheibe brought chefs from around the world to Kendall's in July 2004 as part of the Chef to Chef program.

The friendly, helpful service mirrors the building's sunny exterior. The cheery yellow paint trimmed with burgundy shutters offers street appeal. This feeling is carried through indoors, as the same colors create a happy, casual, restful dining room. Maize table linens with burgundy napkins coordinate with chairs upholstered in burgundy and yellow. Seated at a table near one of the windows, I enjoyed the pleasant spring breeze as it wafted through.

What is today Kendall's Steak & Seafood was once the site of Easton's livery. Built in the late 1800s, the building retains its sloping straw ceiling, today unobtrusive under a coat of white paint. During the Roaring Twenties, Cadillacs and Chryslers replaced horses as G. R. Warner and Brothers operated an automobile showroom on the premises. Two decades later, a glass shop was opened on this site by Albert Smith. For nearly fifty years, Smith provided glass for homes, businesses, and automobiles belonging to Easton residents. His longevity earned him the nickname "the mayor of West Street."

In 1992, the building began its tenure as an eatery, first becoming Bullbrier's Saloon and later operating under the name of Tom's Tavern. Today, the restaurant bears the name of its owner with well-deserved pride. As I was finishing my meal, Karen stepped in just in time to share a dessert of Chocolate Mousse. I was happy that she was able to experience even a small part of Kendall's, and even happier that she liked it just as much as I did.

CURRIED BUTTERNUT SQUASH SOUP

4 tablespoons sweet butter
2 cups finely chopped yellow onions
4 to 5 teaspoons curry powder
2 medium butternut squash
3 cups chicken stock
2 Rome apples, peeled, cored, and chopped
1 cup apple juice
salt and freshly ground pepper to taste
sour cream for garnish
1 small, diced, unpeeled Granny Smith apple for garnish

Melt butter in a pot. Add onions and curry powder. Cook, covered, over low heat for about 25 minutes until onions are tender. Peel squash, scrape out seeds, and chop flesh. When onions are tender, pour in stock, add squash and Rome apples, and bring to a boil. Reduce heat and simmer, partially covered, about 25 minutes until squash and apples are very tender. Pour soup through a strainer, reserving liquid. Transfer solids to the bowl of a food processor fitted with a steel blade, or use a food mill fitted with a medium disc. Add 1 cup of cooking stock and process until smooth. Return puréed soup to pot and add apple juice and about 2 additional cups cooking liquid until soup is of desired consistency. Season with salt and pepper. Simmer briefly to heat through and serve immediately. Garnish with dollops of sour cream and Granny Smith apples. Serves 6.

MARYLAND CRAB CAKES

1 egg
1 teaspoon Worcestershire sauce
1 teaspoon freshly squeezed lemon juice
1 teaspoon Old Bay seasoning
½ cup mayonnaise
1 slice dry toast
1 pound Maryland lump crabmeat, picked

Preheat oven to 425 degrees. Whisk together all ingredients except toast and crabmeat. Gently fold crabmeat into mixture, being careful not to break up lumps. Process toast in a food processor to make breadcrumbs. Gently fold into crab mixture. Scoop 4 portions onto a lightly oiled sheet pan and bake 10 to 12 minutes until golden brown. If preferred, sauté in ½ inch of clarified butter or oil. Another option is to coat in flour, apply an egg wash, and coat in breadcrumbs before deep-frying. Serves 2.

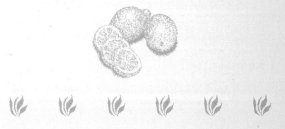

Baldwin's Station

7618 Main Street
Sykesville, MD 21784
www.BaldwinsStation.com
410-795-1041

Sykesville's mayor once stated, "Sykesville may be a small town, but it's not a sleepy one." The historic town has a picturesque, shop-filled Main Street. The 1883 railroad station, known today as Baldwin's Station, is one of the focal points of the community. The station is located along the Patapsco River on the Old Main Line of the B&O Railroad, the oldest railway in the country. Excitement runs high, just as it did in days of yore, when the whistle blows and the railcars rumble past.

The eatery began in the 1990s after thirty tons of coal were removed from the basement in order to allow the installation of modern heating and cooling equipment. Owner Stewart Dearie has since been showered with accolades, including "Best Restaurant" recognition many years running. It's not surprising, given the outstanding cuisine and the variety of activities that take place here, including children's theater performances and live concerts featuring nationally known jazz, folk, and bluegrass artists. Lunch includes starters such as Eggplant Napoleon and Blackened Chicken and Vegetable Soup. Among the popular sandwich and salad selections are the

Thin-Sliced Poached Chicken Wrap, the Atlantic Salmon BLT, and the Apple and Almond Chicken Salad. For dinner, a great choice is the Shrimp Toast, served with five different sauces (Thai Chili, Sun-Dried Tomato, Olive Tapanade, Soft Cheese, and Fennel Marmalade). The Fried Stuffed Artichokes also present a choice within a choice, as the three artichokes each come with a different filling. For her entrée, Karen was drawn to the Honey- and Walnut-Crusted Rack of Lamb with Sweet Potato Purée. Debbie quickly settled on the Vegetable Tower, which consisted of Polenta Cakes, roasted red peppers, portabello mushrooms, grilled zucchini, and grilled squash.

The restaurant bears the name of E. Francis Baldwin, one of the best-known Baltimore architects of his era. He must have had a sense of humor, fashioning the chimneys to look like an 1880s locomotive! The construction is Queen Anne-style with Victorian accents. The jewel-toned stained-glass windows and the high ceilings have been around since the structure's creation. Opened to the public in September 1884, the depot provided Sykesville with passenger service until the 1950s. Freight service continued even later.

Diners enter the station through what was once the ladies' and children's waiting room. Today, it continues as a waiting area and also houses the restaurant's bar. Today's coatroom, just off this area, was once the ticket office, where the stationmaster went about his duties. The restaurant's popular deck was constructed where the original depot platform once stood. The main dining room, once the freight room, features original brick walls and large freight doors. Who knows what trinkets and treasures have come through this room?

ROASTED RED PEPPER AND BRIE SALAD

1 pound arugula, picked and washed
1 pound Brie cheese
3 red peppers, roasted and seeded
salt and pepper to taste
1 to 2 tablespoons olive oil

Dry arugula gently on a towel. Cut Brie into 1-ounce squares, leaving rind. Cut peppers into ¾-inch strips and season with salt and pepper. Wrap each pepper strip around a piece of Brie. To plate salad, place 4 pieces of wrapped Brie at the outer edge of a microwave-safe plate. Heat for 10 seconds in microwave, just to slightly melt Brie. Place a small bunch of arugula in the center and drizzle with oil. Season with salt and pepper. Serves 4.

AMARETTO CHEESECAKE

1¾ cups finely crushed graham crackers
¼ cup chopped walnuts
½ teaspoon cinnamon
½ cup butter
3 8-ounce packages cream cheese, softened
1 cup sugar
2 tablespoons flour
3 tablespoons amaretto
1 teaspoon vanilla
2 eggs
1 egg yolk
¼ cup milk
Peach Sauce (see next column)

Preheat oven to 375 degrees. For crust, combine graham cracker crumbs, walnuts, and cinnamon. Melt butter and stir into crumb mixture. Press mixture onto bottom and 2 inches up sides of an 8- or 9-inch cake pan. In a mixing bowl, combine cream cheese, sugar, flour, amaretto, and vanilla. Beat until fluffy. Add eggs and yolk all at once, beating on low until just combined. Stir in milk. Pour mixture into crust. Place in a water bath and bake for 40 to 45 minutes. Chill at least 4 hours or overnight. Serve with Peach Sauce. Serves 12 to 16.

PEACH SAUCE

¾ pound fresh peaches
juice of ½ lemon
½ cup sugar
½ cup water

In a blender or food processor, purée peaches with lemon juice. Add sugar, then water until mixture reaches desired consistency. Store in refrigerator. Yields about 1 cup.

FIRESTONE'S
Restaurant & Bar

105 North Market Street
Frederick, MD 21701
www.firestonesrestaurant.com
301-663-0330

Visiting Firestone's for lunch one sunny spring day, I found it to be quietly elegant as I sat in the second-floor window and enjoyed the Market Street bustle. Debbie was elsewhere, and I knew she'd be disappointed to miss the unique menu selections. The cuisine is classic American steakhouse, the dishes created from scratch every day. I savored the Barbecued Prawns, served with crunchy and cool Red Onion and Cantaloupe Slaw. I'm sure I would have been equally happy with the Seared Tuna Carpaccio with Cucumber and Ginger Relish or the Duck Trap River Smoked Salmon with Red Onion Mango Salad and Mascarpone Crostinis. The Walnut Chicken Salad Wrap and the Monte Cristo Sandwich—smoked turkey, ham, and Swiss on battered Texas toast, served with maple syrup—were both highly recommended. The special of the day, Fried Oyster Salad with Bacon and Buttermilk Dressing, sounded equally good.

I consulted my server, Jenny, who I discovered makes many of the wonderful desserts. We discussed the merits of Homemade Buttermilk Pound Cake, faithfully prepared according to her grandmother's recipe, Chocolate Truffle Cake, Raspberry Trifle, and Carrot Cake. I'm well known among my friends for tasting every Tiramisu that crosses my path, so when Jenny said that magical word, my decision was made. Firestone's version arrived ensconced in a wafer-thin chocolate shell. Every mouthful was heavenly!

The building was constructed in the early 1900s for Shipley's Sporting Goods. Passersby will notice the name *Shipley* in yellow brick high above the ground-floor windows on the outside of the building. Large windows in wooden frames intricately painted in hues of purple, green, and yellow echo the fanciful eaves and dentil molding. Many patrons remember visiting Shipley's to purchase their first bicycle.

Over the years, the building was also the home of an Irish pub called Donnelly's. Known as a very lively spot, it was the place for a good fistfight as well as a great beer! Despite this history—or perhaps because of it—very little has changed over the years. Patrons still appreciate the original brick walls and tin-tiled ceiling. The wooden floors help to emphasize the long, polished wooden bar with a brass foot rail. The small tables were adorned with white linens, navy-blue napkins, and vases of daffodils the day I visited. Upstairs, the original office has been converted into a mezzanine seating area. This area was extended in 1975 to surround the main dining room on three sides, adding many more tables. The kitchens are located in the basement of the building, so the wait staff certainly has to be fit running up and down several flights of stairs to deliver piping-hot food to each table.

Firestone's has managed to make the perfect transition from the rowdy bar of yesteryear to the quiet family atmosphere I discovered. On

Friday evenings, guests enjoy acoustic guitar, a jazz singer, piano music, or a little something Sinatra. After ten o'clock on Fridays and Saturdays, patrons at the bar enjoy rock-and-roll or perhaps a local blues band. Whatever your choice of entertainment, your meal is sure to be delicious!

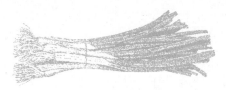

CRAB CAKES

1 egg
¼ cup finely diced red pepper
¼ cup finely diced red onion
¼ cup finely diced scallion tops
1 teaspoon lemon juice
½ teaspoon Old Bay seasoning
½ teaspoon grain mustard
1 tablespoon mayonnaise
dash of Tabasco sauce
1 pound jumbo lump crabmeat, picked
½ cup breadcrumbs
2 tablespoons butter
1 teaspoon olive oil

Combine first 9 ingredients in a medium bowl. Fold in crabmeat and breadcrumbs, being careful not to break up crabmeat lumps. Allow to stand for 5 minutes. Divide mixture into 4 equal parts and form into patties. In a large sauté pan, melt butter and add olive oil. Sauté cakes for about 3 minutes on each side until golden brown. Serve immediately. Serves 2.

CIOPPINO

2 tablespoons clarified butter
4 scallops
1 tablespoon olive oil
1 teaspoon finely chopped garlic
1 teaspoon chopped shallots
6 large shrimp, peeled and deveined
8 topneck clams
8 mussels, cleaned
½ cup white wine
1 cup fish stock
1 cup canned plum tomatoes with juice
2 generous pinches of saffron
1 bay leaf
2 tablespoons chopped Italian parsley
salt and pepper to taste
crusty bread
lemon wedges

Place butter in a large pot over medium-high heat. Brown scallops on both sides. Reduce heat to medium. Add olive oil, garlic, and shallots. Allow to sweat for 45 seconds, then add shrimp, clams, and mussels. Add wine, fish stock, tomatoes, saffron, and bay leaf. Bring to a simmer. Cover and continue to simmer for 5 to 8 minutes. When clams open, Cioppino is cooked enough. Add parsley, remove bay leaf, and season to taste. Divide between 2 bowls and serve with crusty bread and a lemon wedge. Serves 2. Note: Any type of fish may be substituted for the shellfish.

JOHANSSONS
DINING HOUSE

4 West Main Street
Westminster, MD 21157
410-876-0101

The building at 4 Main Street sits at a busy corner. At first glance, its crisp blue-and-white exterior gives onlookers a glimpse into turn-of-the-twentieth-century Westminster. It originally functioned as a clothing store and tailor shop, operating as such until 1940. At that time, it was leased to the G. C. Murphy Company, which maintained its variety store here over the next forty years.

Owner David Johansson's history with the building began in 1987, when he leased the downstairs portion and opened Champs. When the building came up for sale in 1994, David was able to expand his restaurateur dreams to include Johanssons Dining House, Johanssons Microbrewery, and The Down Under Nite Club and Grill. Each of the dining rooms here has a different feel and décor, thanks to David's wife, Wendy. The main dining rooms are quiet and subdued, giving the feel of a hotel lobby from yesteryear. Stained-glass windows are displayed throughout. Some are intact, while others are displayed in pieces, their colors shown to full advantage by creative backlighting.

On the lovely summer evening I visited, I was seated in a glassed-in porch area adjacent to the brewing operation. The rust-red walls were an attractive backdrop for many interesting treasures, including a very old tapestry hanging to my left. Other artifacts including antique fire screens added visual interest throughout the ample restaurant space. The bar area was interesting as well, separated from the rest of the premises by what appeared to be sections of wrought-iron garden fencing, popular in the late 1800s and early 1900s. The ceiling fans whirring overhead in that section of Johanssons were unique in that they were aligned vertically rather than horizontally.

After meandering through the interior, I arrived back at my table to find that a selection of petite white and wheat rolls had been delivered. The menu has something for everyone, so it took a little while to arrive at a decision. The Vegetable Turnover sounded tasty, as did the Tournedos St. Michael, two petite fillets topped with Crab Imperial. Ultimately, I opted for a Spinach Salad and the Barbecued Shrimp. Both were delicious. Others around me enjoyed a wide variety of selections including ample sandwiches such as the Monte Carlo and the Gouda Cheeseburger. A popular choice here is the Combination Dinner, which allows diners to choose two from the list of Jumbo Lump Crab Cake, Baked Stuffed Shrimp, Petite Filet Mignon, Half-Rack of BBQ Ribs, and Fried Shrimp. From that list, I think I'd have to do eenie, meenie, minie, mo! Or maybe I'll just bring Karen next time. Between the two of us, we can enjoy four of the five choices.

When David's father, chef Birger Johansson, made his voyage to America during World War II, David had not yet been born. However, the pieces soon fell into place for a successful Johansson venture in Westminster.

SOUTHWEST CORNBREAD CATFISH

¼ cup flour
¼ cup cornmeal
2 8-ounce catfish fillets
1 egg, beaten
1 teaspoon Southwest seasoning
2 tablespoons butter
8 ounces spinach
½ cup chopped shallots
½ cup chopped sun-dried tomatoes
1 teaspoon minced garlic
2 ounces lump crabmeat, picked

Preheat oven to 400 degrees. Combine flour and cornmeal in a small, flat dish. Dip fillets into egg, then into flour mixture. Sprinkle fillets with seasoning. Melt butter in a large sauté pan and fry fillets for 3 minutes on each side. Transfer fillets to a baking sheet and bake for 8 to 10 minutes. Sauté spinach, shallots, tomatoes, garlic, and crabmeat for 2 minutes; stir gently to avoid breaking up crabmeat. Place sautéed vegetables on 2 plates and place a fillet on top of each. Drizzle fillets with sauce from pan. Serves 2.

CHICKEN MIRANDA

2 tablespoons butter
4 to 5 ounces fresh spinach, divided
2 5-ounce chicken breasts, butterflied
salt and pepper to taste
¼ teaspoon garlic powder
½ teaspoon Montreal chicken seasoning
¼ cup pine nuts, toasted
2 ounces feta cheese
¼ cup flour
2 tablespoons olive oil, divided
¼ cup chopped shallots
2 tablespoons white wine
2 tablespoons brandy
½ cup heavy cream
2 tablespoons marinara sauce

Preheat oven to 400 degrees. In a medium sauté pan, melt butter and sauté spinach. Open each chicken breast and season with salt and pepper, garlic powder, and chicken seasoning. In a small bowl, combine ⁴/₅ of spinach, pine nuts, and feta. Stuff breasts with spinach mixture. Roll chicken in flour. Heat 1 tablespoon oil in a sauté pan and sauté chicken for 3 minutes on each side. Remove chicken from pan, place on a baking sheet, and bake for 10 minutes. In another sauté pan, heat remaining tablespoon oil over medium heat and sauté shallots for 2 minutes. Add remaining spinach. Add wine and brandy and heat until liquid is reduced by half. Add cream and reduce slightly until sauce thickens. Add marinara and stir to combine. Pour sauce over chicken and serve immediately. Serves 2.

the PLUM

6 Rochester Place
Hagerstown, MD 21740
301-791-1717

Milton Kohler began his career with a bench and some tools, carrying on his watchmaking and jewelry business inside a barbershop in Pomeroy, Ohio. After an Ohio River flood, Kohler and his wife ventured east and bought a jewelry store on West Washington Street in Hagerstown. For the next two decades, business thrived to the point that Kohler commissioned the construction of a three-story building adjoining his store. A 1901 Hagerstown trade publication shows its unique domed roof with large bay windows just below it on the second and third floors. The eclectic structure with Romanesque influences features a decorative frieze that incorporates lion's heads. The tiled entryway, framed with a Greek key design, still bears the Kohler name. As local residents remarked about the building, "Everything typifies elegance." The quality of Kohler's merchandise, workmanship, and service created that perception.

The space to the rear of the structure was used as a carriage house. The wealthy citizens served by Milton Kohler & Sons Jewelry needed somewhere to park their carriages while being waited upon by the attentive staff. It is that carriage house that today houses The Plum, a delightfully cozy eatery open for breakfast and lunch. The high ceilings and large windows curtained in lace create an airy feel. Just inside the door is a large board with menu items and a high counter where guests can place their orders before proceeding to one of the green-and-cream-plaid cloth-covered tables. The restaurant has three separate dining rooms, the tiniest of which is upstairs in the old hayloft. Throughout the dining space, quilts hang from old brick walls and stenciled vines, whimsical flowers, and unobtrusive plum knickknacks add a decorative touch.

The lunch menu offers a large selection of hot and cold sandwiches. From the hot list, the Chicken Pita Fajita sounded quite tasty, as did The Floridian, with bacon, cheddar, avocado, bean sprouts, spinach, mayo, and whole-wheat bread. A lover of egg salad who rarely makes it herself, Debbie thought hard about selecting the Crack of Dawn, consisting of Egg Salad, bacon, spinach, and tomato on a croissant. We started our early lunch by sharing the Lettuceless Salad, a simple but creative combination of diced vegetables, fruit, and cheese, topped with Buttermilk Dressing and sunflower seeds. Debbie then sampled The Woodley, a concoction of roast beef, provolone, portabello mushrooms, caramelized onions, lettuce, tomato, and Horseradish Sauce on a French club roll. Karen considered The Florentine, served hot with bacon, spinach, cream cheese, feta, and tomato piled high on a croissant, before choosing The Downtowner, stuffed with sautéed mushrooms, red, green, and yellow peppers, red onions, and zucchini and topped with provolone and mozzarella. Just before we went on our way, owners Sarah Ardinger and Jennifer Kane presented us with Trail Mix Bars to enjoy on the road. The recipe is a well-guarded secret, and rightly so. Those bars alone were worth the trip!

LETTUCELESS SALAD

1 head cauliflower
2 large bunches broccoli
1 large cucumber
3 stalks celery
3 carrots, peeled
1 green pepper, seeded
½ red onion
2 Red Delicious apples
1 Granny Smith apple
½ pound cheddar cheese
½ cup raisins
Buttermilk Dressing (see below)
½ cup sunflower seeds

Dice vegetables, apples, and cheddar into bite-sized pieces. Combine with raisins in a large bowl. Drizzle with Buttermilk Dressing and top with sunflower seeds. Serves 4 to 6.

BUTTERMILK DRESSING

1 egg
3 teaspoons Dijon mustard
2 teaspoons dill seed
½ teaspoon marjoram
½ teaspoon thyme
1 cup buttermilk
1 clove garlic, minced
¼ teaspoon pepper
½ teaspoon celery seed

½ teaspoon basil
⅓ cup vegetable oil
4 cups mayonnaise

Combine all ingredients in a large container, whisking until well mixed. Store in an airtight container in the refrigerator. Yields 5 cups.

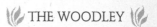

THE WOODLEY

¼ cup butter, divided
2 yellow onions, sliced thin
4 large portabello mushrooms, sliced
¼ cup soy sauce
1 pound rare roast beef, sliced
8 slices provolone cheese
4 club rolls
4 leaves lettuce
1 tomato, sliced
horseradish sauce to taste

In a medium skillet, melt 2 tablespoons butter and caramelize onions. Remove from pan and set aside. Add remaining butter and sauté mushrooms. Add soy sauce. Allow to cool. Layer ¼ pound roast beef, ¼ of the onions, ¼ of the mushrooms, and 2 slices provolone on the bottom half of each roll. Broil until cheese is melted. Top with lettuce, tomato, horseradish sauce, and other half of roll. Serves 4.

Gardel's
Supper Club

29 South Front Street
Baltimore, MD 21202
www.gardels.com
410-837-3737

A dance floor and a sound system on each floor distinguish Gardel's as a supper club instead of just a restaurant. It definitely has the feel of a 1940s or 1950s spot for dinner and dancing. The building that houses Gardel's was once the Baltimore City Life Museum, so the space is vast and open, allowing plenty of room for guests to fully enjoy the music. We stopped in unexpectedly one afternoon and were graciously given a tour by Zeb Blair, the marketing coordinator. Apparently, it's fairly standard for folks to pop in and want to look around.

The first floor is painted in a rich burgundy trimmed in cream. Large columns throughout divide the dining area from the dance space. Copper-colored Corinthian caps add architectural interest and dramatic flair. The copper is carried through in a unique sculpture that reminded us of wind chimes; the sculpture hangs above the dance floor. Guests can also view an enormous picture of Carlos Gardel, heralded as "the king of tango." Also known as *El Zorgal Criollo* or "the songbird of Buenos Aires," Gardel is said to have begun the era of tango when he recorded

"Mi noche triste" in 1915.

A wide wooden staircase with brass and iron railings leads to the second and third floors. The second floor is where the building's former use as a museum is most evident. Murals depicting various Baltimore scenes have been retained, including one of the Centre Market. Also on the second floor is a real White Tower eatery. Having once served Baltimore residents, it was dismantled and then reconstructed inside the museum. The third floor functions as a nightclub. Globe chandeliers from the building's earlier days light an open space painted in vivid colors. Large arched windows provide a fabulous view toward downtown and the Inner Harbor. The club specializes in tango, salsa, and cha-cha, providing dance lessons for guests to improve their steps.

All this and an interesting menu, too. Appetizers such as Coconut-Encrusted Shrimp Tamales, Sumac-Dusted Diver Scallops, Cinnamon-Grilled Quail, and Shredded Duck Flautas make one visit insufficient to sample all of the creative offerings. Entrées of Roasted Rack of Lamb with Apple and Chestnut Crust and Wood-Fired Brook Trout with Jalapeño Rice and Tropical Fruit Compote would pique our interest (and our taste buds) anytime. The influence is certainly Latin. For example, the traditional Roasted Chicken is served with Coconut and Sweet Potato Purée, and the Oven-Roasted Duck is highlighted by Allspice Chianti Cream.

Carlos Gardel was quoted as saying, "The tango is like a lullaby. It gets in your ear and never goes away." We certainly did a dance step or two on the way to the car, and hummed and drummed the melodies we heard for the rest of the day.

GRILLED PINEAPPLE WITH VANILLA RUM SAUCE

1 large pineapple
1 piece lemon grass
4 cups water
4 cups sugar
2 vanilla beans, halved lengthwise
1 stick cinnamon
2 cups dark rum
1½ teaspoons chili flakes
6 slices angel food cake
6 generous scoops coconut sorbet or ice cream

Peel pineapple but leave whole. Smash lemon grass and cut on a bias. Place pineapple, lemon grass, water, sugar, vanilla beans, cinnamon, rum, and chili flakes in a large saucepan or pot over high heat. Bring to a boil. Reduce heat and simmer 30 minutes, turning pineapple halfway through. Remove pot from heat and allow pineapple and liquid to cool. Place mixture in refrigerator and allow pineapple to marinate in liquid for 24 hours.

The next day, remove pineapple from liquid, reserving liquid. Cut pineapple into ¾-inch slices. Punch out core of pineapple with a metal cutter. Strain 2 cups liquid and reserve as Vanilla Rum Sauce. Return pineapple to remaining liquid and store in refrigerator until ready to use. Pineapple can be stored for up to 14 days.

When ready to serve, grill pineapple. Warm Vanilla Rum Sauce. Place angel food cake on plates with a scoop of coconut sorbet or ice cream. Top with 2 or 3 pineapple slices. Spoon sauce over top. Serves 6.

TOMATILLO SALSA

12 tomatoes, peeled and diced
3 jalapeño peppers, seeded and diced fine
3 plum tomatoes, seeded and diced fine
1 red onion, peeled and diced fine
1 teaspoon garlic purée
½ cup washed and chopped cilantro
2 tablespoons extra-virgin olive oil
zest of 3 limes
juice of 3 limes
1 tablespoon salt
1 teaspoon cayenne pepper
1 teaspoon coriander seeds, toasted and ground
½ cup orange syrup
½ cup honey
½ cup red wine vinegar

Combine all ingredients in a large bowl. Gently mix until thoroughly combined. Let sit until flavors blend. Yields 4 cups.

310 East Green Street
Westminster, MD 21157
www.maggieswestminster.com
410-848-1441

Once upon a time, this building was a blacksmith shop dating back to 1903, when Maggie and Levi Zahn operated the business. The blacksmith shop was actually in the back, while Maggie ran a barroom in the front. In addition, the Zahns sold tools and farm implements, sometimes backpacking through the woods and valleys around Westminster to make deliveries. Until Prohibition interrupted the selling of alcohol, Maggie and Levi kept the business pretty much the same as the day it was founded.

Sometime after Prohibition, the name was changed to the Green Street Inn. That establishment was known far and wide for having the best steamed crabs ever sold. In a state like Maryland, where everyone takes their crabs very seriously, that's quite a statement. Ownership fluctuated throughout the mid-1900s until the eatery was purchased and reopened as Maggie's in 1976. The name was selected because the new owner had childhood memories of the original Maggie, the most vivid of which was her ever-present black apron. During the remodeling of the former blacksmith shop into a dining room,

the fireplace and hearth were styled so they were reminiscent of the kind Levi Zahn once used. Another item incorporated to remind guests of yesteryear was the *Ivan Gambler* nameplate. No one knew who that was, but employees hung it on the wall anyway. The mystery was solved one day when a ninety-year-old man walked in and introduced himself. Ivan Gambler had been an employee of Levi Zahn's until the advent of the automobile, when he switched from working as a blacksmith to repairing automobiles. Curious about what had transpired at his old workplace, he had come in to check it out and was pleased with the result.

The menu here could be described as "upscale down-home" or perhaps "continental with a touch of Maryland." Dishes like Maggie's Crab Cakes, Chicken and Shrimp Madagascar, Veal Madeira, and Seafood Cassolette are representative of the dinner menu. While Debbie was busy elsewhere, I stopped in for a quick lunch and thoroughly enjoyed the Homemade Chicken Pot Pie, though I would have been equally happy with Maggie's Omelet, a spinach, bacon, and cheese omelet served souffléed in traditional French style, or the quiche du jour with scallions and bacon. The Crab Crostinis are very popular, as are the Shrimp Salad Sauté and the Texas Tortilla Salad. Be sure to save room for a homemade dessert, though, like me, you will have difficulty in making a choice among Turtle Pie, Chocolate Mousse in a Puff Pastry Cuff, English Trifle, Amaretto Italian Layer Cake, Maggie's Napoleon, and New York Cheesecake. The staff members at Maggie's pride themselves on making almost everything from scratch. They assured me that nothing here is ever frozen or prepackaged!

The creamy walls adorned with antiques and memorabilia and the terra-cotta floor make for a charming dining room. With delicious foods and delightful surroundings, you have the perfect recipe for an enjoyable meal.

 CHICKEN CHAMPAGNE

1½ pounds boneless chicken breasts
⅓ cup flour for dredging
⅓ cup oil
4 tablespoons butter
4 medium carrots, peeled, julienned, and
   blanched
½ pound mushrooms, sliced
8 shallots, sliced
1 cup champagne
½ cup dry sherry
1½ cups whipping cream
salt and pepper to taste
fresh parsley, if desired

Trim chicken of fat and cut into 1½-by-3-inch strips. Dust strips lightly with flour. Heat oil in a skillet. Add chicken and sauté about 2 minutes on each side. Remove to a warm platter. Drain oil from skillet and add butter. Sauté carrots, mushrooms, and shallots until tender. Turn heat to high and add champagne and sherry. Boil until reduced by half. Add cream and stir to blend. Lower heat, return chicken to pan, and cook until sauce lightly coats a wooden spoon. Add salt and pepper. Plate chicken and drizzle with sauce. Garnish with parsley. Serves 6.

 CHOCOLATE MOUSSE

½ pound semisweet chocolate
3 egg yolks
3 tablespoons sugar
3 tablespoons dark rum
2 cups heavy whipping cream
additional whipped cream for garnish
fresh strawberry slices for garnish

Slowly melt chocolate in a bowl over hot water. Do not simmer. Set aside to cool slightly. Beat yolks until fluffy. Add sugar and rum, beating until well blended. Slowly add cooled chocolate until well blended. In a separate bowl, beat heavy cream until fluffy. Fold in chocolate mixture. Divide mousse among 4 serving bowls. When ready to serve, garnish with additional whipped cream and sliced strawberries. Serves 4.

 CRAB DIP

8-ounce package cream cheese
1 teaspoon granulated garlic
dash of lemon juice
½ teaspoon Old Bay seasoning
dash of salt
1½ cups loosely packed chopped spinach
3 ounces crabmeat, picked
toast points
assorted crackers

In a mixing bowl, beat cream cheese until smooth. Add garlic, lemon juice, Old Bay, and salt. Mix well. Fold in spinach and crab until well blended. Place in an oven-safe dish and bake 12 to 15 minutes until heated through and bubbling. Serve with hot toast points and crackers. Serves 4 as an appetizer.

Isabella's

Taverna & Tapas Bar

44 North Market Street
Frederick, MD 21701
www.isabellas-tavern.com
301-698-8922

The Mutual Insurance Company of Frederick City built the structure at 44 North Market Street in 1888. It started as the home of the *Daily News*, a precursor of the *Frederick News Post*. Like most businesses in the Market Street area, it changed hands a few times. One of its longest inhabitants was Hendrickson's Dry Goods, known far and wide for its variety of household items. Today, the building is still known as the Hendrickson Building. Among other businesses, it houses Isabella's Taverna & Tapas Bar.

The red bricks and green paint on the building's exterior complement the large green awning. Inside is a warm and welcoming space. Original brick walls line the long, thin room, which has polished wooden floors and its original tin-tile ceiling painted hunter green. The cheery terra-cotta and turquoise paint is enhanced by the gaily colored tablecloths. Fresh flowers in blue vases and Spanish posters on the walls complete the look. Sitting in the raised area in the front window, I knew that Debbie would have enjoyed this Mediterranean dining experience in Frederick.

The cuisine is definitely Spanish, with an exclusive Spanish wine list to match the sophisticated array of tapas. Tapas originated more than a hundred years ago. Visitors to Andalusia, the home of sherry, were given pieces of bread to cover their glasses. The word *tapa* means lid or cover. Over a long period of time, innkeepers added other foods such as ham, sausage, seafood, and cheese to make the bread more interesting. This evolved into a large array of small dishes served at all times of the day and night. Isabella's has created an extensive selection of delectable small dishes to tempt even the most finicky appetite. There are even entrée selections for the conservative among us. This is the sort of place to visit with a group of friends, so you can try a large number of tapas selections.

It was hard to chose among the salads, soups, cold tapas, and hot tapas. I eventually opted for a Fresh Asparagus and Cilantro Omelet and Catalan-Style Grilled Bread with Fresh Vine-Ripe Tomatoes and Olive Oil. Both were excellent. However, I'm sure I would have been equally delighted with the Baked Purple Potato with Roasted Garlic and Melted Blue Cheese Butter, the Andalusian-Style Gazpacho with Olive Oil-Roasted Croutons and Vegetable Brunoise, or even the Leaf Spinach with Pine Nuts and Malaga Raisins. Patrons around me were clearly enjoying the Braised Wild Boar with Caramelized Onions and the Grilled Chicken Breast with Savory Chocolate Sauce and Toasted Sesame Seeds. Quite a few opted for the Mediterranean Seafood Stew, which includes shrimp, mussels, clams, calamari, and chorizo, simmered in Saffron-Tomato Broth.

The desserts here are also delectable. My

favorite was the Hazelnut Ice Cream with Chocolate Sauce. The Peach Sherbet in a Natural Peach Shell and the Classic Spanish Custard with Caramel Sauce were close runners-up. This Spanish aficionado certainly found the cuisine and atmosphere *muy bien*!

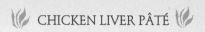

MUSHROOM EMPANADILLAS

2 tablespoons olive oil
4 tablespoons minced garlic
¼ pound serrano ham
1 pound mushrooms
1 cup walnuts
⅓ cup sherry
salt and pepper to taste
6 sheets puff pastry

Preheat oven to 350 degrees. Warm oil in a large frying pan over medium-high heat. Add garlic. Sauté for 2 to 3 minutes before adding ham. Sauté ham an additional 2 to 3 minutes. Add mushrooms and walnuts and continue cooking until walnuts start to boil. Add sherry and reduce. Let mixture cool, then blend until smooth. Season with salt and pepper. Roll puff pastry about ⅛ inch thick and cut into rounds. Place a small amount of filling into rounds, fold in half, and seal. Use a fork to make a decorative edge. Bake 15 to 30 minutes until golden brown. Serves 10.

CHICKEN LIVER PÂTÉ

1 medium onion, chopped
1 tablespoon oregano
¼ cup sherry
4 tablespoons extra-virgin olive oil, divided
1 pound chicken livers
1 tablespoon thyme
2 tablespoons minced garlic
¼ cup brandy
10 hard-boiled eggs, peeled
1½ cups butter
salt and pepper to taste
capers for garnish
toast points or crackers

Sauté onions, oregano, and sherry in 2 tablespoons olive oil. In a separate pan, sauté livers, thyme, garlic, and brandy in remaining oil. Chill both mixtures, then blend in a food processor. Add eggs and continue blending until smooth. Add butter a little at a time. Season with salt and pepper. Put into a loaf pan lined with wax paper. Chill for 4 hours. Garnish with capers and serve with toast points or crackers. Serves 16 as an appetizer.

CHAPTER 5

Gone but Not Forgotten

Gabriel's Inn

Ghosts, apparitions, spirits—something or someone from the past that just doesn't seem to want to go away. Some say they're here because of unfinished business. Others feel they're like guardian angels, watching over a place they loved dearly. People who have experienced them describe a wide variety of sensations, from viewing lifelike bodies to seeing soft lights to feeling cool blasts of air. Far from frightening, they are to most people intriguing. Without them, the buildings in this chapter wouldn't have nearly the character they do today.

true

a pure dining experience

at The Admiral Fell Inn
888 South Broadway
Baltimore, MD 21231
www.admiralfell.com
410-522-7377

During my meal, Livingston the Ghost came to my table. He's employed by the hotel to tell guests about the ghosts of The Admiral Fell Inn. Frequently, he takes on the persona of one of them, telling their story. There are eight documented spirits here. Two of them have been nicknamed Bitsy and Grady, who are known for thumping. Guests occasionally call the front desk asking that the guest in the room above them be asked to settle down. Frequently, upon investigation, it is discovered that no guest is checked into the room in question. My favorite story was born during Hurricane Isabel. The hotel was evacuated, only a few of the management staff remaining. On consecutive nights, the assistant hotel manager, Iwona Diaz, and the hotel manager, John Lowe, were alone in the lobby. Both heard footfalls and noise, as if a party were going on above. Since everyone else who remained on the premises was having dinner in the dining room, the only explanation was that the ghosts were celebrating the fact that guests were gone and the hotel was all theirs!

The inn is comprised of eighty guest rooms and suites fashioned from eight connecting buildings whose construction dates from 1770. In 1889, The Anchorage, a legendary seamen's hostel, was established by the Woman's Auxiliary of the Port Mission. The hope was to maintain a boardinghouse for seamen while at the same time providing Christian influence. In 1929, the Young Men's Christian Association took over The Anchorage and expanded it into a 105-bed YMCA. The rooms were so small that the hostel was nicknamed "the Doghouse." As many as fifty thousand sailors per year were given lodging.

The lowest level, which today houses the inn's restaurant, was once the site of a vinegar-bottling factory. When it closed in the mid-1970s, the site remained empty until the inn's creation in 1985. Today, the large stones of the foundation are juxtaposed with the more modern arched ceiling and recessed lighting to create a very pleasing décor. Wrought-iron sconces and curtained nooks finish the room with an Elizabethan overtone.

The specials the evening I dined included Lamb Chops and Mahi-Mahi. I was tempted to choose the Warm Crab and Brie, baked in light puff pastry and served with seasonal berries. The Pumpkin Ravioli, garnished with shavings of black truffles, was also something I'd definitely enjoy. Ultimately, I opted for the Chesapeake Bay Rockfish with Raspberry Chipotle Glaze, a decision I'd make again. The desserts were equally appealing. Had she been with me that night, Karen would have selected the Poached Pear with Ginger Crème Brûlée. I chose the sinful Chocolate Volcano topped with Orange-Butterscotch Crème Anglaise.

Before visiting, I wondered about the restaurant's name. I discovered that it reflects the philosophy here. The restaurant strives to be true to the ideal of providing healthy meal options. It strives to be true to the seasons in providing fresh ingredients and true to the region by supporting local suppliers. Ultimately, it stays true to its customers by providing a truly memorable experience.

ATLANTIC LOBSTER AND SALMON SAUSAGE

10-ounce salmon fillet
4 ounces lobster
1 tablespoon cognac
1 slice white bread, crumbled into breadcrumbs
1 tablespoon chopped fennel
salt and pepper to taste
scant ½ cup heavy cream
1 egg
20 inches pork casing

Cut fillet into 1-inch pieces. Place in a bowl and add lobster. Add cognac, breadcrumbs, fennel, and salt and pepper. Marinate for a couple of minutes. Add heavy cream. Run through a meat grinder, then process in a food processor until smooth. Add egg. Pass mixture through a sausage maker into pork casing. Tie off 4 links. Poach links in a medium saucepan for about 8 minutes until done. Serves 4.

 WHITE TRUFFLE RISOTTO

1 large shallot
2 tablespoons butter
1½ cups arborio rice
1 cup white wine
4 cups chicken stock
2 tablespoons shredded Parmesan cheese
1 tablespoon white truffle oil
salt and pepper to taste

Chop shallot. Heat a medium saucepan over high heat. Add butter, shallots, and rice. Cook for 2 minutes, then reduce heat to medium. Add wine and cook until all wine is absorbed. Slowly add chicken stock 1 cup at a time until absorbed, stirring frequently. Continue cooking, stirring constantly, until rice is tender but not overcooked. Add Parmesan and white truffle oil. Season with salt and pepper. Serves 4.

Gabriel's Inn

4730 Ijamsville Road
Ijamsville, MD 21754
www.gabrielsrestaurant.com
301-865-5500

As we traveled through Maryland, Gabriel's Inn was a destination recommended time and again. The restaurant specializes in traditional French provincial cooking, using only the freshest ingredients. One of the interesting things about the approach of owners Shirl and Sean DeLawder is the option to dine either in the French or the American tradition. The American style includes a salad, followed by an entrée accompanied by the vegetable du jour. The French style includes a full-course presentation beginning with hors d'oeuvres and continuing with soup, an entrée with a vegetable, salad, cheese, and dessert.

I opted for the leisurely French style and was amazed when the selections for my first course arrived on a three-tiered cart. I sampled the Salmon Pâté, the Country Pâté, and the unique and delicious Kidney Bean Salad, so popular that it's available for carry-out. The Mushroom Soup that followed was absolutely the best I've ever had. The entrée choices were extensive, including Frog Legs or Shrimp prepared either in the Bordelaise or the Provençal style. Traditional chicken selections such as Coq au Vin and Poulet a l'Estragon in Tarragon Cream Sauce are quite popular. After I made my choice of the Salmon Couilibac—a concoction of salmon, crab, wild rice, and mushrooms wrapped in puff pastry—Shirl told me that it and Beef Wellington are Gabriel's most-requested items. As I continued my meal with a salad and the cheese course, I wished Karen were there to enjoy it, too. The grand finale was a scrumptious Crème Brûlée.

The property where the inn sits is part of what is known as the Duvall Tract, established in 1659. In the mid-1700s, William Iiam, a colonial agent of Lord Baltimore, settled the South River in Annarundel County. Iiam's descendants began using the name Ijams and subsequently founded the area now known as Ijamsville. In 1831, Plummer Ijams gave the B&O Railroad right of way through his land. On March 13, 1832, all two hundred or so Ijamsville residents turned out on the hillside above the tracks to watch the first journey of America's original railroad as four cars, each drawn by a single horse, passed by on their way from Baltimore to Frederick.

Built in 1862, the building that houses Gabriel's was occupied by Welsh families who worked in the quarries that helped establish the town. In 1896, Dr. George H. Riggs founded the Riggs Cottage Sanitarium here for the treatment of women with nervous ailments. All accounts indicate that it was a warm, nurturing environment where patients were provided fresh air, lush surroundings, plenty of exercise and activities, and excellent care. During his tenure, Dr. Riggs treated a total of 1,030 patients from every state in the union. Also the community's general practitioner, he treated local residents and delivered 1,004 babies.

With so much history here, it's not surprising that Gabriel's has resident spirits that are frequently sighted. Shirl and Shawn host Ghost Dinners in October, giving guests in-depth insight into these phenomena.

The sanitarium closed in 1965. In 1968, Guy Gabriel created Gabriel's French Provincial Inn. Not only did he nurture a family of seven children, he also raised much of the produce and some of the meats used at the restaurant. In 1998, the DeLawder family took the helm with every intention of keeping the tradition begun by Guy Gabriel and adding a few wonderful touches of their own.

HOT CRAB DIP

2 8-ounce packages cream cheese
½ cup shredded Gruyère cheese
2 tablespoons dry sherry
juice of ½ lemon
8 ounces lump crabmeat, picked
Old Bay seasoning for garnish
crackers or French bread

Place first 4 ingredients in a heavy-bottomed sauce pan. Heat on medium heat, stirring frequently so as not to burn. When mixture is melted and hot, add crab and stir to warm through. Remove to a serving bowl and sprinkle with Old Bay. Serve with crackers or French bread. Serves 6 as an appetizer.

COQUILLES SAINT JACQUES PROVENÇAL

1 tablespoon olive oil
12 sea scallops
2 cloves garlic, minced
1 tomato, diced
2 teaspoons basil
¼ cup white wine
2 tablespoons sliced black olives
2 tablespoons sliced green olives
salt and pepper to taste

Heat oil in a sauté pan. Add scallops and sear on each side to give a nice brown caramelized color. Remove scallops to a plate and set aside. Add garlic, tomatoes, and basil to sauté pan. Stir for about 1 minute. Add wine and olives and cook for another minute. Return scallops to pan and season with salt and pepper. Heat through. Serves 2.

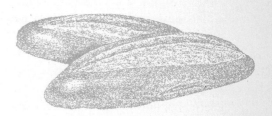

RAMS HEAD
SAVAGE
TAVERN
where great minds meet

at Savage Mill
8600 Foundry Street
Savage, MD 20763
www.ramsheadtavern.com
301-604-3454

Historic Savage Mill was once a thriving textile mill. Today, this fabulous old building has been renovated to house specialty retail stores, craft studios, art galleries, and several eateries. Rams Head Tavern patrons enter through the brick gateway, past the old paymaster's office and the carding house. It's easy to imagine wagons coming and going in this courtyard, picking up textiles and making deliveries of supplies.

The dining room is located up what is known as "the tower stairs." The banisters were worn smooth by the hundreds of workers who climbed these stairs over the course of almost two hundred years. In the early 1900s, children were employed to run up and down the stairs exchanging full bobbins for empty spools, moving swiftly between the spinning floor and the weaving floor. If you look carefully, you can find the places where spikes were impaled on the banisters to stop the children from sliding down. It is interesting to check out the unevenness of the steps here, built long before regulations were established for such things. One of the women

mill workers is reputed to have died here. According to local legend, she now appears frequently to guests using the staircase. Staff working in the paymaster's office are occasionally visited by a ghost who appears out of the computer. Guests here can thus partake of an exciting past and an intriguing paranormal present.

Amos Williams and his three brothers built the mill in 1820. Amos was an enterprising young man. He persuaded his friend John Savage to lend him twenty thousand dollars to start a textile-weaving business, an enormous sum in those days. John Savage must have been a very good friend indeed. No wonder Amos named the mill after him. Construction of the mill took about two years. The enormous thirty-foot waterwheel built to power the weaving machines functioned from 1822 until World War II finally put a stop to the need for the woven cotton used for such items as clipper-ship sails, Civil War tents, and silent-movie screens.

The lovely dining area has pale yellow brick walls reaching to the original beams supporting the next floor. Towering wooden columns hold the beams in place. The room's bistro feel is softened by the profusion of schoolhouse lights and the large glass jars of flowers. The two other floors here house the tavern and the Rams Head Rathskeller, which specializes in nightly live entertainment.

Beer aficionados will be very happy with the terrific selection of Fordham lagers, ales, and stouts. The specials on the menu the day we visited included Creamy Beef Stew, Jumbo Baked Shrimp with Crab Imperial, and Pico Beef Rib-Eye, served over Mashed Potatoes. Karen was tempted by the Steel Pulse Sauté—chicken tenderloins sautéed in Caribbean jerk spice—while Debbie was more interested in the Honey- and Roasted Almond-Covered Brie with Fresh Fruits. The staff at the Rams Head takes pride in the menu items, prepared from scratch every day. The Rams Head Tavern at Savage Mill serves delicious food, interesting history, and unique ambiance in equal quantities.

 BEER BATTER

2¼ cups ale
3 eggs
2 cups all-purpose flour
1½ teaspoons salt
½ teaspoon white pepper

In a food processor, combine half of ale with eggs. Add half the flour and an additional 1 cup of ale slowly. Mix well to avoid lumps. Add seasonings, remaining flour, and remaining ale, mixing well. Place in refrigerator to chill before using. Yields about 2½ cups batter. Note: Rams Head Tavern uses Fordham Copperhead Ale. It uses this batter for shrimp, onion rings, fresh fish fillets, and veggies.

SHRIMP SALAD

1 teaspoon kosher salt
1½ pounds Gulf shrimp
½ cup chopped celery
¼ cup mayonnaise
1 tablespoon chopped parsley
3 teaspoons Old Bay seasoning
¼ tablespoon garlic powder
2 tablespoons breadcrumbs
2 tablespoons lemon juice
salt and white pepper to taste

In a medium saucepan, bring kosher salt and 6 cups water to a boil. Peel and devein shrimp. Add shrimp to boiling water and cook for 5 minutes. Drain shrimp and plunge into an ice bath to stop cooking process. After 2 minutes in ice bath, drain shrimp and repeat ice bath to insure shrimp are cold. Combine remaining ingredients in a medium bowl. Drain shrimp and pat dry with paper towels. Chop coarsely. Add shrimp to mayonnaise mixture and stir well. Cover and refrigerate until ready for use. Serves 4.

Old Field Inn

485 Main Street
Prince Frederick, MD 20678
www.oldfieldinn.com
410-535-1054

It was difficult to choose what to have for dinner. Debbie pondered over the Sautéed Crab with Prosciutto, served in a puff pastry basket with asparagus and Lemon-Thyme Cream Sauce, before opting for the three-course prix fixe special of the evening, featuring Crab Cakes. Karen vacillated between the Grilled Portabello Mushroom Napoleon, which consisted of layers of grilled mushrooms, wilted spinach, roasted red peppers, and chèvre, and the Filet Mignon, wrapped in bacon and served with Béarnaise Sauce on the side. Debbie's meal began with the Old Field Salad, a refreshing combination of leafy greens tossed with shrimp, mandarin oranges, toasted coconut, and Mango Chutney Dressing, while Karen enjoyed a cup of Cream of Crab Soup. Both of our entrées were perfectly prepared and presented. An autumnal Pear Tart was the third course of Debbie's prix fixe. However, Karen is quite fond of pears, so she took the tart and Debbie luxuriously ended her repast with Betty Cake, a chocolate muffin with a center of cream cheese and molten chocolate chips.

The cake is named for Betty Briscoe, long-time mistress of the home. Betty, her husband, Dr. Everard Briscoe, and their family moved to Prince Frederick after receiving urgent pleas from the citizens of Calvert County for Dr. Briscoe to return from Baltimore and walk in the footsteps of his father, who had been a physician in the area. Unfortunately, Betty's husband met an untimely death in 1944 after an accident at the hospital.

Dr. and Mrs. Briscoe had purchased the property from another prominent Briscoe, Judge John Parran Briscoe, chief judge of the Seventh Circuit Court of Maryland. When Judge Briscoe bought the land and constructed the house in the 1890s, the tract was known as Williams Old Fields because the Williams family, the original owners, believed it was no longer suitable for planting. The judge subsequently donated a portion of his purchase to Calvert County to build a courthouse, then built his family a fine home, which he called Old Field.

Old Field was home to Betty Briscoe for fifty-eight years. A noted local citizen, she founded garden clubs and was a charter member of the Calvert County Historical Society. In 1954, she began writing a weekly newspaper column entitled "Know Your County," which she continued until her death in 1981. In addition, she was known as a gracious hostess who entertained with an open-door policy. Today's owners, Brendan and Ashley Cahill, have once again captured this feel.

We were seated in the Bay Room, a lovely dining room that once functioned as the home's parlor. The pale yellow plaster with white trim provided a casually elegant backdrop. The small Tiffany lamps on each table and the Glenn Miller music playing quietly overhead recaptured the aura of Betty's day. Across the hall is the lovely Blue Room, which the Cahills unwittingly decorated with blue china, just like Betty had done. When the Briscoes' daughter, Betsy, came to the restaurant for a recent visit, she was amazed at the similarities and offered some of her mother's teacups to add to the collection. That isn't the only influence of Betty Briscoe still felt here. Employees have seen apparitions and witnessed a presence that they feel is Betty, still the gracious hostess at Old Field today.

 VEAL OSCAR

¼ cup clarified butter
2 4-ounce pieces thinly sliced or pounded veal
¼ cup flour
4 asparagus spears
6 ounces jumbo lump crabmeat, picked
2 shots sherry

Heat butter in a skillet until very hot. Dust veal in flour and place in skillet. Cook 2 minutes and turn. Place asparagus and crabmeat in skillet. Add sherry and cook until crabmeat is hot. Serve immediately. Serves 2.

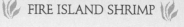 FIRE ISLAND SHRIMP

10 21-25 count shrimp, peeled, tails removed
5 teaspoons horseradish
3⅓ slices bacon
leaf lettuce
Thousand Island dressing

Preheat oven to 450 degrees. Butterfly the shrimp. Place ½ teaspoon horseradish on each shrimp. Cut each slice of bacon into thirds. Wrap shrimp with bacon and place on a baking sheet. Bake for 15 to 20 minutes until bacon is browned. Serve on a bed of lettuce with a ramekin of Thousand Island dressing on the side. Serves 2 as an appetizer.

Kent Manor Inn & Restaurant
Circa 1820

500 Kent Manor Drive
Stevensville, MD 21666
www.kentmanor.com
410-643-7716

A lengthy driveway winds its way toward the attractive front entrance of Kent Manor Inn & Restaurant. The front of the building is impressive with its myriad white-painted porch balustrades and wide red steps leading to the main doors. Guests entering the building will enjoy the Victorian furnishings and the cozy dining rooms. We sat in the enclosed rear porch overlooking the Garden House, an enormous glass-enclosed gazebo, some of the mile and a half of waterfront, and the surrounding grounds.

The Cream of Crab Soup and the Seafood Chowder were both excellent. From the entrée selections, Debbie chose the Eastern Shore Spinach Salad with orange segments, red onions, black walnuts, and applewood-smoked bacon with tangy Raspberry Sherry Vinaigrette, while Karen nibbled on the Grilled Salmon Club Sandwich with applewood bacon, pepper Jack cheese, and Basil Herbed Mayonnaise on a ciabatta roll. Too full to even think about sampling desserts, we decided to take a quick peek at the dessert tray. Servings of Crème Brûlée, White Chocolate and Raspberry Layer Cake, and Chocolate Decadence Cake sat side by side with Carrot Cake and Chocolate Truffle Cake. We sighed regret-

fully and decided that we ought to restrain ourselves.

The property on which Kent Manor Inn sits was granted to Thomas Wetherall in 1651. He sold the land to Dr. John Smyth at the turn of the eighteenth century. The estate, then known as Smithfield, remained in the Smyth family for about 150 years. During that time, the original wing of the house was built. It included a living room, dining room, kitchen, and pantry on the first floor, four reception rooms on the second floor, and two large rooms on the third floor. Many local men were employed in its construction.

In 1843, Sarah Smyth bequeathed 307 acres of the property to her son Alexander Thompson. It was Thompson who oversaw the construction of the center part of the inn, which is even more lavish than the original section. Of particular note are the Italian marble mantels on the first and second floors and the eight-window cupola on the roof. It is said that Thompson could view his entire acreage from the cupola. Local legend has it that there still exists an unusual odor in Alexander Thompson's old bedroom. A faint aroma of his pipe tobacco supposedly lingers there despite all efforts to remove it over the past 150 years. Thompson is said to spend a great deal of time in his room during the day and then gallop his horse up the long driveway at night. We were disappointed not to see him when we visited, but maybe next time. The entire history of the property is too extensive to tell here, but a copy of that history is available in the entranceway for guests to enjoy when they visit.

ROAST QUAIL

¼ cup pecans
2 tablespoons butter
1 small leek, diced
¼ medium onion, diced
1 stalk celery, diced
salt and pepper to taste
¾ teaspoon thyme
1 small Granny Smith apple, diced
¼ cup raisins
¼ teaspoon grated fresh nutmeg
¼ teaspoon ground cloves
4 quail
favorite glaze

Preheat oven to 400 degrees. Spread pecans on a baking sheet and toast in oven for 10 minutes, turning frequently. Reduce temperature to 350 degrees. Melt butter in a skillet and sauté leeks, onions, and celery until transparent but still crisp. Season vegetables with salt and pepper and thyme. Toss mixture with apples, raisins, toasted pecans, nutmeg, and cloves to make stuffing. Stuff quail with mixture and place in a deep roasting pan. Bake for 20 minutes. Remove from oven and ladle favorite glaze over quail. Return to oven for an additional 5 to 10 minutes. Serves 4.

PORTABELLO MUSHROOM SANDWICH

1½ cups olive oil
6 tablespoons red wine vinegar
salt and pepper to taste
pinch of oregano
pinch of basil
pinch of parsley
pinch of thyme
4 portabello mushroom caps, cleaned
4 leaves lettuce
4 slices tomato
4 sandwich rolls

In a medium bowl, combine oil, vinegar, and seasonings. Stir until well mixed. Marinate mushroom caps in mixture for 30 minutes, turning caps over at least once. Place a mushroom cap, a lettuce leaf, and a slice of tomato on each roll. Serves 4.

33 West Street
Annapolis, MD 21401
www.ramsheadtavern.com
410-268-4545

The Rams Head Tavern is a delightful two-story building in brown and hunter green along one of the main roads into Annapolis. Part of the structure is located below ground in what was the original Sign of the Green Tree tavern from 1794. This intimate room is now known as the Down Bar. Guests who look above the barman's head will see a curious wooden object protruding through the ceiling. It is in fact the bottom of a bedpost pushed through from the room above. Any of the staff will tell the tale of Amy, who worked above the tavern. The rooms there were reputed to be a brothel, and Amy was one of the ladies of the night. Supposedly, Amy died one night at the hands of one of the gentlemen availing himself of the facilities. Apparently, he was so vigorous that he pushed the bed through the ceiling. Amy now haunts the building and is known for playing tricks on the staff.

Today, the tavern occupies all the floors at 33 West Street and has incorporated several other buildings as well. Various rooms in the tavern are named for the businesses that previously oc-

cupied the space. We sat in the room overlooking the brew house and enjoyed the large windows and Victorian lighting. The staff and management state on the menu that the tavern serves the freshest food in town. The beef is hand-cut each morning, the burgers are freshly ground, and the seafood is delivered fresh daily. The desserts are handmade by local pastry chefs and delivered to the tavern. We found no holes in this statement during our visit. Debbie's Chicken Breast with Golden Raisin and Granny Smith Apple Curry Sauce was excellent, as was Karen's Jackson Burger with Blackened Shrimp and Melted Gorgonzola. The extensive menu offers many choices of soups, salads, burgers, and sandwiches. The Three Amigos Fish Tacos sounded delicious—battered, fried cod with Chipotle Pepper Mayonnaise and Cilantro Slaw in flour tortillas. Visitors can select favorite dishes made with veal, chicken, beef, pork, and seafood. As expected, there are more delectable seafood selections than anything else. Do save room for dessert. From the many wonderful items on the menu, we highly recommend Paula's Peanut Butter Pie. It appears to be a favorite with everyone.

The Fordham Brewing Company brews most of the beers served here. Fordham is historic in its own way. An Englishman, Benjamin Fordham, started the company in Annapolis in 1703. He went on to become a city alderman. Many of his descendants still live in Annapolis. Today, visitors can enjoy the golden Fordham Lager, Copperhead Ale, and the dark Genius Stout among many other choices. To get the most from your beer-tasting experience, we suggest you try the Beer Sampler, which includes five signature brews and the current seasonal beer on tap. Cheers!

🌿 PONZU SAUCE 🌿

½ cup soy sauce
1½ teaspoons lemon juice
1 tablespoon chopped shallots
¼ cup olive oil
¼ cup fresh orange juice
1 tablespoon sugar
½ teaspoon crushed red pepper flakes
1½ teaspoons minced fresh ginger
¼ cup rice wine vinegar
2 tablespoons chopped scallions

Place all ingredients in a medium bowl and mix well. Cover and chill at least 1 hour to allow flavor to develop. The Rams Head Tavern uses this to marinate tuna steaks and as a dipping sauce for beer-battered items. Yields 1¼ cups.

🌿 MARYLAND ROCKFISH SALAD 🌿

4 6-ounce rockfish fillets
salt and pepper to taste
4 ears white corn
1 cup chopped applewood-smoked bacon
1 cup chopped red onions
1 tablespoon chopped shallots
1 tablespoon minced garlic
1 cup diced plum tomatoes
1 teaspoon cracked black pepper
¼ cup olive oil
½ cup chopped fresh basil

Place fillets on an ovenproof baking tray. Season to taste. Broil fillets, turning once, for about 4 minutes until fish flakes easily. Shuck kernels from corncobs. In a medium sauté pan, render bacon slowly until well browned and crisp. Add onions, shallots, corn, and garlic and sauté for 3 minutes. Remove from heat. Add remaining ingredients and mix well. Serve vegetables over top of broiled rockfish. Serves 4.

🌿 🌿 🌿 🌿 🌿 🌿 🌿 🌿 🌿 🌿 🌿 🌿

The Kitty Knight House

14028 Augustine Herman Highway
Georgetown, MD 21930
www.kittyknight.com
410-648-5200

Kitty Knight was born about 1775. She grew up in the high society of the day and became a beautiful and accomplished young woman. Various records describe her as tall and graceful. Others refer to her hair being dressed in the most up-to-date fashion, while still others relate that she danced with none other than George Washington at a ball held in Philadelphia during a session of the Continental Congress.

When the British invaded this area during the War of 1812, their mission was to burn down houses and communities close to the shore. This effort removed hiding places for American soldiers, allowing the British to move about the Chesapeake region safely. Of course, all able-bodied men had marched to fight, leaving behind old men, women, and children to protect the area. The British burned Fredericktown—the lower part of Georgetown—and were approaching a hill where two brick houses were located. There, they were met by Miss Kitty Knight. Even though she owned neither of the houses on the hill, Miss Kitty pleaded with Admiral George Cockburn not to torch them. Legend reports that Kitty Knight stamped the flames out twice. Other versions relate that she met the admiral with a broom and a bucket of water in hand. Regardless, she managed to convince the admiral not to continue his destruction. She did later pur-

chase one of the houses, so today's inn and restaurant bear her name.

After spending the night, we had a quick bite of breakfast before continuing on our way. Karen chose the Eggs Sassafras, which consisted of poached eggs, crab, and asparagus perched atop an English muffin. Debbie opted for the French Toast, unique in the fact that it is made with pan-fried croissants coated in a batter flavored with Grand Marnier and vanilla. Other diners enjoyed the Belgian Waffles, the breakfast sandwiches, and the Eggs Benedict.

Lunch and dinner lean strongly toward seafood, which is not surprising, since the structure sits above the Georgetown Yacht Basin. Chesapeake Oyster Stew is a local favorite. Oysters appear again in the Chicken and Fried Oysters Salad, a unique twist on a popular luncheon choice, as is the Crisp Calamari Oriental Salad. Many of the lunch items are available at dinner, along with additions such as Shrimp and Scallops Penne, Low Country Shrimp and Scallops, and Chicken Scaloppine Chesapeake.

The history of the houses doesn't end with Kitty. The home next door was reputed to be a stop on the Underground Railroad. Today, it houses a tavern named to honor Admiral Cockburn and the decision he made that day. An alley that used to separate the two dwellings has been enclosed and converted into a parlor. It's been said that, from that parlor, Kitty Knight continues to watch over the houses she once protected so fiercely. A painting hanging over one of the fireplaces in the dining room beautifully commemorates the legend.

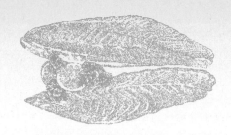

CEDAR PLANK SALMON
WITH TOMATO COULIS

4 8-ounce salmon fillets
2 medium tomatoes, diced
1 tablespoon minced garlic
¼ cup chopped fresh basil
¼ cup sugar
¼ cup red wine vinegar
¼ cup olive oil

Preheat oven to 425 degrees. Place each fillet on an individual cedar plank. Bake for 10 to 15 minutes until done. Place tomatoes, garlic, basil, sugar, vinegar, and olive oil in a blender and purée. Top each fillet with ¼ of Tomato Coulis. Serve immediately. Serves 4.

¼ cup olive oil
12 shrimp
12 scallops
3 andouille sausages, chopped
2 bell peppers, julienned
½ cup frozen corn
1 teaspoon minced garlic (optional)
4 cups Bloody Mary mix
2 chicken bouillon cubes
1 teaspoon cayenne pepper
salt and pepper to taste
¼ cup cornstarch
½ cup water

In a large sauté pan, heat oil and sauté shrimp and scallops for about 1 minute until cooked. Toss in sausages, bell peppers, corn, and garlic and cook until peppers are soft. Add Bloody Mary mix, bouillon cubes, cayenne, and salt and pepper. Bring to a boil. In a small bowl, combine cornstarch and water to form a slurry. Add cornstarch mixture slowly to boiling mixture, stirring well, until desired thickness is reached. Serves 2.

Venuti's Ristorante

16 East Patrick Street
Frederick, MD 21701
www.venutis.com
301-668-2700

As I chatted with Michael Everett and my server, Alex, it was obvious that they both take a great deal of pride in this venture. Everett operates the restaurant with his wife, Patty, who has a rich Italian heritage. Son Mike is the executive chef. As I read reviews of Venuti's, the Seafood Manicotti and the Veal Scaloppine were revered again and again. This restaurant has been voted "Best Italian" in Frederick on multiple occasions. After my experience, I can see why.

Venuti's is well known for its Garlic Rolls. When I arrived for a late lunch and asked Alex what she recommended, she said one of her favorite meals is Garlic Rolls with a glass of wine. Although Venuti's has a very fine wine list, I had to pass, since Karen and I had additional driving to do that day. I took Alex's advice on the Garlic Rolls, however. When they arrived, they were absolutely and utterly unique, not at all what I expected. Fashioned from homemade dough rolled with fresh garlic, Parmesan, and mozzarella, they looked similar to muffins. I ordered three, over which I ladled Marinara Sauce, then

savored each bite. Two were quite filling, so I saved the third for Karen. I wasn't aware she'd sampled hers until later, when I heard a resounding "Yum!"

Other antipasta options include Calamari Fritti, Bruschetta Florentine, and Portabello Grigliata, a grilled portabello mushroom stuffed with spinach, smoked salmon, and fresh mozzarella. The multiple salad selections are all accompanied by homemade dressings. The sandwiches, listed under "Paninis," are divided into northern Italian mild varieties and southern Italian spicy sandwiches. Venuti's offers baked pastas and stuffed pastas, including the delicious-sounding Lobster Ravioli. The numerous entrée choices for those wanting something other than pasta include Veal Con Cognac, a combination of veal cutlets, mushrooms, and spinach in Cognac Butter Sauce.

The desserts are outstanding, too. The Chocolate Rum Cake is an award-winning selection, and the Lemon Mousse Cheesecake has collected its own rave reviews. The pastry chef is quite creative, a fact that was prominently on display during my visit. A gnarled tree sat on the counter near my table. Upon reading the placard, I discovered that it was made entirely of chocolate and decorated with flowers and petals made of sugar. The workmanship was unbelievable.

I was told that the building was once a grain-storage facility. Michael Everett pointed out the old grain elevator shaft at the front of the building and told me that the original elevator works are still in place on the third floor. The heavy support beams typical of such structures are still visible today, wrapped in ivy accented by grape clusters to give an Italian feel. Michael also told me about the resident spirit that once removed the curtains at the front of the restaurant.

Located near the Weinberg Theater, this eatery is a frequent pre- and post-theater stop, partly thanks to its popular piano bar. No wonder Venuti's has been hailed. Ambiance, great food, and entertainment—what else could anyone want?

THICK FOCACCIA BREAD

3¼ cups lukewarm water
1 teaspoon sugar
¼-ounce package yeast
1 medium baking potato, peeled, boiled, and diced
5½ cups bread flour
1 teaspoon table salt
5 tablespoons olive oil, divided
1 tablespoon coarse salt

Place water in the bowl of an electric mixer fitted with a hook attachment. Add sugar and yeast and allow to sit for about 5 minutes until foamy. Add potatoes, flour, table salt, and 3 tablespoons olive oil and combine with dough hook until a soft dough is formed. Dough should be slightly sticky. Form dough into a ball and transfer to an oiled bowl. Cover with plastic wrap and set aside in a warm place to rise for 60 to 90 minutes until dough is doubled in size.

Preheat oven to 400 degrees. Knock down dough and place on an oiled sheet pan. Press into a rectangle about 15 by 10 inches. Cover loosely with plastic wrap and set aside in a warm place to rise for about 60 minutes until dough is doubled in size again.

Dimple dough, making ¼-inch-deep indentations with fingertips. Brush top of bread with remaining oil and sprinkle with coarse salt. Bake in bottom third of oven for 30 to 40 minutes until golden brown. Let bread cool in pan on a rack. Serve warm or at room temperature. Yields 1 loaf.

CROSTINI ALL'AGLIO ARROSTO

3 whole heads garlic
1 tablespoon olive oil
3 tablespoons unsalted butter, softened
1 baguette, sliced ½ inch thick
1 tablespoon Italian herbs
fruit or cheese

Preheat oven to 375 degrees. Cut off papery tips of garlic heads. Brush garlic liberally with oil. Place in a garlic roaster or wrap heads tightly in foil and place in a shallow baking dish. Bake about 2 hours until garlic is very soft but not browned. Remove from oven and allow to cool. Squeeze garlic bulbs over a small bowl until garlic comes out. Discard any paper from the mix. Mash garlic with a fork. Lightly butter bread slices and place on a baking sheet butter side up. Season with Italian herbs. Bake in oven for 7 or 8 minutes until crispy and lightly browned. Spread toasted bread with mashed garlic. Serve with fruit or cheese. Serves 4.

The Wharf Rat Fells Point

801 South Ann Street
Baltimore, MD 21231
www.thewharfrat.com
410-276-9034

Fells Point is reputed to have the peculiar distinction of housing more bars per square mile than anywhere else in the United States. It is interesting to note that there are actually fewer bars here today than there were a hundred years ago. One of them is The Wharf Rat, located on Ann Street. This is a favorite neighborhood location—one might almost say an institution—for locals and tourists. The building is over two hundred years old. Although it has spent most of that time as a tavern, there are myriad tales about the ladies of the evening who've plied their trade here over the years.

The original brick walls and wide plank floors speak to the building's age. The plain wooden tables and bentwood chairs allow patrons to sit in comfort and take in the nautical flavor of the place. Antique ship pictures and knotted ships' ropes festoon the walls and columns, giving a nod to the seamen of yore who doubtless bellied up to the bar during their few days ashore. The exposed wooden beams on the ceiling are covered with a vast collection of bar towels and beer coasters. Over the years, the tavern was patronized by merchants, shipbuilders, captains, privateers, immigrants, and freed slaves. Some just passed through, while others stayed and prospered together with the port. A vast amount of history awaits those who visit The Wharf Rat and the surrounding homes in this eclectic neighborhood. Given such a background, it is to be expected that apparitions haunt the area. A former owner of the tavern who was cut down in his prime is said to appear from time to time.

Thoughts of paranormal phenomena are never enough to sway us from our main objective—trying the food. Delicious offerings from the Seafood Bar included Coconut Shrimp with Raspberry Sauce (always a favorite with Debbie), Beer-Battered and Deep-Fried Calamari, Crab Cakes, and Oysters on the Half Shell, to name but a few. In the Galley, patrons were enjoying Roast Beef and Smoked Turkey Sandwiches, Cheddar-Battered Broccoli Florets with Honey Mustard Dipping Sauce, Sweet Southern Hush Puppies, and Jalapeño Poppers. We settled for The Wharf Rat's Crab and Artichoke Dip for two, served in a sourdough bread bowl. It was hard to beat with a side of Waffle-Cut Fries smothered in melted cheese, Ranch Dressing, and chives.

Bill Oliver, the owner, is renowned for brewing excellent British-style ales. Oliver Ironman Pale Ale and Oliver Irish Red are favorites here. Oliver Scottish Ale is reputed to be particularly uplifting on a cold winter day. It has a smoky toasted-malt flavor and a slightly fruity aroma. Whatever your choice, the nearly twenty Oliver beers won't leave you disappointed. Beer aficionados should try the Special Beer Tasting, three different beers for an exceptionally low price. Whatever your choice, it's sure to be exceptionally good!

SAVORY SHRIMP SALAD

1 pound 26-30 count shrimp
1/3 cup mayonnaise
2 stalks celery, chopped
1 tablespoon Old Bay seasoning
1 teaspoon celery seed
½ teaspoon dill weed

Boil shrimp until pink and firm; don't overcook. Shock shrimp in an ice-water bath until thoroughly cold. Chop shrimp into 1/3-inch pieces. In a separate bowl, combine mayonnaise, celery, Old Bay, celery seed, and dill weed. Add shrimp. Yields 2 cups. Note: The Wharf Rat serves this salad on a lightly toasted kaiser roll with potato chips and a dill pickle.

CRAB AND ARTICHOKE DIP

1 clove garlic
1 cup chopped artichoke hearts
2 8-ounce packages cream cheese, softened
1 cup fresh Maryland lump crabmeat, picked
1 cup mayonnaise
1 cup Parmesan cheese
1 sourdough boule

Mince garlic in a food processor. Add artichoke hearts and pulse until chopped fine. Slowly blend in cream cheese. Scrape into a large mixing bowl. Add crabmeat, mayonnaise, and Parmesan and mix well. Hollow out sourdough boule. Save center and dice. Pour dip into center of boule. Place diced bread around boule. Serve. Yields 6 cups dip.

3733 Old Columbia Pike
Ellicott City, MD 21043
www.tiberrivertavern.com
410-750-2002

Fried green tomatoes, I believe, are an acquired taste. We had them often in the summers of my childhood, but it was a food that no one else I knew ever had. Because they were unusual, fried green tomatoes certainly weren't on my list of favorites way back when. Quite a bit has changed since then, including my appreciation of this side dish. Fried green tomatoes appear on many menus throughout Maryland, and I took advantage of several opportunities to sample dishes that featured them.

At the Tiber River Tavern, Fried Green Tomatoes appear on the list of appetizers and as a salad, served with Black-Eyed Pea Salsa. After a cup of creamy Mushroom Bisque, I thoroughly enjoyed Tiber River's salad version. On another occasion, I might try the Muffaletta, which was popular with other guests, or perhaps the Sandtrap Fillet, which consists of twin petite Filet Mignons topped with alfalfa sprouts and Béarnaise Sauce on an English muffin. Karen was at an appointment of her own, but had she been along, she may have tipped her hat to her English heritage and ordered the Fish and Chips, or

she might have enjoyed the ample Spinach Calzone. During dinner, seafood exerts a larger influence on the menu in dishes like Classic Surf and Turf, Chesapeake Filet Mignon, and Maryland Crab Cakes. I liked the sound of the Pecan-Crusted Rainbow Trout and the Nantucket Rockfish, topped with cornmeal-dusted oysters and Corn Chowder Sauce.

The restaurant was fashioned from what was once an old barn. The horses of shopkeepers were stabled here on the hill as their owners plied their trades in the stores along the town's main street down below. The iron fittings, sliding doors, and crisp white trim on the exterior reflect the building's original use. Inside, an original stone wall makes a lovely backdrop. However, the overall atmosphere is that of a bistro, with crisp linens and simple furnishings.

The town of Ellicott City was founded by three Quaker brothers by the names of John, Andrew, and Joseph Ellicott. The trio arrived in 1772 and chose a spot to establish a flour mill in what was then wilderness. Their enterprise led Ellicott City to become one of the greatest milling and manufacturing towns in the East. The brothers also helped revolutionize area farming. They convinced farmers to plant wheat rather than tobacco and introduced fertilization to help replenish the soil that long-term tobacco farming had stripped of its nutrients. Charles Carroll, a signer of the Declaration of Independence, was one of their earliest converts.

The National Road runs through the center of Ellicott City, and the town boasts the B&O Railroad Station Museum, housed in the oldest railroad terminal in America. Built in 1831, the station saw a great deal of activity during the

Civil War. Ghost tours through the community stop at the Tiber River Tavern, trying to spot a woman in a white dress frequently seen at the upstairs windows. No one is quite sure of her origin, but the kitchen staff, having felt her presence on more than one occasion, verifies that she keeps a close eye on them. Designated a historic community in 1973, Ellicott City has much to offer.

 BLACK-EYED PEA SALSA

10-ounce can black-eyed peas, drained
1 tomato, diced
1 red pepper, diced
1 small cucumber, diced
1 bunch parsley, chopped
4 cloves garlic, chopped
juice of 2 lemons
¼ cup olive oil
salt and pepper to taste

Combine first 8 ingredients. Season with salt and pepper. Yields about 3 cups.

 GREEN CHILI STEW

¼ cup oil
3 roasted poblano peppers, diced fine
3 stalks celery, diced fine
1 large onion, diced fine
2 carrots, diced fine
1 large potato, diced fine
¼ cup chopped garlic
12 cups chicken stock
4 cups heavy cream
1 tablespoon cumin
1 teaspoon cayenne pepper
1 bunch cilantro, chopped
salt and pepper to taste
½ cup butter
½ cup flour

Heat oil in a large sauté pan. Sauté vegetables and garlic in oil until tender. Add chicken stock and cream. Stir in cumin, cayenne, and cilantro. Season to taste. Allow soup to simmer. Melt butter in a small saucepan. Whisk in flour to make a roux. Whisk roux into soup mixture with a wire whisk until all of roux is incorporated. Simmer for 20 minutes while soup thickens. Serves 12.

CHAPTER 6
Hearth and Home

Restaurant Columbia

What do elaborate mansions and simple log cabins have in common? Each, for someone, was home. Every individual has a slightly different definition of that word, perhaps influenced by reflecting on the one they experienced growing up or looking toward the one they'll create. Each of the eateries in this chapter was created in what was once a home. The chefs and owners share a bit of their own definition through the décor, ambiance, and menu as they extend their hospitality by welcoming guests into their "home."

Quills at The Catoctin

3619 Buckeystown Pike
Buckeystown, MD 21717
www.catoctininn.com
301-874-5555

George Buckey established a tannery in the late 1700s, utilizing a natural spring on his property. Just up the hill from the tannery was his home, which forms the back portion of today's Catoctin Inn. Across the street, George's brother, John, operated a tavern. Ultimately, the community was named for this enterprising family.

During the 1800s, Daniel Baker and his wife, Kitty, lived in the structure. By that time, the Buckeys' brick house had become too small to suit their needs. They raised the roof, enlarged the building, and remodeled the entire house. The north sitting room was where much of the Bakers' family life unfolded. I had dinner in that room with general manager Rita Barrett Waltz and Michele Mauro Small, the Catoctin's corporate events manager.

The property remained in the Baker family for 123 years until it was purchased by Ella King Prime in 1955. Several owners have come and gone since then. The restored carriage house has been used as an antique shop now and again. Four other permanent structures—the stables, the staff cottage, the smokehouse, and the manor house—dot the property.

The wide front porch of the manor house, with its simple Doric columns, welcomes guests as they arrive along Buckeystown Pike. Once inside, they can't help feeling the elegance of yesteryear as they enter the gracious center hall flanked by parlors painted in cream and taupe. Large windows afford sweeping views of the historic village of Buckeystown and the Catoctin Mountains. Guests staying at the inn are invited to partake of a full country breakfast served in the elegant dining rooms or on the sun porch. Visitors just stopping by can also enjoy breakfast, Sunday brunch, lunch, and dinner. Whatever meal takes your fancy, it's sure to be tasty and served promptly by informative wait staff in colonial costume.

Without Debbie on this occasion, I knew that choosing from the delicious-sounding options on the menu was going to be difficult. However, Rita and Michele generously allowed me to taste their choices, so I wouldn't miss anything. I began with Blue Crab Corn Chowder and can say without hesitation that it was the best I've ever had. Among the interesting entrée choices was Catoctin Brook Trout, smoked in English Tea and served with Cranberry Wild Rice, and Concord Partridge, rubbed with rosemary and served with Baked Apple Stuffing. My selection of Seneca Red Jacket Duck in Bing Cherry Sauce was superb, as were the Crab Cakes with Apricot-Pecan Rice. Rita told me that a gentleman guest had sampled the duck two days earlier and found it so delicious that he returned the next day bringing a large group of friends with him to savor the selection again!

The dessert menu is short, but every item is homemade and quite wonderful. I sampled the

Amaretto Citrus Custard with caramelized sugar and the Apple Cobbler with homemade Vanilla Ice Cream. Ever a sucker for chocolate, I pronounced the Milk Chocolate Boat filled with Chocolate Mousse my favorite. Whatever you choose when visiting Quills, you're sure to find a favorite, too!

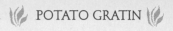

SENECA RED JACKET DUCK IN BING CHERRY SAUCE

2 6-ounce duck breasts
salt and pepper to taste
2 tablespoons oil, divided
2 cups Bing cherries
2 cups cherry brandy
2 tablespoons butter
2 shallots, chopped
2 large sweet potatoes, peeled, diced, and blanched
2 tablespoons orange liqueur
2 tablespoons chopped walnuts, toasted

Preheat oven to 350 degrees. Season duck with salt and pepper. In a medium ovenproof sauté pan, heat 1 tablespoon oil and sear duck on both sides. Place pan in oven and bake for 15 minutes. Remove pan from oven. Remove duck from pan and set aside. Add cherries and brandy to pan and cook on stove about 10 minutes until liquid is a syrup consistency. Add butter and swirl until melted to finish Bing Cherry Sauce. Heat remaining oil in a large sauté pan and sweat shallots until translucent. Add sweet potatoes and season to taste. Cook about 5 minutes until thoroughly warm. Finish with orange liqueur and sprinkle walnuts on top. Serves 2.

POTATO GRATIN

1 tablespoon butter, softened
1 cup heavy cream
1 teaspoon salt
$1/8$ teaspoon pepper
pinch of grated nutmeg
2 pounds potatoes, peeled and sliced thick
1 large clove garlic, peeled and minced
½ cup Parmesan cheese

Preheat oven to 350 degrees. Rub bottom and sides of a 5- to 6-cup gratin dish or shallow baking dish with half the butter. In a medium saucepan, bring cream, salt, pepper, nutmeg, potatoes, and garlic to a boil over medium-high heat, stirring continuously. Reduce heat and simmer for 3 to 5 minutes until liquid thickens. Stir in Parmesan. Pour potato mixture evenly into prepared dish. Gently press down potatoes until submerged in liquid and dot with remaining butter. Bake for 20 minutes, stirring twice. Continue baking another 15 to 25 minutes until potatoes are done and top is golden brown. Remove from oven, let rest 5 minutes, and serve. Serves 4 to 6.

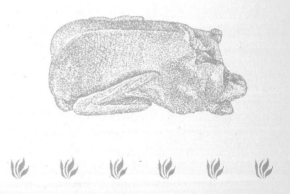

Tersiguel's

FRENCH COUNTRY RESTAURANT

8293 Main Street
Ellicott City, MD 21043
www.tersiguels.com
410-465-4004

Owners Fernand and Odette Tersiguel have been serving their unique version of French food for over twenty years in Maryland. The menu at Tersiguel's is reflective of the cuisine at their original home in Brittany, France. It's a cuisine that changes with the seasons, an authentic French cuisine with rustic overtones. Their son, Michel, the youngest chef ever to be awarded the title Grand Master Chef of America, is now responsible for Tersiguel's continuing acclaim.

The restaurant is located in the heart of historic Ellicott City. The city, founded in 1772 by Quakers John, Joseph, and Andrew Ellicott, became one of the greatest milling and manufacturing towns in the East. The charming nineteenth-century three-story structure that houses Tersiguel's is painted white with dark shutters. It features two large dormer windows overlooking Ellicott City's historic Main Street. Once the home of the first mayor of Ellicott City, the restaurant now houses six separate dining rooms.

Alone for lunch on a windy spring day, I was looking forward to a delicious meal. I entered through the front door and spent a few moments looking at all of the awards that Fernand, Odette,

and Michel have accumulated over the years. I was seated in the Hunt Room, so called because of all the hunting pictures lining the walls. My server, Vickie, carefully explained the menu and the specials of the day. Patrons may choose the prix fixe menu, order à la carte, or, if they're feeling adventurous, try the Chef's Tasting Menu.

The homemade Sausage with Warm Potato Salad sounded lovely, as did the Pan-Seared Scallops with Cauliflower Sauce. The Ruby Trout with Black Butter is one of the house specialties and almost always appears on the menu. However, the special of the day, Pan-Roasted Grouper with Crayfish and Wild Mushroom Sauce, piqued my interest, as it contained three of my favorite things to eat. Cooked to perfection, the grouper did not disappoint, and I savored every mouthful. On another visit, I might opt for the Pan-Seared Kobe Beef Sirloin with Wild Porcini Mushroom Ragout or perhaps the Grilled Filet Mignon with Foie Gras Mashed Potatoes and Truffle Sauce. A large number of fabulous salads, crepes, and hors d'oeuvres are also offered.

Full almost to the brim, I consulted Vickie about Les Delices de la Maison—or, in other words, dessert! My choices were Chocolate Mousse, Chocolate Triple Layer Cake, Tiramisu, Pear Tarte, Apple Tarte, and homemade ice cream. The Poire Tarte Tatin was extremely good. I decided that I had better take a long walk around town to work off those calories.

Next time I visit, I'm going to bring Debbie along to enjoy the experience. The Tersiguels grow many of their own herbs, fruits, vegetables, and edible flowers. They even raise their own goats and make a very creamy chèvre that I know will be a favorite of Debbie's. This is definitely a place for delicious food, flavorful wines, and attentive service!

🌿 RUBY TROUT WITH BLACK BUTTER 🌿

4 small fillets ruby or red trout
salt and pepper to taste
½ cup flour
4 tablespoons oil, divided
3 tablespoons sweet butter, softened
juice of 1 lemon
1 rounded tablespoon capers
4 fingerling potatoes, parboiled
1 shallot, diced fine
8 asparagus spears, blanched

Season trout with salt and pepper, then dredge in flour. In a large sauté pan, heat 2 tablespoons oil and sauté trout over medium heat until golden on both sides. In a medium saucepan, cook butter about 5 minutes until dark brown solids form. Remove saucepan from heat and allow to cool. Add lemon juice and capers and reheat to serve. In a medium sauté pan, sauté potatoes in remaining oil. When potatoes have colored slightly, add shallots and asparagus and heat through for about 3 minutes. To serve, place potatoes, shallots, and asparagus around plate, place trout in center, and spoon sauce over trout. Serves 2.

🌿 PAN-ROASTED SCALLOPS 🌿 WITH GINGER AND LEMON GRASS JUS

2 tablespoons olive oil
1 tablespoon chopped lemon grass
1 tablespoon chopped ginger
1 shallot, chopped
1 clove garlic, chopped
salt and pepper to taste
½ cup chicken stock
4 tablespoons sweet butter, divided
16 sea scallops
16 snow peas
1 tomato, chopped
1 tablespoon chopped parsley

In a medium sauté pan, heat oil and sauté lemon grass, ginger, shallots, and garlic. Season with salt and pepper. Add chicken stock and bring to a boil. Reduce heat and simmer until reduced by half. In a separate pan, heat 2 tablespoons butter and sauté scallops about 6 minutes until golden on both sides. Remove scallops from pan and set aside. Add snow peas, tomatoes, and lemon grass mixture to pan. Add remaining butter and swirl to create sauce. Divide vegetable mixture between 2 plates and place scallops on top. Garnish with parsley. Serves 2.

28 South Washington Street
Easton, MD 21601
www.restaurantcolumbia.com
410-770-5172

The two-and-a-half-story Federal townhouse that functions as Restaurant Columbia was once the home of Judge Tharpe, a well-known bachelor of his time. The judge still makes his presence known from time to time. Perhaps he's holding court, or just making sure his old home is in good hands.

The structure was built around 1795, but the third floor was added at a later date. The addition is clearly marked by a change in the brickwork from the earlier Flemish bond brick. The most notable portion of the townhouse may well be its balcony-style porch with side steps. Chamfered posts adorned with ornate brackets support a low hip roof. The balustrade across the front is an excellent example of nineteenth-century ironwork made by a famous ironworker of the day.

Indoors, many features from the home's bygone era still exist. The stairway with turned balusters and a heavy newel is but one example. The mantelpieces in each of the dining rooms are another. I was seated at a cozy table for two nestled into a nook right beside the fireplace in the Blue Room, where the two-tone walls are offset by crisp white trim, white table linens, and flickering white candles. In the front dining room, the taupe walls create a subdued mood.

The décor here has been described in many write-ups as minimalist. One review went so far as to say that the fresh food prepared by chef-owner Stephen Mangasarian provides a décor of its own. From my experience, I'd have to agree. I began my meal with Summer Squash and Zucchini Double Soup. It arrived in a shallow soup bowl, the Zucchini Soup forming the center and the Summer Squash Soup forming an outer ring. Regardless of how my spoon moved through the dish, the two didn't mix. Instead, they created an ever-changing pattern of swirls. All in all, my starter was attractive and delicious down to the last bite. Although the menu changes every three weeks, the Rack of Lamb with Pistachio and Raspberry Sauce is always one of the entrées. Because it's the signature dish, I was very tempted to try the lamb but was ultimately drawn to the Crab and Lobster Cakes. I was sorry Karen wasn't with me to enjoy the Ahi Tuna in Corn Sauce with Chili Pepper Relish. I'm sure it would have been every bit as delicious as my choice was. Since everything here is made fresh on the premises, I decided to splurge. The dessert choices on any given night might range from Ginger Ice Cream in Crisp Lemon Phyllo to a traditional French Napoleon. I savored the Blood Orange Sorbet that late-summer evening, its tartness the perfect follow-up to my seafood entrée.

Not only is Stephen creative in the kitchen, his artwork adorns the walls of the restaurant. Restaurant Columbia is quite a successful endeavor considering that Stephen started out with an undergraduate degree in psychology, followed by a master's in education. He got into the kitchen after meeting a noted French chef through a mutual friend. Why don't you continue your own culinary education by enjoying dinner at Restaurant Columbia? *Bon appétit!*

ROASTED RACK OF LAMB WITH PISTACHIO AND RASPBERRY SAUCE

1 tablespoon chopped fresh rosemary
1 tablespoon chopped fresh parsley
1 tablespoon chopped fresh thyme
2 tablespoons minced onion
2 teaspoons minced garlic
2 tablespoons balsamic vinegar
3 tablespoons olive oil
1 teaspoon freshly ground pepper
1 teaspoon kosher salt
14- to 16-ounce rack of lamb (chine bone removed), trimmed and frenched
2 cups fresh raspberries
1 tablespoon sugar
1 tablespoon framboise or Chambord liqueur
1 cup chicken stock
½ cup chopped pistachios

In a large bowl, combine rosemary, parsley, thyme, onion, garlic, vinegar, olive oil, pepper, and salt. Add lamb and coat with mixture. Refrigerate for 4 hours, turning every hour to ensure uniform soaking. Meanwhile, purée raspberries, sugar, and liqueur in a blender until smooth. Force through a fine sieve to remove seeds. Preheat oven to 375 degrees. Heat a heavy-bottomed skillet to the point where a drop of water sizzles immediately. Place lamb in pan and sear about 2 minutes until dark brown. Place lamb in a roasting pan bone side down and pour purée over meat. Add chicken stock to pan and place in oven for 14 to 16 minutes for medium-rare. Remove lamb from pan and allow to rest for 5 minutes before serving. Add remaining purée to juices in roasting pan. Skim off any fat and pour this sauce over lamb, reserving some for table use. Garnish with pistachios. Serves 4.

CHOCOLATE MOUSSE

5 egg yolks
¼ cup superfine sugar
6-ounce package semisweet chocolate, melted
2 cups heavy cream, whipped
1½ teaspoons amaretto
1½ teaspoons dark rum
1½ teaspoons Kahlua

Combine egg yolks and sugar and cook in the top of a double boiler until slightly thickened. Remove from heat and add chocolate in a smooth stream while stirring. When chocolate is completely incorporated into egg mixture, add whipped cream in 3 equal amounts while stirring. When mixture is smooth, add amaretto, rum, and Kahlua. Pour mousse through a sieve into a serving dish and refrigerate at least 2 hours. Serves 4.

ABACROMBIE

FINE FOOD AND ACCOMMODATIONS

58 West Biddle Street
Baltimore, MD 21201
www.abacrombie.net
410-244-7227

Operagoers streamed in the night that I visited Abacrombie Fine Food. Judging by the greetings from the staff and patrons at other tables, many of them must have been regulars. Located in the heart of the cultural district right across the street from the Meyerhoff Symphony Hall, Abacrombie would certainly be my choice of a dinner destination prior to enjoying a concert or a show. The restaurant's white linen table coverings, modern lighting, and old brick walls painted with a faux finish create an upscale, yet relaxing, atmosphere.

Had Karen been with me, we may have chosen the six-course Menu of the Moment, the selections for each course a surprise until they arrive at your table. Many of those seated around me chose the three-course prix fixe menu, which can be ordered with or without accompanying wines. Selections for the prix fixe might include Cream of Corn Soup served with a Sauvignon Blanc, followed by Oven-Roasted Rack of Lamb accompanied by Paringa Shiraz, then topped off by Caramel Flan, a Cinnamon Churro, and Span-

ish Hot Chocolate with a dessert wine of Santa Julia Tardio. There are also wine dinners and themed dinners throughout the year, providing diners myriad opportunities to experience all that Abacrombie has to offer.

The menu changes frequently to take advantage of fresh seasonal ingredients. On another occasion, I may choose the Gazpacho Salad with Avocado Sorbet and Crunchy Dried Corn. However, I opted for the Orange-Glazed Beets with lettuce, Maytag Blue Cheese, and Pear-Port Reduction as an unusual, tasty way to begin my meal. I followed that with the White Truffle-Crusted Scottish Salmon, accompanied by Mashed Potatoes, Asparagus, and a *vin blanc*. Perfectly prepared, the meal was outstanding. Although I was quite satisfied, I gave in to my curiosity and sampled the Banana Spring Roll, a creative twist on the longtime favorite Bananas Foster. Witnessing my obvious enjoyment, two gentlemen at the table next to me followed suit and also declared their approval.

Melanie and Sonny Sweetman are the proprietors of Abacrombie. Sonny is also the chef responsible for the delicious creations that have won a great many accolades. Abacrombie was named Best Restaurant in Baltimore in 2003 and has found its way onto the top-fifty list for the state of Maryland on multiple occasions. One of Sonny's recipes was featured in a 2004 issue of *Bon Appétit*, which declared Abacrombie an "in spot" for dining. Sonny won the Chesapeake Seafood Challenge with the recipes we've featured here. Known not only for its food but also for its accommodations, the establishment has been recognized as the best bed-and-breakfast in Baltimore.

The property that today houses Abacrombie began as the city residence of Colonel Chapman Biddle, who served in the Union army and was a member of the prominent Philadelphia Biddle family. The street that runs along the front bears their name. No doubt, he would be quite proud of the prominence achieved here now.

 CORIANDER CABBAGE

4 strips bacon, diced
¼ onion, diced
½ cup cream
2 tablespoons butter
¼ cup crab stock
¼ head Savoy cabbage, shredded
¼ teaspoon coriander
salt and pepper to taste

Render bacon in a medium skillet. Add onions and cook until tender. Drain fat. Pour cream into skillet and slowly reduce by half. Add butter to finish. Pour crab stock into a medium saucepan. Add cabbage and cover. Turn heat to high and shake saucepan over heat to steam cabbage and prevent sticking; steam for 2 minutes. Add coriander. Pour cream sauce over cabbage and toss to coat. Season to taste. Serves 2 as a side dish or 4 as a garnish.

 PUFF PASTRY-WRAPPED MARYLAND ROCKFISH WITH CORN-CRAB SAUCE

2 ears corn, cooked
1 package puff pastry
4 6-ounce Maryland rockfish fillets
1 clove garlic, roasted and minced

2 cups crab stock
1 cup cream
1 egg
1 tablespoon water
6 tablespoons butter
½ teaspoon turmeric

Preheat oven to 400 degrees. Remove kernels from corncobs and set aside. Using half a sheet of puff pastry for each fillet, butcher-wrap fillets. Refrigerate for 5 minutes. While pastry is chilling, combine garlic, crab stock, and cream in a medium saucepan. Reduce by half over medium-low heat. While sauce is cooking, combine egg and water to make an egg wash. Remove fish from refrigerator, brush with egg wash, and bake for 8 minutes. Finish sauce with butter. Add turmeric and corn. Spoon sauce onto plates and top with fillets. Serves 4.

 SMOKED PEPPER FLAN

1 tablespoon butter
1 roasted red pepper
2 tablespoons paprika
1 cup heavy cream
4 eggs

Butter 4 custard cups and set aside. Preheat oven to 325 degrees. Purée red pepper. Add paprika and cream. Add eggs and process to combine. Pour into custard cups and bake for 13 minutes. Turn out of custard cups and serve. Serves 4.

301 South Union Avenue
Havre de Grace, MD 21078
www.vandiverinn.com
800-245-1655

During the Revolutionary War, this area was visited multiple times by the renowned General Lafayette. During one of his sojourns, he suggested that the community reminded him of Le Havre, a well-known French seaport. From that comment, the town's name, Havre de Grace—"Harbor of Grace"—was derived. Later, during the search for a capital city for the young United States of America, Havre de Grace was strongly considered, losing out to Washington, D.C., by the narrowest of margins—a single vote.

History tells that during the War of 1812, British ships sailed up the Chesapeake Bay. After burning Washington, D.C., and then being staved off at Baltimore, the Brits arrived at Havre de Grace. Most of the townspeople fled, leaving only Lieutenant John O'Neill to defend the town single-handedly. After being wounded and captured, O'Neill was imprisoned aboard one of the British ships while everything in town save two houses and a church were burned. Accounts indicate that O'Neill's fifteen-year-old daughter, Matilda, pleaded with the admiral of the fleet to

spare her father's life. Apparently, Matilda was quite persuasive, because Admiral George Cockburn released O'Neill and presented Matilda with his personal sword and gold snuffbox. O'Neill went on to become the keeper of the lighthouse built at Concord Point in 1827. The position of lightkeeper remained in the O'Neill family until the lighthouse was automated in the latter part of the twentieth century.

The history of this town is rich and interesting. Many, many of its historic buildings have been preserved for use as shops and bed-and-breakfasts. One such structure is the Vandiver Mansion, built in 1886 by Murray Vandiver as a wedding gift for his wife, Anna. Located along Union Avenue, it's just a few blocks from the bay and downtown. Vandiver served as the mayor of Havre de Grace and as Maryland's state treasurer. The home remained in the family until sometime in the late 1960s or early 1970s. Today, it functions as the Vandiver Inn, specializing in romantic getaways, weddings, and corporate events. To our benefit, the inn also hosts themed dinners by reservation several times a year. In April, John and Susan Muldoon host an "I Got Dem Tax Payin' Blues" dinner, featuring a blues-and-jazz trio and a Southern blues-inspired menu. Starters of Spicy Shrimp on Cheddar Cheese Grits and Tomato and Green Bean Salad with Creole Buttermilk Dressing capture both the flavor of the event and the attention of the dinner guests. Entrées for the evening include Barbecued Pork Ribs in North Carolina Barbecue Sauce and Cornmeal-Crusted Catfish in Mustard Sauce. Both are served with Maple-Glazed Sweet Potato Rounds and Pineapple Coleslaw, which is as tasty as it is unique. Desserts such as Mini Rum Cakes in Pineapple and Coconut Sauce finish off an evening that definitely relieves the annual stress of mid-April. Mother's Day brunch, wine-tasting dinners, and monthly jazz dinners are also on the schedule. Go and add your endorsement to the list of rave reviews of The Vandiver Inn.

ROASTED TOMATO AND GARLIC BISQUE

28-ounce can Italian plum tomatoes in juice
6 cloves garlic, peeled
1 large onion, sliced
4 cups water or chicken stock
¼ cup sherry
1 cup heavy cream
cayenne pepper to taste
salt and pepper to taste

Preheat oven to 400 degrees. Put tomatoes and juice, garlic, and onions in a roasting pan. Roast for at least 1 hour until tomatoes are slightly shriveled and browned. Transfer contents of roasting pan to a large saucepan. Add water or stock and bring to a boil. Turn down heat to low and simmer until all vegetables are soft. Purée with an immersion blender or in a food processor until smooth. Transfer back to saucepan. Add sherry and cream. Simmer for about 10 minutes. Season to taste with cayenne and salt and pepper. Serves 6.

SMOKED DUCK AND MUSHROOMS

1 cup grated Parmesan cheese
2 smoked magret duck breasts
½ pound white mushrooms, cleaned and sliced thin
½ pound assorted mushrooms (shiitake, oyster, porcini)
½ cup plus 1 tablespoon olive oil, divided
salt and pepper to taste
1 large onion
¼ cup balsamic vinegar
4 cups mixed greens

Preheat oven to 400 degrees. Spray a baking sheet with cooking spray. Create 8 circles to make Parmesan crisps by spooning Parmesan into 2-inch circles on baking sheet. Bake for 8 to 10 minutes until lightly browned. Remove from oven and cool on a wire rack. Julienne the duck breasts, removing any fat and membrane. Sauté mushrooms in 1 tablespoon oil until just cooked through. Season with salt and pepper. Combine mushrooms and duck and warm through in sauté pan. Keep warm. To make Caramelized Onion Vinaigrette, dice onion and sauté in remaining olive oil until golden and tender. Add vinegar, stirring briskly to incorporate. Season to taste. Toss greens with a small amount of vinaigrette. Portion salad onto 4 plates. Place ¼ of duck mixture on top of greens. Drizzle with remaining vinaigrette and top with Parmesan crisps. Serves 4.

The Inn at Buckeystown

3521 Buckeystown Pike
Buckeystown, MD 21717
www.innatbuckeystown.com
301-874-5755

The snow had fallen heavily and was cling-ing to the branches of the stately trees around the inn. The effect was beautiful, adding to the charm and grandeur of this 1897 Victorian trea-sure. The home was built by a Mr. Keller, who operated the lime kilns nearby. The lovely stair-case that leads to the second and third floors is registered with the Smithsonian. Made of Mary-land chestnut, it cannot be replaced due to the fact that chestnut trees were blighted at the turn of the twentieth century. During recent mainte-nance, proprietress Janet Wells discovered that the doors, covered in layers and layers of paint, are also made of the same wood. No doubt, af-ter much elbow grease, that feature of the house will also be returned to its original splendor. One of the most interesting features is the stained-glassed windows on the front wall of the home. During our research, we found some indication that they were completed by students of Louis Comfort Tiffany.

We relaxed in the Music Room, just to the right of the main hall. Perched upon a settee in front of a welcoming fire, we enjoyed the ambi-ance created by the high ceilings, the tall, thin windows, and the antique instruments lining the walls. Just to the back of the Music Room is the Morning Room, where breakfast for overnight guests is served. Each bedroom has a distinct personality. For example, The Homefront is a Civil War-themed room, The Victoriana is deco-rated according to that period, and Teddy's Place is full of antique toys and dolls.

After our tour, we settled ourselves across the hall in the dining room. Our table for two in front of the fire was perfect for that particular evening. We started our five-course meal with an *amuse-bouche* of Lobster in Lobster Butter Sauce. The second course was a choice of French Onion Soup or Buffalo Hot Wing Soup. Of course, we tried both. Chunks of blue cheese and streaks of buffalo-wing sauce punctuated the creamy soup. Karen thoroughly enjoyed the Pick-led Vegetable Salad, since it featured beets, of which she is incredibly fond. Debbie found the Asian Salad with Shrimp deliciously flavored with ginger. We duly enjoyed our entrées of Mushroom- and Herb-Stuffed Chicken and Po-tato-Crusted Salmon. The outstanding Flourless Chocolate Cake, served with ice cream on a bed of Raspberry Coulis, was equaled by the Soufflé with Baileys Irish Cream.

The Inn at Buckeystown is open for lunch, dinner, and tea by reservation only. The tea here has been voted the favorite of the Afternoon Tea Society on multiple occasions. Offerings such as Wild Rice Chicken Soup, Stuffed Plum Tomatoes, Cheese Broccoli Puffs, Egg Salad in Mint Puff Pastry, and Carrot Slices with Herbed Cream Cheese are just a few of the items guests might be offered. The selection of teas is incredible—

it's six pages long! South African Vanilla Rooibos, Chinese Keemun, and flavored teas such as Peach Melba and Tiramisu are among the myriad choices. The chef's creations coupled with Janet's enthusiasm have created a definite success at The Inn at Buckeystown.

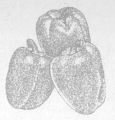

CHAMPAGNE VINAIGRETTE DRESSING

½ cup olive oil
2 tablespoons Dijon mustard
1½ cups champagne vinegar
1 large shallot, minced fine
salt and pepper to taste
½ teaspoon sugar
2 teaspoons fresh herbs of your choice

Whip oil into mustard in a deep bowl. Add vinegar to thin as needed to keep dressing from breaking up. Add remaining ingredients. Yields 2 cups.

JAMAICAN FRICASSEED CHICKEN

¼ cup flour
4 chicken breasts, cut in half
2 tablespoons butter
1 onion
1 bunch green onions
1 green pepper
1 tomato
2 serrano peppers
2 cloves garlic
2 tablespoons soy sauce
2 tablespoons hot sauce
2 tablespoons Worcestershire sauce
½ cup coconut milk
1 cup orange juice
1 teaspoon thyme

Flour the chicken and sauté in butter until brown on 1 side. While chicken is browning, dice onion, green onions, and green pepper. Set aside. Peel, seed, and dice tomato. Seed and dice serrano peppers. Mince garlic. Add vegetables and garlic to pan with chicken. Sauté until onions are soft. Add liquids and thyme. Continue to simmer for 12 to 18 minutes until chicken is done. Add water to sauce as necessary to maintain desired thickness. Serves 4.

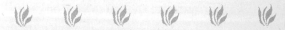

208 Talbot

208 North Talbot Street
St. Michaels, MD 21663
www.208talbot.com
410-745-3838

This block along Talbot Street in downtown St. Michaels is the only one in town on which every structure is brick. In years past, a brickyard and kiln sat just behind this row of structures. It is believed that the buildings in the 200 block of North Talbot Street belonged primarily to individuals working at the brick company, and that 208 was the company owner's residence. Today, most of the structures might not be immediately recognized by the brickyard employees, since they are awash in color—blue, white, taupe, yellow—adding to the charm of this quaint village.

The building at 208 Talbot is the taupe one, trimmed in burgundy awnings and black shutters, which work together to create an exterior that speaks of subdued elegance. In the interior, red-brick walls, brick floors, and tiny original fireplaces are juxtaposed with crisp white table linens and classic stemware. The walls are painted a very pale sage and adorned with brass sconces and multiple botanical prints, creating a soothing, restful atmosphere.

We were fortunate enough to visit on opening night, after the restaurant had been closed for the off-season. The majority of diners were local residents, who chatted amiably with Candace Chiaruttini as they were seated. Candace and her husband, chef Paul Milne, are the owners of 208 Talbot. No doubt, the locals like to sneak in and get their fill of Paul's creations before having to compete with tourists for reservations.

The specials that evening were a creamy Seafood Chowder and a Pan-Seared Shad Roe entrée served atop a bed of spinach with Chardonnay Cream Sauce. We'd recently read an article in a local magazine lamenting the decline of restaurants serving shad roe. Hopefully, the author will discover its availability here. Many of the options were appealing, making it difficult to choose. Wild Mushroom Ravioli with Rosemary Cream, Sautéed Shrimp on a Soft Corn Tortilla, and Grilled Quail with Salad of Frisee, Bacon, Red Grapes, and Almonds highlighted the list of starters.

Each entrée is served with a choice of either a salad or a sorbet. As a change of pace, we both opted for the latter, thoroughly enjoying the Passion Fruit Sorbet. The salads that evening were dressed in either Creamy Blue Cheese or Dijon Parmesan Vinaigrette, both made in-house. The Cassoulet of Lobster, Monkfish, Shrimp, Clams, and Mussels with Shellfish Cream Sauce was a popular entrée selection throughout the dining room. Karen chose the Salmon on Hash Brown Potatoes, while Debbie enjoyed the Pan-Roasted Halibut with Lobster Mashed Potatoes and Lobster Cream Sauce. Both were quite delicious.

Although we left ourselves no room for dessert, the choices were creative and appealing—Strawberry Rhubarb Crisp, White Chocolate

Bread Pudding, Butterscotch Pot de Crème, Banana Cheesecake with Chocolate, Key Lime Tart, Caramel Espresso Ice Cream Float, fresh raspberries topped with a wide variety of options ranging from Crème Anglaise to liqueurs. Next time, definitely!

OYSTERS WITH CHAMPAGNE SAUCE

1 tablespoon minced shallots
½ cup dry champagne
2 tablespoons champagne vinegar
½ cup heavy cream
4 tablespoons unsalted butter
salt and white pepper to taste
20 oysters, shucked
¼ cup thinly sliced prosciutto
¼ cup chopped pistachios
1 cup rock salt
4 sprigs fresh parsley

Place shallots, champagne, and vinegar in a small saucepan over medium heat. Bring to a boil and cook to reduce by ⅓. Add cream and cook to reduce again by ⅓. Remove pan from heat but keep the burner on low. Cut butter into small pieces and whisk into sauce 1 piece at a time. Return pot to burner for a few seconds if sauce cools too much to melt butter. Season with salt and white pepper, adding just the minimum. Strain through a fine-mesh sieve and keep warm over hot water. Preheat oven to 450 degrees. Place oysters on a baking sheet and bake for 3 to 4 minutes until edges begin to curl. Julienne prosciutto into ¹⁄₁₆-inch slices. Spoon Champagne Sauce over oysters and top with prosciutto and pistachios. Return oysters to oven for 45 seconds to warm sauce. Divide rock salt equally among 4 plates. Place 5 oysters atop rock salt. Garnish with parsley. Serves 4.

COFFEE-BUTTERFINGER CRUNCH ICE CREAM

1 tablespoon instant coffee powder
2 tablespoons hot water
2 cups half-and-half
2 cups heavy cream
8 egg yolks
¹⁄₃ cup sugar
3 or 4 Butterfinger candy bars, chopped coarse

Combine coffee with hot water and set aside. Place half-and-half and cream in a heavy medium-sized saucepan. Bring mixture to a boil over medium heat, stirring occasionally to make sure it doesn't boil over. In a medium bowl, beat yolks and sugar until mixture is fluffy and pale in color. Add ¼ of the cream mixture to eggs, then pour mixture back into saucepan. Whisk dissolved coffee into mixture in pan. Place pan over low heat and stir constantly with a wooden spoon until mixture thickens so that a line drawn on the back of the spoon does not fill in. Be careful not to let custard boil, or yolks will curdle. Strain through a fine-mesh sieve and cool in a bowl set over ice cubes. Freeze mixture in an ice-cream machine according to manufacturer's instructions. When mixture is almost frozen, stir in candy pieces. Continue to freeze until hard. Serves 6 to 8.

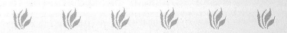

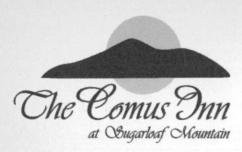

The Comus Inn
at Sugarloaf Mountain

23900 Old Hundred Road
Dickerson, MD 20842
www.TheComusInn.com
301-349-5100

The Comus Inn came to our attention through word of mouth, which is our favorite and most reliable method of research. The inn had just reopened after extensive renovation, so we might have missed it altogether if it hadn't been for that chance comment. Once we heard about it, we were bound and determined to seek it out despite an unexpected snowstorm and winding country roads. What we discovered at a crossroads in rural Montgomery County was a white farmhouse-style structure with a red tin roof. Inside, we were greeted by the cheery yellow vestibule and the incredibly helpful sommelier, David M. Dantzic. Even though we arrived unannounced, he readily gave us a tour of the lovely restaurant. The hues of yellow and gold throughout gave the dining rooms a warm, restful ambiance.

The large dining room to the rear of the restaurant has an expansive wall of windows designed to capture the view of Sugarloaf Mountain. A quaint barn and nearby pond at the back of the property also provide a pleasant backdrop. To the front of the restaurant is the chef's tasting room, called the Happy Choice Room. A window allows guests to view the activity in the ultramodern kitchen, whereas the log beams from the original 1862 structure refer to the days when cooking was not nearly so enjoyable. The dining room overhead, also part of the original two-story cabin made of hand-hewn chestnut logs, was Debbie's favorite because of its coziness.

The first construction on the property was done by Robert Johnson. A second period of construction occurred around 1885 courtesy of Hamilton Wolfe and well-known local builder William T. Hilton, whose addition gave the inn its current configuration. The central hall with straight stairs and turned balusters was added at that time. The built-in cabinetry in one of the dining rooms also dates to that period.

The restaurant is open for lunch, dinner, and Sunday brunch. Sandwiches and salads dominate the lunch menu. Choices include Yellow Bowl Shrimp Salad and Crabtini, which consists of jumbo lump crab served with Lemon Sabayon on a bed of watercress and Italian parsley. Karen agreed that she'd be quite happy with that most days of the week! The Ham Sandwich is served on focaccia bread with roasted asparagus and Brie. A different Po-Boy is available every day, and each is quite a handful. The uniquely organized dinner menu gives diners options for three, four, and five-course menus. Curried Winter Oysters with Wilted Spinach and Champagne is listed in the "Creamy and Soothing" section, while Smoked Salmon on Goat Cheese Johnny Cake is listed in the "Piquant and Smokey" column. The Seared Beef Tenderloin with Foie Gras on Parmesan Polenta, found in the "Bold and

Aggressive" menu section, can't be beat. With so many choices and so much history, the future of The Comus Inn is as bright as its well-chosen hues.

SEARED SEA SCALLOPS WITH PARMESAN CUSTARD

4 cups heavy cream
1½ ounces Parmigiano Reggiano, grated fine
1 ounce Pecorino Romano
1 tablespoon fresh basil
scant 1 cup granulated sugar
7 eggs
8-ounce package cream cheese, room temperature
1½ gelatin leaves or ½ packet gelatin, softened in warm water according to package directions
1 tablespoon butter
½ to ¾ cup clarified butter
24 sea scallops
⅛ teaspoon fresh lemon juice
Lemon Sabayon (see next column)
cooked baby beets, sliced

Combine cream, cheeses, and basil in a medium saucepan. Bring to scalding over medium-high heat. Remove from heat and let sit, allowing mixture to infuse. Whisk together sugar and eggs until light and smooth. Strain hot cream mixture through cheesecloth. Return to heat and bring back to a scalding temperature. Gradually add hot cream to sugar mixture, whisking constantly. Fold in cream cheese and gelatin mixture. Strain again. Preheat oven to 350 degrees. Grease ovenproof ramekins with 1 tablespoon butter and place in a deep baking dish. Fill ramekins ¾ full of mixture. Add hot water to baking dish until it is about ¾ of the way up outside of ramekins. Fill ramekins to top with any remaining custard mixture. Bake for about 35 minutes until custard is set. Allow custard to cool completely, then unmold.

Heat clarified butter in a sauté pan until very hot but not burning. As foam begins to settle, place scallops in pan. Sear for 2 minutes on 1 side. Turn scallops over and cook for 1 more minute or to an internal temperature of 150 degrees. Remove scallops and place in a small pan with additional butter and lemon juice. Let rest in a warm place.

To serve, reheat custard in a warm oven until heated through. Plate scallops and top with Lemon Sabayon. Broil for about 30 seconds. Arrange custard, scallops, and beets attractively on plates. Top with additional Lemon Sabayon. Serves 8.

LEMON SABAYON

¼ cup plus 2 tablespoons dry sherry
1 teaspoon Creole mustard
½ teaspoon grated orange zest
1 teaspoon fresh tarragon
juice of 1 lemon
5 egg yolks
1 cup clarified butter
salt and pepper to taste

Combine sherry, mustard, orange zest, tarragon, and lemon juice in a medium saucepan. Bring to a rolling boil over medium-high heat and reduce by ⅔. Place yolks in a large double boiler. Add sherry syrup and combine well. Whisk mixture until it has a ribbonlike consistency. Remove from heat and slowly whisk in butter. Season to taste. Yields about 1 cup.

the
INN at
EASTON
CIRCA 1790

28 South Harrison Street
Easton, MD 21601
www.theinnateaston.com
410-822-4910

Starters such as Soft-Shell Clam Chowder, Korean-Style Steak Tartar, and Seared Calf's Liver with Fried Shallot Rings all portend good things to come. My attention was grabbed by an entrée called Char-Grilled Moreton Bay Bugs. I've eaten many unusual dishes through the years, but this was completely uncharted waters, as it were. As tempting as it was to try the "bugs," I chose the Sweet Corn Soufflé with Nuggets of Lobster and Applewood-Smoked Bacon with Bourbon Sauce, followed by a salad with shaved Parmesan and a light Vinaigrette. My entrée—Tempura of Soft-Shell Crab with Caramelized Coconut Juice— was one Debbie would have loved if she had been with me. The dessert choices were equally unique—Lumpia of Banana and Chocolate with Rum Currant Ice Cream and Cold Wattle Seed Soufflé with Kahlua Sauce. My British heritage took over as I selected the Sticky Fig and Ginger Pudding, served with Caramel Sauce and English Double Devon Cream.

I'd like to be able to say that this is the way I dine at home for every meal, but that would be untrue. Even on the other side of the Atlan-tic, meals like this are a rare treat. Chef and owner Andrew Evans prides himself on changing the menu often and using the freshest local ingredients. Looking at the menu, it's easy to see the influence of the many and varied kitchens he has worked in at different corners of the globe.

My sumptuous meal was certainly befitting of the backdrop against which it was served. The Inn at Easton was fashioned from an elegant Federal-style mansion that was formerly one of Maryland's most prominent homes. It was built in stages over the course of more than a hundred years, from 1790 to 1894. Guests enjoy the clever way that the historical integrity of the house has been preserved amidst the atmosphere of a sophisticated, chic hotel. The polished wooden floors blend perfectly with the beautiful fireplaces, ornate moldings, and high ceilings. The white-linen-covered tables are given an unusual touch with a small glass bowl filled with water, blue glass stones, and an exotic fish. I thoroughly enjoyed the relaxed atmosphere as I checked out the collection of artwork by acclaimed Russian impressionist painter Nikolai Timkov.

The village of Easton is charming, one of those places where you feel completely comfortable just strolling around and soaking up the scenery. During the early 1900s, one of the last silent films, *The First Kiss*, starring Gary Cooper and Faye Wray, was filmed in Easton. Whether you're sharing your first kiss or one of a million others, The Inn at Easton is the perfect place for romance. Do be sure to make a reservation, though, since some evenings are à la carte and some are prix fixe.

STICKY FIG AND GINGER PUDDING

1 tablespoon baking soda
1 tablespoon powdered ginger
18 ounces dried figs, chopped
3½ cups boiling water
¾ cup butter
1½ cups brown sugar
3 teaspoons vanilla
3 eggs
scant 4 cups self-rising flour
6 ounces chocolate, chopped (optional)
Butterscotch Sauce (see next column)
Fig and Ginger Compote (see next column)
English Double Devon Cream

In a medium-sized stainless-steel bowl, toss together baking soda, ginger, and figs. Add boiling water and set aside to steep until completely cool. Preheat oven to 350 degrees. In a large bowl, cream butter, brown sugar, and vanilla. Add eggs 1 at a time and beat well. Fold in flour until well combined. Pour off any remaining liquid from figs and add figs to pudding batter. Spoon mixture into 12 muffin tins. For a final touch, insert chocolate chunks or chips into center of batter. Bake in a water bath covered with tinfoil for 30 minutes, then reduce heat to 315 degrees and bake for 60 minutes. Cool in molds and reheat in microwave as needed. Serve with Butterscotch Sauce, Fig and Ginger Compote, and English Double Devon Cream. Serves 12.

BUTTERSCOTCH SAUCE

scant 1 cup sugar
¼ cup water
1 cup whipping cream
1 tablespoon unsalted butter

Place sugar and water in a small saucepan and bring to a boil, stirring often. Reduce heat and continue to simmer until mixture turns a deep golden brown. Remove from heat and add cream, then stir in butter. Yields about 1 cup.

FIG AND GINGER COMPOTE

8 ounces dried figs, julienned
2 knobs fresh ginger, julienned fine
½ cup honey
½ cup sauterne

Place all ingredients in a noncorrosive saucepan and simmer gently for 15 minutes. Yields about 1½ cups.

Bistro
ST. MICHAELS

403 South Talbot Street
St. Michaels, MD 21663
www.bistrostmichaels.com
410-745-9111

It was cold and wet outside, the sort of evening when enjoying a long, leisurely meal inside is most appealing. We sat at a small table in what was the front parlor of this 130-year-old Victorian house. The intimate atmosphere was reminiscent of a smart Parisian café. The structure has served as a home for most of its existence, although it was a realty office for a while before Phil and Sue Stein turned it into an authentic two-story bistro.

The Steins visited Paris in the early 1990s and discovered that the best food and the most fun could be found at the little street cafés located throughout the great city. Their son, David, was already a popular and accomplished chef in Maryland, so it was a natural progression to find a property that could be re-created as a bistro, where David could cook. Downstairs, guests may sit at the zinc bar festooned with glasses and sip on an apéritif. The closely placed green marble tables are lit with tiny white tea lights. The bistro flavor is continued in the green-and-white-striped draperies hung on brass rods across the bottom half of the windows. There are

wooden beams across the ceilings and antique French posters around the walls. The closeness of the tables is deliberate, creating an atmosphere of enjoyment as people laugh, talk, drink, and eat together. Upstairs, where there is slightly more elbow room, lighting is provided by small brass wall sconces. The polished wooden floors and the crisp white linens make for a softer and warmer feeling. Guests can peer over the wrought-iron balustrade to the bar below.

As we received our Black Bean Soup with Andouille Sausage, Cheese, and Roasted Corn, we settled back and enjoyed the conversations all around us. Karen followed the delicious soup with a Hearts of Romaine Salad loaded with shaved Pecorino Romano, toasted pine nuts, Croutons, and grape tomatoes, bathed in Black Pepper Dressing. Debbie's Baby Spinach and Bibb Salad contained Cornbread Croutons, apples, Spiced Pecans, tasso tam, and tasty Buttermilk and Blue Cheese Dressing.

Selecting an entrée was extremely difficult, as there were many delectable items to choose from. The Grilled Duck, the Broiled Halibut, the Pan-Seared Lamb, the Crispy Flounder, and the Grilled Entrecôte Steak all sounded wonderful. Bistro St. Michaels also boasts a seafood bar with many more choices. Karen chose the Sautéed Jumbo Shrimp with Roasted Garlic and Lime, served with Curried Vegetables and Orzo with Pesto. Debbie opted for the Apricot Mustard-Glazed Beef Brisket with Mushroom Brown Rice and Sautéed Rapini, served with Rhubarb Chutney. Both were most enjoyable.

The dessert menu is short, but everything is mouth-wateringly delicious. We were told that David's lovely wife, Indra, inspires the desserts.

Who can choose among Lemon Sorbet with Cookies, Crème Caramel with Fresh Fruit, and Fruit Tart with Apricot Preserves? We'll have to come back and have a large helping of the Warm Coffee Cake with Hot Fudge Sauce, Crème Anglaise, and Vanilla Ice Cream on another occasion.

CRAB WITH OLIVES

4 tablespoons sherry vinegar
8 tablespoons olive oil
1 teaspoon Dijon mustard
¼ cup pitted green olives
¼ cup pitted black olives
½ cup chopped roasted red peppers
1 tablespoon capers, rinsed
¼ cup chopped parsley
1 teaspoon cracked black peppercorns
1 pound jumbo lump crabmeat, picked

In a small bowl, whisk together vinegar, oil, and mustard to make vinaigrette. Set aside. In a medium bowl, combine green olives, black olives, peppers, capers, parsley, and peppercorns. Add crabmeat and stir gently to avoid breaking up lumps. Dress with vinaigrette and serve. This dish is excellent spooned over grilled fish or served as a dip with chips or crostinis. Serves 2 to 4, depending on use.

CORN PUDDING WITH CRAB

¼ cup sugar
3 tablespoons flour
2 teaspoons salt
1½ teaspoons baking powder
6 eggs
2 cups milk
½ cup butter, melted
6 cups fresh corn kernels
¼ cup chopped parsley
1 teaspoon red pepper flakes
1 pound jumbo lump crabmeat, picked

Preheat oven to 350 degrees. In a small bowl, combine sugar, flour, salt, and baking powder. Set aside. In a large bowl, beat eggs with milk and melted butter. Add corn, parsley, and red pepper flakes, stirring well. Add dry ingredients and mix well. Add crabmeat, stirring gently to avoid breaking up lumps. Lightly grease a 13-by-9-by-2-inch casserole dish. Pour in pudding and bake for about 45 minutes until golden brown. Serves 12.

924 North Charles Street
Baltimore, MD 21201
www.brasselephant.com
410-547-8480

Baltimore magazine has voted The Brass Elephant "the best place in Baltimore to wear a slinky black dress." Winner of both the prestigious DiRoNA Award and the Wine Spectator Award, this is a splendid place to dine. From the outside, this nineteenth-century row house looks very similar to many others in this part of town. Inside, however, the glorious architecture and blend of Eastern and European styles will appeal to the eye as much as the exquisite cuisine will delight the palate.

Charles Morton Stuart built the house in 1861. Its second owner, George Wroth Knapp, enhanced the décor. A trader who traveled extensively across China and India, Knapp acquired many exotic sculptures and lavish Eastern furnishings. The main dining rooms on the lower floor are ornately paneled and lit by brass elephant sconces. The ornamental hand-carved white marble fireplaces are topped by intricately carved wooden moldings and gilt-edged mirrors. Upstairs, the lovely Tusk Lounge has comfy chairs and crystal chandeliers that light up the

fabulous ceiling painted to look like a cloudy sky. Having dined at The Brass Elephant ten years ago, I was thrilled to be back, although without Debbie on this occasion. I sat at the bar, sipped a ginger ale, and settled back to read the menu.

The White Bean Soup with Crispy Prosciutto and Roasted Duck sounded delightful. I was equally tempted by the Artisan Cheese Plate, which includes a selection of unusual cheeses, a Poached Pear, Spiced Pecans, and Port Syrup. I'm very fond of smoked salmon. The Brass Elephant's version is served with fresh wasabi, mascarpone, and Ciabatta Crostinis. Among the variety of wonderful salads, the Watercress and Apple Salad, served with grilled red onions, shiitake mushrooms, and Roasted Red Apple and Sesame Vinaigrette, was most appealing. How to choose among Herb-Crusted Lamb Loin with Mushroom and Truffle Flan, Roasted Game Hen with Pistachio-Studded Sausage, and Kurobuta Pork Osso Buco with Herbed Risotto? Every choice sounded good.

I decided to be guided by my server, so I finished my drink and headed downstairs to a table in the Atrium. From there, I had a great view of Charles Street and was thoroughly entertained by the passersby while I awaited my chosen entrée of Fusilli with Jumbo Lump Crabmeat and Gulf Shrimp in Spicy Marinara Sauce. This pasta dish was unbelievably good. Too full for dessert, I had to pass on the Chocolate Ginger Truffle Torte, the Warm Pear and Currant Galette with Pistachio Ice Cream, and the many other offerings.

A meal at The Brass Elephant has always been wonderful, but under the new management of executive chef Christopher Lewis, the cuisine has moved from continental Italian to a more contemporary American style. The magnificent cuisine and the efficient and deferential service are sure to make even the fussiest diner relax and enjoy the evening. It's definitely an experience to remember.

SEAFOOD GAZPACHO

2½ English cucumbers
2 large tomatoes
½ green pepper
¼ red onion
¼ cup tequila
4 scallions
½ teaspoon minced garlic
8 cups tomato juice
¼ cup red wine vinegar
½ tablespoon cumin
½ tablespoon white pepper
4 drops Tabasco sauce
1 tablespoon kosher salt
1 pound jumbo lump crabmeat, picked

Peel cucumbers and cut into large chunks. Quarter tomatoes and remove seeds. Quarter pepper and remove seeds. Slice onion. Warm tequila in a small saucepan to burn off alcohol; be careful not to flame. Add cucumbers, tomatoes, peppers, onions, scallions, garlic, tequila, and tomato juice to a food processor; this may be done in batches. Purée long enough to chop ingredients finely but do not liquefy. In a large bowl, combine chopped vegetable mixture with next 5 ingredients. Stir well to combine. Chill for at least 1 hour. Garnish with lump crabmeat and serve. Serves 10 to 12.

EGGPLANT MANICOTTI

3 eggs
1¼ cups whole milk
4 to 5 tablespoons butter, melted, divided
½ cup flour, sifted
pinch of salt
pinch of mixed herbs
3 eggplants
1 shallot, diced and sautéed
2 tablespoons ricotta cheese, plus extra for
   garnish
1 tablespoon basil
salt and pepper to taste
tomato sauce

In a medium bowl, combine eggs, milk, and 1 tablespoon butter. Add flour, salt, and herbs. Stir until there are no lumps. Heat a small non-stick pan and add a small amount of butter. Add 2 tablespoons batter. Cook on one side, then tip out of pan onto wax paper. Mixture should make 10 crepes.

Preheat oven to 350 degrees. Cut eggplants in half and score insides. Lay cut side down in a shallow baking pan. Add 2 cups water to pan and bake for about 30 minutes until eggplants are soft. Remove from oven, drain, and allow to cool. Scoop out cooked eggplant and place in a medium bowl. Add shallots, 2 tablespoons ricotta, and basil. Stir to combine. Season to taste. Place ¼ cup eggplant mixture on each crepe. Roll crepes and place in a baking tray. Bake for 10 minutes. Top each crepe with a dollop of ricotta and serve with tomato sauce. Yields 10 crepes.

The Kings Contrivance

10150 Shaker Drive
Columbia, MD 21046
410-995-0500

As we turned into the drive leading to The Kings Contrivance, solitary candles in the third-floor windows shone, welcoming us to dinner. The conversion of this Federal-style mansion to a restaurant commenced in 1962. Great care was taken to re-create the aura and ambiance of an earlier era. To that end, graceful furnishings, brass chandeliers, swag draperies, and lovely accessories appoint the seven spacious dining rooms. Walls painted in muted shades provide a backdrop for the creativity of local artists. Fireplaces add a further touch of elegance.

We were led to a seating area on what was once the porch. The large window wall overlooked the property's gardens. White fans hung from a ceiling of sea-foam green, adding to the springlike atmosphere. Guests can choose from the regular menu or select the three-course prix fixe option. Because we arrived for an early dinner, the cost of the prix fixe menu was comparable to the entrée prices, so we decided to experience all that The Kings Contrivance has to offer.

After pondering starters such as Pheasant Pâté, Smoked Fish Plate, and Cajun Seafood Crepe, Karen began her meal with the Mussels appetizer, a real treat she rarely has an opportunity to enjoy. Debbie opted for the Mesclun Salad with Goat Cheese, which was quite tasty. She followed that with the superb Crab Cake entrée, served with a side of Green Bean Salad. Karen had the Chicken Oscar, as recommended by our server. The Sautéed Black Grouper in Coconut-Red Pepper Sauce sounded wonderful, as did the Roquefort-Covered Filet Mignon. We'll look forward to those on another occasion. Not surprisingly, we dithered over the dessert selections, pausing at the Crème Brûlée and the Chocolate Torte but ultimately deciding on the English Trifle and the Key Lime Pie in a Coconut-Graham Cracker Crust, served with Coconut Ice Cream.

The history of the property dates back to a land grant from one of the Lords Baltimore to the Reverend James McGill in 1730. The property remained in the family until 1961. James McGill was one of the first Episcopal ministers appointed to serve in the province of Maryland. At some point during the eighteenth century, a residence was built on the present site of the restaurant. It burned but was subsequently rebuilt. Sources we found indicated that the reconstruction was probably linked to the marriage of one of the Reverend McGill's descendants, Richard. Richard injured himself fairly significantly on barbed wire one day at the estate. The attractive Rachel Clark nursed him back to health and ultimately agreed to be his bride, providing the impetus for the rebuilding. Perhaps it is Rachel's ghost that is seen from time to time on the graceful, curving staircase. Maybe she is still a caregiver here, ensuring that guests receive the same careful attention she once lovingly gave her family.

ENGLISH TRIFLE

2 cups milk
¾ cup plus 2 tablespoons sugar, divided
2 egg yolks
1 egg
2 tablespoons plus 2 teaspoons cornstarch
2 tablespoons butter
1½ teaspoons vanilla extract
1 cup whipped cream
2 10-ounce packages frozen strawberries
9-inch pound cake
¼ cup water
½ cup dry sherry
12-ounce jar strawberry preserves
½ cup raspberry preserves
½ pint heavy cream
½ cup walnuts, broken

In a small saucepan, bring milk and ¼ cup sugar to a boil to dissolve sugar. Remove from heat. Combine yolks, egg, cornstarch, and an additional ¼ cup sugar. Temper egg mixture by slowly adding hot milk until mixture is combined. Return mixture to heat and let boil, stirring constantly. When thickened, remove from heat. Stir in butter and vanilla. Cool in a covered shallow pan. Fold in whipped cream 1 tablespoon at a time. Chill. Thaw and drain strawberries. Set aside. Slice cake into thirds horizontally and lay first slice in bottom of a 9-inch glass bowl that is 3½ inches deep; cut cake as necessary to fit. Boil water with ¼ cup sugar until it becomes a syrup. Add sherry to syrup and use ⅓ of mixture to lightly soak cake slice. Combine strawberries, strawberry preserves, and raspberry preserves and spread ⅓ of mixture over cake slice. Next, spoon on half of chilled cream mixture. Cover with a second slice of cake and repeat layers. Place the third cake slice on top and cover with remaining syrup and remaining strawberry mixture. Whip heavy cream with 2 tablespoons sugar and place a dollop on each serving. Refrigerate. Serves 12 to 15.

CRAB LOUIS

1 pound baby spinach, washed
4 hard-boiled eggs
2 medium tomatoes
Louis Dressing (see below)
2 ripe avocados, peeled and halved
1½ pounds jumbo lump crabmeat, picked

Clean and dry spinach and arrange on 4 plates. Peel and quarter eggs and tomatoes. Arrange eggs and tomatoes atop spinach and drizzle with Louis Dressing. Place an avocado half in center of each plate and fill with crabmeat. Top with additional dressing. Serves 4.

LOUIS DRESSING

1 cup mayonnaise
½ cup heavy cream, whipped
¼ cup chili sauce
2 tablespoons grated onion
2 tablespoons chopped parsley
dash of cayenne pepper

Combine ingredients in a medium bowl. Cover and refrigerate. Yields 2½ cups.

Blair Mansion Inn

7711 Eastern Avenue
Silver Spring, MD 20902
www.mansionmysteries.com
301-588-6646

When I got married, I got things like can openers, bathroom towels, china, and crystal. When Abner Shoemaker's niece, Abigail, married Charles Newman in the 1890s, Shoemaker gave them a gift that entitled them to vote—a piece of land straddling the boundary between Washington, D.C., and Maryland. At that time, residents of D.C. couldn't vote, so the fact that a portion of the property was over the line granted the privilege to the newlyweds. Shoemaker was a descendant of the Pierce family, who had received the original land grant from King Charles II in 1685. As generations passed, the Pierces expanded their holdings, acquiring over four thousand acres in the D.C. area and approximately a hundred thousand acres in Virginia and Kentucky.

A fine Colonial-style mansion designed by renowned architect Stanford White was built for the Newmans on their twenty acres. Both the stone and the timber came from nearby sources. In fact, the only portion of the house that didn't come from Washington, D.C., was the furnishings, which were imported from France at a cost in excess of a hundred thousand dollars. Unfortunately, the new husband was of the ne'er-do-well variety and swiftly gambled away the home and its property. Although originally owned by the Newmans, the house became known as Blair Mansion because of its proximity to property owned by the Blair family, for whom many local landmarks were named.

In 1959, the mansion underwent extensive renovations. The addition of the semicircular Terrace Room was the only significant structural change. Today, the structure functions as Blair Mansion Inn, a restaurant specializing in murder-mystery dinner theater. As guests arrive, clues abound. Dinner guests serve as suspects, judge, and jury. Brochures describe it as an interactive form of theater that starts with a basic premise but goes on to blend script with improvisation. From the reports and pictures we've seen, it looks like lots of fun.

Unfortunately, Debbie was elsewhere, so I opted for an à la carte luncheon. I spent a quiet time enjoying my Club Sandwich, preceded by a cup of Fruit Cocktail. The meal was also served with one of Blair Mansion's specialties, Pineapple Fritters, which were fabulous. I sat in the old family parlor, which has an interesting mural of the state capitol on one wall. Painted on the ceiling is a street map of Annapolis depicting the major historic buildings throughout the town. The Stars and Stripes hangs next to the original fireplace along with a framed copy of the Gettysburg Address. Every room has its own theme, each as interesting and unique as the one where I dined.

I marveled at the many exceptional antiques throughout the home. The foyer houses a piano that stood in the White House during Woodrow Wilson's presidency. Also in the foyer is a grandfather clock that won the grand prize at the 1915 Pan-Pacific International Exhibition. There's so much to see and do here that it requires an additional visit. When Debbie's around or when I'm in town with my family, I'll certainly return to experience even more of what Blair Mansion Inn has to offer.

🌿 CRAB IMPERIAL 🌿

1 egg yolk
6½ tablespoons mayonnaise, divided
⅛ teaspoon Old Bay seasoning
½ teaspoon capers
1 pound backfin crabmeat, picked
3 egg whites

Preheat oven to 375 degrees. Add egg yolk, 2 tablespoons mayonnaise, Old Bay, and capers to crabmeat. Mix until well combined. Using an electric mixer, beat egg whites until stiff, then gently fold in remaining mayonnaise. Stir until mixed. Divide crab mixture into 6 equal portions and place on a greased cookie sheet. Ladle egg-white mixture evenly over top of crabmeat and bake for 10 minutes. Serves 6.

🌿 PINEAPPLE FRITTERS 🌿

3 eggs
1 cup milk
1 cup sugar
2 tablespoons vanilla
4 cups flour
1½ tablespoons baking powder
1½ cups crushed pineapple, drained
1½ cups vegetable oil
1 cup powdered sugar

Combine first 4 ingredients, stirring until mixture has a rough, wavy consistency. Add flour, baking powder, and pineapple. Mix to incorporate. Heat oil to 350 degrees in a deep fryer. Drop well-rounded tablespoons of batter into oil. When fritters pop to surface, tap with a spoon until they turn over. Cook other side to a golden brown. Remove, drain on paper towels, and keep warm until all batter is used. Roll fritters in powdered sugar. Yields about 40 fritters.

CHAPTER 7

The National Road

The Casselman Inn

The National Road, known as the National Pike in its early days, was authorized by Congress in 1806 during the Jefferson administration, becoming the first highway built entirely with federal money. The chosen route closely paralleled the military road forged by George Washington and General Edward Braddock in 1754 and 1755. Construction began in 1811 in Cumberland, Maryland. By 1818, the road had been completed all the way to the Ohio River at Wheeling, which was still in Virginia at the time. During the road's heyday, daytime traffic was very heavy. Every type of vehicle could be seen on the road. It is estimated that there was about one tavern per mile to service those travelers. The National Road evolved into US 40. That route continued to be a prime spot for travel-related businesses, some of which remain today.

The Casselman Inn

113 Main Street
Grantsville, MD 21536
www.thecasselman.com
301-895-5055

Grantsville was named after Daniel Grant, an English engineer who originally owned more than a thousand acres along the National Road, now US 40, a historic road crossing the Appalachian Mountains. Once an Indian trail known as Nemacolin's Path, it was renamed several times. At one time, it was named after General Edward Braddock, who in 1755 widened the road from six to twelve feet so it could be used as a military supply line during his march from Cumberland to Fort Duquesne. Later known as the Old National Trail, it became the country's first federally funded highway, stretching from Cumberland to Wheeling, then part of Virginia.

The Casselman Hotel, built in 1824, was one of many constructed along this stretch of the Old National Trail to accommodate Americans traveling west. Traffic along the road included Conestoga wagons, stagecoaches, men on horseback, slaves, mail delivery, and livestock. At one time, as many as fourteen stagecoaches a day passed in each direction, the travelers stopping often to change horses and eat.

This hotel was constructed of handmade bricks fired on the land. A fireplace in each of the main rooms furnished heat and provided a means for cooking. The Federal-style hotel has served the traveling public under a variety of names. It began under original owner Solomon Sterner as Sterner's Tavern, a popular stop for cattle drovers. It was renamed Drover's Inn. At that time, a large corral on the premises allowed the drovers to pen their animals overnight. The building went on to become Farmer's Hotel, Dorsey's Hotel, and The Casselman Hotel.

In 1964, the Ivan Miller family bought the old Casselman Hotel. The sale was instigated by thirteen-year-old Philip Miller, who thought it would be a marvelous opportunity. A large family of Mennonite farmers, the Millers developed the old hotel into a thriving family business. They reopened the restaurant, which had been closed for over twenty years, and added a modern kitchen and bakery. Many other inns and hotels nearby have been demolished or have simply closed down, but The Casselman Inn continues to flourish, providing substantial country food prepared from a wide variety of Mennonite recipes.

Ever a sucker for homemade baked goods, I opted to stop here for breakfast while Debbie investigated other parts of the town. I ate in the main dining room, a comfortable carpeted room with a huge stone fireplace. Old photographs and oil-lamp sconces were scattered around the walls, and a large rack of antique kitchen utensils hung next to the fireplace. Everyone in the room agreed that whether you opted for the homemade Cinnamon Rolls, the Sausage Gravy over Homemade Biscuits, or the delectable French Toast (made from one of the delicious breads baked on the premises), breakfast was certainly a value for the money! Dinner here features a variety of steak, chicken, and ham selections. Visitors are always impressed by the variety of homemade soups and dressings. In fact, travelers driving along this historic route always have, and probably always will, find a warm welcome at The Casselman Inn.

 SHOO-FLY PIE

1 teaspoon baking soda, divided
¾ cup boiling water
½ cup dark corn syrup
½ cup light corn syrup
9-inch pie shell
1 cup flour
½ cup brown sugar
¼ cup shortening

In a small glass bowl, dissolve ½ teaspoon baking soda in boiling water. Stir well to be sure soda is completely dissolved. Add syrups and stir to combine. Set aside and allow to cool. Preheat oven to 375 degrees. Pour syrup mixture into pie shell. In a separate bowl, combine flour, brown sugar, and rest of baking soda. Using your fingers, rub shortening into flour mixture until crumbly. Spoon over top of syrup mixture. Bake for 35 minutes. Yields 1 pie.

BAKED BEANS

2 cups dried navy or Great Northern beans
½ cup brown sugar
¼ cup ketchup
½ small onion, chopped fine
⅛ teaspoon dry mustard
pinch of ginger
½ cup chopped ham
12-ounce can tomato juice

Soak beans in cold water for several hours or overnight. Preheat oven to 325 degrees. Place beans and water in a large saucepan and cook until beans are almost soft. Drain water. Add remaining ingredients and stir well. Tomato juice should cover mixture. Pour contents of pan into a 3-quart casserole and bake for 45 minutes. Serves 8.

APPLESAUCE NUT BREAD

2 eggs, slightly beaten
1¼ cups applesauce
3 tablespoons oil
¾ cup sugar
¾ cup chopped nuts
2 cups flour
1 tablespoon baking powder
1 teaspoon salt
½ teaspoon baking soda
¾ teaspoon cinnamon
½ teaspoon ground cloves

Preheat oven to 375 degrees. In a large bowl, combine ingredients in order listed. Do not overbeat. Pour into a greased bread pan and bake for about 1 hour until tester comes out clean. Yields 1 loaf.

PENN ALPS
RESTAURANT

125 Casselman Road
Grantsville, MD 21536
www.pennalps.com
301-895-5985

When reading the many pages of research we'd gathered on Penn Alps Restaurant, we were struck by the sentence, "Penn Alps Restaurant and Craft Shop are housed in the last log hospitality house on the National Pike still serving the traveler." That kind of longevity excites us. Constructed in 1818, the old stagecoach stop was once called the Inn at Little Crossings. The site is within walking distance of the Casselman River Bridge, the largest stone arch in America at the time of its construction in 1813.

The tavern once hosted thirty prominent Native Americans en route to see President Andrew Jackson. The group was served beef and boiled potatoes, then continued to feast on turkeys that had been prepared for a group of stagecoach passengers who didn't show. On the way to Washington, they were in native dress. On the return journey, they arrived here in broadcloth suits, which starkly illustrates their lack of success in dealing with Jackson and the government's policy of assimilation.

In 1957, Alta Schrock decided to provide marketing opportunities for local craftsmen. Her enterprise began at the foot of Mount Davis, the highest mountain in Pennsylvania—thus the moniker Penn Alps. The operation was moved to its present site in 1959. When a restaurant soon followed, an increasing number of folks pulled off US 40 to enjoy hearty country fare, just as those Native Americans had pulled off the highway's predecessor so many years before.

For lunch and dinner, the restaurant serves up a popular German Vegetable Soup, as well as a choice du jour. The Barbecued Ham Sandwich is one of the house specialties. For heartier appetites, choices such as Liver, Cabbage Rolls, Roast Pork and Sauerkraut, and Herb-Roasted Chicken come with the soup-and-salad bar and a side dish. I was intrigued by the Penn Alps Special, which featured Smoked Sausage, Dried Corn, and Dutch Fries.

I arrived for breakfast on an unseasonably warm winter day. As I looked around the rooms that were part of the original log cabin, I was most interested in the triangular fireplace with openings on two sides, allowing a wider distribution of heat throughout the room. Simple furnishing, light fixtures, and window treatments help preserve the ambiance of earlier days. I quickly decided on one of the homemade Sweet Rolls and ordered scrambled eggs, bacon, and orange juice to go with it. The Sweet Roll was superb—warm and tender and slathered with Maple Icing.

Freshly baked goods are available in the restaurant lobby, as are wares made by the artisans working in the adorable houses and cabins throughout the property. Visitors can watch potters, weavers, woodcarvers, and soap makers fashion their creations. Because of the early hour and the time of year, many of them weren't working, so I decided to return with Karen later in the season for some shopping and another taste of Penn Alps' home cooking.

 EGG CUSTARD

4 cups milk
9 eggs
¾ teaspoon salt
1 tablespoon vanilla
½ cup sugar
nutmeg to taste

Preheat oven to 350 degrees. Scald milk in a pan. In a large bowl, beat eggs, salt, and vanilla together. Gradually add sugar while still beating. Slowly add some hot milk to egg mixture, then add all remaining milk. Put into baking cups or a Pyrex dish. Sprinkle with nutmeg. Set baking cups or dish in an ovenproof pan. Pour hot water around cups or dish. Bake for about 60 minutes until set. Serves 8.

NUT BROWN PUDDING

1 cup margarine
2 cups sugar
½ teaspoon salt
1 teaspoon nutmeg
2 teaspoons cinnamon
1 teaspoon ground cloves
2 eggs
1½ teaspoons baking soda
¼ cup warm water
½ cup flour
3¼ cups milk
4 cups bread cubes
1 cup raisins
¾ cup chopped nuts

Preheat oven to 300 degrees. In a large mixing bowl, cream margarine, sugar, salt, and spices. Add eggs and beat until smooth. Dissolve baking soda in warm water and add to egg mixture. Add flour. In a separate bowl, pour milk over bread, raisins, and nuts. Allow to sit for 15 minutes. Combine 2 mixtures and pour into a greased 9-by-13-inch pan. Bake for about 1 hour until knife inserted in center comes out clean. Serves 12.

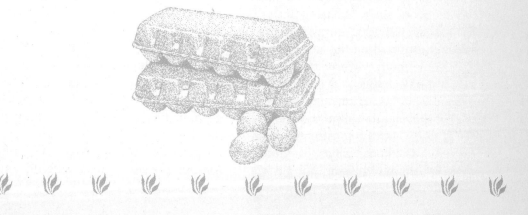

60 East Main Street
Frostburg, MD 21532
301-689-9600

The town of Frostburg probably would not exist but for the development of the National Pike, the principal route along which western migration took place during the first half of the nineteenth century. The National Pike was surveyed in 1811. Just one year later, a small town had grown up in this location. In 1812, Meshach and Catherine Frost built a house that they later rented to the Stockton Stagecoach Company. Known as Highland Hall, it accommodated as many as three hundred guests and forty stagecoaches a day as travelers poured across the state of Maryland.

Alas, the building no longer exists. But in its place alongside US 40 sit St. Michael's Rectory, Church, School, and Convent. This collection of buildings was constructed on the site between 1871 and 1906. On the far right of the site is a tiny building in the same style as the others. This was the stonemason's house, where tombstones were made. Small stone steps lead up to a tiny brick terrace, the walkway constructed from tombstone rejects. The stone building has Gothic arched windows and large wooden double doors with ornate black hinges. The cornerstone states

that the building was constructed in 1882. Inside, a small bar, a corner fireplace, tables set with white linens, and walls and furnishings in hues of maroon and purple proclaim this to be an unusual place to dine.

We came across the Tombstone Café quite by accident as we passed through Frostburg on our way back to Pennsylvania after a week of driving around Maryland. It was fate, we were hungry, and the café was open for Sunday brunch. We sat outside among the tombstones and enjoyed the shade of the overhanging maple tree. Chef and owner John W. McConnell has received rave reviews for his innovative use of regional ingredients in his healthy and nourishing menu choices. He is proud to see that every dish is given individual attention and is the very best that can be produced.

The couple next to us was busy with the Strawberry-Banana French Toast, served with Hash Browns and bacon—and jolly delicious it looked, too. Opposite, a large family was enjoying several flatbread pizzas. The intriguing variety of toppings such as Smoked Tomatoes, Roasted Mushrooms, Spicy Italian Sausage, Duck Leg Confit, and Roasted Garlic Cream Sauce made our mouths water. The café offers a delicious selection of unique salads, overstuffed artisan sandwiches, and fondues. The Welsh Rarebit Fondue—made with English cheddar, Guinness, Turkey Kielbasa, Beer-Battered Pearl Onions, and Rye Croutons—sounded particularly good. In the mood for something savory, Debbie opted for a bowl of Mushroom and Salmon Soup, which she pronounced very tasty indeed. Making a beeline for the desserts, Karen reluctantly passed by the Rocky Road Fondue with

Ladyfingers and Poached Meringue and the Double Chocolate Cake with Fresh Berries in favor of a Cinnamon Poached Pear in White Chocolate. Yummy! Whatever your choice, it is sure to be delicious.

AMERICAN BOUNTY VEGETABLE SOUP

2 tablespoons vegetable oil
1 cup chopped onions
1 cup chopped carrots
1 cup chopped celery
1 cup chopped turnips
1 cup chopped parsnips
1 cup broccoli florets
1 cup cauliflower florets
1 cup green beans, cut into 1-inch pieces
1 cup asparagus, cut into 1-inch pieces
½ tablespoon basil
½ tablespoon oregano
1 teaspoon cracked coriander
kosher salt and white pepper to taste
12 cups vegetable stock

Heat oil in a large stockpot. Add onions, carrots, celery, turnips, and parsnips and sweat for 5 minutes. Add broccoli, cauliflower, green beans, and asparagus and cook until vegetables are done; do not overcook. Add basil, oregano, and coriander and season with kosher salt and white pepper. Add vegetable stock and bring to a slow boil. Simmer for 10 minutes. Taste and adjust seasonings. Serves 10 to 12.

WARM CHICKEN SALAD

1 to 2 tablespoons vegetable oil
¼ cup finely diced red pepper
¼ cup finely diced green pepper
¼ cup finely diced orange pepper
¼ cup finely diced yellow pepper
¼ cup minced onion
2 tablespoons minced garlic
1 teaspoon cumin
1 teaspoon red pepper flakes
1 teaspoon chili powder
1 tablespoon finely chopped rosemary
1 tablespoon finely chopped tarragon
1 pound cooked chicken leg meat, diced
¼ cup cream cheese, softened
2 tablespoons mayonnaise
toasted baguette or bread bowls
root vegetable chips
whole-grain mustard

Heat oil in a large skillet. Add peppers, onions, and garlic and sweat for 10 to 15 minutes until onions are translucent. Stir in cumin, red pepper flakes, chili powder, rosemary, and tarragon. Reduce heat and add chicken. Continue cooking about 20 minutes until chicken is heated through. Remove from heat. Fold in cream cheese and mayonnaise until ingredients are blended. Serve on toasted baguette or in bread bowls with root vegetable chips and mustard. Serves 2.

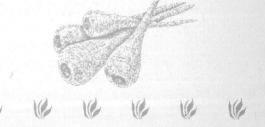

JB's Steak House

12901 Ali Ghan Road NE
Cumberland, MD 21502
www.edmasons.com
301-777-7005

We were on our way through Maryland, traveling Interstate 68 on a sunny afternoon, when our attention was drawn to a white house just off Exit 46. Within its walls are two distinct restaurants—JB's Steakhouse on the main floor and Uncle Tucker's Wood-Fired Pizza Cellar nestled in the basement. We descended the well-worn stairs to a dining room defined by old stone walls, hand-hewn beams, and patterned brick floors. At one end of the room, guests can watch an adept young man pat and stretch the pizza dough before topping it with a wide variety of choices and sliding it into the wood-fired oven. We selected the Marylander Pizza, a combination of Creamy Crab Sauce, cheeses, fresh spinach, tomatoes, and shrimp. We enjoyed it thoroughly but would have been equally happy with the Sante Fe Pizza or the Philly Cheese Steak creation. Burgers, Reubens, and club sandwiches are also available, and the Crab Cake Sandwich has been voted the best in Maryland. Upstairs in JB's Steakhouse, many of the items from the pizza cellar are available alongside such choices as

Prime Rib, Filet Mignon, Jumbo Lump Crab Cakes, and Lobster. Save room for the Mud Pie, which comes highly recommended.

Each of the three dining rooms provides a distinctly different ambiance for visitors to JB's. To the left of the entry hall is the German Room, which has cute booths, a fireplace, an antique mirror pocked with age, and quite a few old black-and-white photos. The collection includes portraits of Mr. and Mrs. Ed Mason, the current owners, decked out as if they were around during the home's early years. The Industrial Room pays tribute to the National Road and other hallmarks of progress. The third dining option is the Presidential Room, a cozy room with wide-plank flooring, gold walls, and stained-glass windows. Ed Mason was once a Maryland senator, and his memorabilia lines the walls. Gavels, pens, and pictures with such notables as Gerald Ford provide visual interest around the room.

The house was built in 1819. Erected as a tavern, it was known for its interior woodwork, some of which is still visible today. The property has frequently been referred to as Turkey Flight Manor, after the tract of land the home was built upon. The Civil War battle at Folck's Mill took place so close by that the house was hit by a cannonball. This battle stopped the advance of Confederate troops marching into Cumberland. After the fray, wounded soldiers were brought to this house, which became a makeshift hospital.

Ed Mason's history as a restaurateur doesn't quite go back to 1819 or the Civil War, but it does date to 1954. Over the years, it has included the Frosty Mug Snack Bar, Snackologist Ed's, and Mason's Barn. We encourage you to go and enjoy JB's Steak House and Uncle Tucker's, his casual, friendly ventures of today.

 BUFFALO-STYLE PIZZA

pizza dough for a 12- to 14-inch pizza
½ cup extra chunky blue cheese dressing
7 ounces baked chicken breast, diced
¼ cup plus 2 tablespoons hot sauce
2 tablespoons butter, melted
1 cup 5-cheese blend (mozzarella, provolone, cheddar, Parmesan, asiago)
2 teaspoons parsley flakes

Preheat oven to 450 degrees. Roll dough into a 12- to 14-inch circle. Spread dressing evenly over dough. Combine chicken, hot sauce, and butter and place on top of dressing layer. Top with 5-cheese blend. Sprinkle parsley flakes over top. Bake for 10 to 15 minutes until cheese is melted. If using a wood-fired pizza oven, bake at 665 degrees for 4 minutes. Serves 4.

CRAB CAKES

1½ cups Hellmann's mayonnaise
3 tablespoons Old Bay seasoning
1 tablespoon Worcestershire sauce
3 eggs
juice of ½ lemon
1 tablespoon hot sauce
2 pounds backfin crabmeat, picked
2 pounds jumbo lump crabmeat, picked

Preheat oven to 425 degrees. Fold together first 6 ingredients. Add crabmeat, folding gently. Form into 16 patties. Bake for 8 minutes, then broil until golden brown. Serves 8.

Town Hill Hotel

Bed and Breakfast
31101 National Pike
Little Orleans, MD 21766
www.townhillbnb.com
301-478-2794

We were driving cross-country on a lovely late-fall afternoon, as we're wont to do. As we crested a hill, we came across a lovely creamy yellow structure sitting proudly in the afternoon sun. The place was quiet—serene, if you will. That's one of the reasons folks like to visit.

This establishment started as a fruit stand, selling produce from the mountaintop orchard established by the Mertens Cooperative Land Development Project. Thanks to increasing automobile traffic, it became a bustling hotel in 1922. In fact, it was the first tourist hotel in the state of Maryland designed to accommodate automobile travelers. The dirt road out front was frequently in poor condition. Imagine climbing to an elevation of sixteen hundred feet along such a road, bouncing along at thirty miles per hour. Obviously, the hotel's ambiance and the vastness of the view were well worth the effort, because an annex was soon constructed, followed by the Town Hill Garage and Gas Station, completing the resort, which became known as "the beauty spot of Maryland." Rooms went for $1.50 per

night, as indicated by the sign displayed in today's lobby area. The restaurant's specialty was chicken dinners, which cost $0.95. For coffee, guests had to ante up an additional nickel.

After World War II, locals Walter White, Louise Brigham, and Norman Haust took ownership and added many features, including the overlook canopy and telescopes. In those days, there were also benches, picnic tables, and even amusement rides. By that time, the road out front had been paved and designated US 40, and neon signs had been added to welcome guests day and night. The hotel prospered until Interstate 68 was built nearby, significantly reducing the traffic that passed this way and resulting in closure in 1965.

Restoration efforts began in 1971, but it wasn't until 1991 that the hotel was reopened to guests. In 2001, Donna and Dave Reusing took the helm. Today, the Town Hill Hotel functions primarily as a bed-and-breakfast, offering a breakfast the likes of which we've rarely seen. Breakfast Pizza, Baked Oatmeal, Biscuits, Muffins, Waffles, and the two recipes featured below are typical fare. The doors are opened to the general public for Sunday brunch once a month, at which time Donna dishes up Prime Rib, Oven-Fried Chicken, Corn Pudding, Glazed Carrots, and Garlic Mashed Potatoes to appreciative guests.

For those who live too far away to drive just for a meal, the hotel's twenty guest rooms offer a pleasant place for a getaway. The view from the front porch—a great place to curl up with a good book—is lovely. Soaking up the scenery and bird-watching are favorite pastimes here. Don't miss the opportunity to experience the sunrise over seven counties, or to watch the sunset over three states. There certainly aren't many places where you can do that!

We had the good fortune to visit Town Hill as our very last stop during research for this book. Although Pittsburgh was several hours away, it was as if we'd already come home. Donna and Dave treat their guests like family. Their warmth and sincerity will simply envelop you.

 CARAMEL CREAM FRENCH TOAST

2 tablespoons light corn syrup
½ cup butter
1 cup brown sugar
1½ loaves cinnamon bread, sliced
6 eggs
2 cups milk
2 cups light cream
1 tablespoon vanilla
½ teaspoon salt
fruit, nuts, whipped cream, or syrup, if desired

In a microwave-safe dish, heat corn syrup, butter, and brown sugar until melted and combined. Pour into a 9-by-13-inch casserole dish. Overlap bread slices in 3 rows, using about 7 slices per row. Set aside. In a large bowl, beat eggs, milk, cream, vanilla, and salt. Pour slowly over bread. Cover with foil and refrigerate overnight. Bake at 350 degrees for 45 minutes. Uncover and bake an additional 15 minutes. Invert onto a large serving plate. Top with fruit, nuts, whipped cream, syrup, or other toppings. Serves 10 to 12.

ALABAMA TOMATO PIE

9-inch piecrust
3 tomatoes, sliced
1 onion, sliced
salt and pepper to taste
½ cup cheddar cheese
½ cup Parmesan cheese
1 cup mayonnaise

Preheat oven to 350 degrees. Place piecrust in bottom of a round baking dish and bake for 6 minutes. Remove from oven. Place a layer of tomatoes in dish, then a layer of onions. Sprinkle with salt and pepper. Repeat tomato and onion layers. Sprinkle with cheddar. Combine Parmesan and mayonnaise. Carefully spread across top. Bake for 30 minutes. Serves 6 to 8.

Old South Mountain Inn

6132 Old National Pike
Boonsboro, MD 21713
www.oldsouthmountaininn.com
301-371-5400

High atop a mountain midway between Middletown and Boonsboro sits the imposing stone structure known as Old South Mountain Inn. The inn has been welcoming visitors since 1732. It is believed that General Edward Braddock passed this way twenty years later, accompanied by his army. Also along was a young lieutenant by the name of George Washington. All were on their way to an encounter with the French and Indians at Fort Duquesne, a campaign that would prove fatal for Braddock.

By the late 1700s, west-bound traffic passed by quite steadily. The inn served as both a wagon stand and a stagecoach stop. The road was quite treacherous until it was paved in the 1820s. Quite a few prominent visitors came this way, including Daniel Webster and Henry Clay. Clay, considered the father of the National Road, enjoyed regular visits here.

In the latter half of the nineteenth century, the inn was part of two significant events related to the Civil War. In 1859, it was captured and held overnight as an outpost and staging point for the raid on Harpers Ferry by followers of John Brown. Then, in 1862, it was used as the headquarters of Confederate general D. H. Hill during the Battle of South Mountain, which took place just prior to the Battle of Antietam.

Business at the tavern declined after the Civil War, as the rise in railroad traffic decreased the importance of the National Road. In 1876, the tavern became the private residence of Madeline Vinton Dahlgren, the wealthy widow of Admiral John A. Dahlgren. Mrs. Dahlgren made improvements to the property while honoring the history and importance of the structure. She also built the Dahlgren Chapel across the street from the inn.

In 1925, the home became a tavern once again. It continued in operation as a pub until it was purchased in 1971 by Charles and Dorothea Reichmuth, who chose to operate their establishment as a fine-dining restaurant with historic ambiance and gracious hospitality. Subsequent owners Russell and Judy Schwartz and Chad and Lisa Dorsey have continued that tradition.

We liked chatting with our amiable server, Andrew, as much as we enjoyed our Sunday-evening meal. Although we were tempted by starters like Japanese-Style Green Mussels, Foie Gras with Dried Cranberry Salad, and Corn and Crab Chowder, we decided to have just an entrée before continuing on our way. The Blackened Tuna with Saffron Lobster Sauce sounded delicious, as did the Filet Mignon Lisa. It's a tasty cut of beef served with Cabernet Sauvignon Demi-Glace and topped with blue cheese. Karen chose the Wasabi-Encrusted Salmon with Ginger-Sage Reduction and proclaimed it to be a wonderful combination of flavors. Debbie decided to go traditional on this occasion, enjoying what was purported to be a petite cut of Prime Rib but was a very generous portion nonetheless. We were sorely tempted to sample the Fresh Strawberries au Chemise and the Peach Melba but ultimately restrained ourselves. After all, they're something to look forward to on our next visit!

 ROCKFISH CHESAPEAKE

1 pound rockfish fillets, skin on
salt and white pepper to taste
1/3 cup flour
1/4 cup clarified butter
1 teaspoon butter
2 ounces country ham, cut into 1/4-inch strips
pinch of Old Bay seasoning
1/2 cup heavy cream
1/4 cup thinly bias-cut celery
2 ounces jumbo lump crabmeat, picked

Preheat oven to 375 degrees. Season fillets with salt and white pepper and coat with flour. Heat clarified butter in a sauté pan. Sear fish skin side down for 2 to 3 minutes until browned. Turn over and finish in oven for 4 to 6 minutes until cooked through. Heat 1 teaspoon butter in a sauté pan. Add ham and Old Bay. Cook until lightly browned. Add cream and reduce until thickened. Add celery and crabmeat. Heat through. To serve, spoon sauce onto plates and place fillets on top. Serves 2.

HORSERADISH-ENCRUSTED SALMON

1/4 cup shredded fresh horseradish
2 tablespoons chopped fresh parsley
1 teaspoon oregano
1/2 teaspoon rosemary
salt and pepper to taste
dash of garlic salt
1 tablespoon water
1 egg
2 8-ounce salmon fillets
1/3 cup flour
1/4 cup clarified butter

Preheat oven to 375 degrees. Combine first 6 ingredients. In a shallow container, combine water and egg to make an egg wash. Coat salmon on bone side with flour, then with egg wash, then with horseradish mixture. Heat butter in a sauté pan. Sear salmon skin side down for 2 to 3 minutes. Turn over to breaded side and cook until breading is lightly browned. Turn back over and finish in oven for 4 to 6 minutes until cooked through. Serves 2.

HAGAN'S TAVERN

5018 Old National Pike
Braddock Heights, MD 21714
www.haganstavern.com
301-371-9189

John Hagan's Tavern is known for its warm and gracious welcome. I was lucky enough to visit this unique establishment twice—once without Debbie for lunch and again later the same week with my husband as he met a business colleague for dinner. Hagan's is easy to find, situated on the Old National Pike. It looks exactly as a tavern should—stone construction, shuttered windows, and the biggest tree you've ever seen lending shade to the front stoop.

Built about 1785, the structure was owned by James Nixdorf. It was not until around 1830, when the tavern was taken over by John Hagan, that it began to make a name for itself. Popular with locals and travelers, Hagan's was a preferred place to stop for the wagoners traveling from Baltimore to Ohio with passengers or with goods to sell. Over the years, many stories about Hagan's have made the rounds. Locals claim that several presidents, including George Washington, have dined here. Both Union and Confederate officers stayed at the tavern. One of the lesser-

known skirmishes of the Civil War came about when a group of Union soldiers took on several Confederates who were in the midst of enjoying "the comforts of the tavern."

One of John Hagan's indentured servants, John Bear, described the tavern as a place where "the old bloats of the neighborhood would gather on Saturdays to run horses, fight chickens, drink bad whiskey, and black each other's eyes." Hagan's survived those times. After serving as a private home, resort, restaurant, tavern, and speakeasy, it has settled once again into being a place where travelers and locals love to eat!

Inside, the tavern pleases the eye. The original wooden floors and the polished wooden tables and chairs allow the beautifully stenciled walls and the murals to speak for themselves. The scrolled menus are tied with ribbon. The lighting is appropriately subdued, provided by candles and pewter chandeliers.

All the food here is made from scratch, so guests are definitely in for a treat. Wait staff in colonial costume are happy to ask the chef to prepare dishes to your own personal taste. We sampled the Warmed Brie with Fruit and Butter Pecan Sauce and the Asparagus with Lump Crabmeat and Key Lime Poppy Seed Vinaigrette. Both were delicious and generous in size for appetizers. From the entrées, we sampled the Crab Cakes, the Oven-Roasted Salmon Fillet with Tangerine Beurre Blanc, the Chicken Chesapeake with Mushrooms and Peppers in Old Bay Sherry Cream Sauce, and the Raspberry-Marinated Duck Breast with Ancho Chili Rub. It was impossible to pick a favorite. They were all fabulous.

The desserts were equally tempting. The

Blueberry Cobbler, the Carrot Cake with Cream Cheese Frosting, and the Lemon Cheesecake with Raspberry Coulis vied for attention on the dessert tray. Guided by our server, my husband and I opted to share a serving of Hagan's signature dessert, Pecan Raisin Bread Pudding. Always on the menu, it was unbelievably good. Owners Jeff and Dee Reinhard were generous enough to give me the recipe. I could barely wait to make it for Debbie's family!

BROCCOLI SOUP
WITH BRIE AND ALMONDS

1 onion, chopped
1 pound broccoli spears, chopped
1 large zucchini, chopped
1 carrot, chopped
1 medium potato, chopped
2 tablespoons butter
2 tablespoons extra-virgin olive oil
8 cups chicken stock, divided
2 cups heavy cream
salt and pepper to taste
4½ ounces Brie cheese, cut into small cubes
½ cup sliced almonds, toasted

Place vegetables in a large pot with butter, oil, and 4 cups chicken stock. Bring to a boil. Reduce heat, cover, and simmer for 15 minutes. Add remaining stock, bring back to a boil, and simmer about 30 minutes until all vegetables are very soft. Place vegetables in a food processor and purée. Return puréed vegetables to pan. Add cream and season to taste. Bring soup back to the boiling point. Stir in Brie and serve immediately, topped with almonds. Serves 6.

PECAN RAISIN BREAD PUDDING

2 cups heavy cream
¼ cup brandy
2 tablespoons vanilla
1 loaf sliced bread, crusts removed, cubed
3 eggs
1¼ cups sugar
½ cup golden raisins
½ cup raisins
1 cup pecans
½ cup brown sugar
1 tablespoon cinnamon
¼ cup butter, melted
whipped cream or ice cream

Preheat oven to 350 degrees. Grease a 9-by-13-by-2-inch baking pan. In a large bowl, combine cream, brandy, and vanilla. Add bread cubes and toss to coat completely. In an electric mixer, beat eggs and sugar until ribbons form. Fold egg mixture into bread mixture. Add raisins and stir to mix thoroughly. Pour mixture into baking pan. In a small bowl, combine pecans, brown sugar, cinnamon, and butter. Spread pecan mixture evenly over top of bread mixture. Bake for about 1 hour until a knife inserted in center comes out clean. Serve with whipped cream or ice cream. Serves 8.

CHAPTER 8
Here's to History

John Steven, Ltd.

In his *Canterbury Tales*, Chaucer wrote of the Friar, "He knew his taverns wel in every toun." Back then, it was necessary to know the best taverns in order to be sure of securing acceptable food and drink and to find respite on long and arduous journeys. Many centuries later, not much has changed in that respect. As folks travel from place to place, concern for creature comforts invariably arises. The establishments in this chapter provide sustenance just as they did in days of yore.

Washington Street PUB

RAW BAR

20 North Washington Street
Easton, MD 21601
www.wstpub.com
410-822-9011

The building that houses the Washington Street Pub is one of Easton's oldest brick structures. It was supposed to be three stories high, but most of the construction crew left Easton on Friday, April 1, 1898, to join Theodore Roosevelt's Rough Riders unit during the Spanish-American War and were never heard from again, so the building remains a two-story edifice with decorated eaves and creamy stoneware banding. It has served the town as a clothing store, as an auto dealership, and even as a speakeasy operated by notorious town merchant Chisholm Hurt.

Inside, the pub is long and thin, its exposed-brick walls giving it a warm and friendly feel. The original hardwood floors have been restored, and the tin-tile ceiling has been painted cream. Showcases from Lomax's Jewelry Store have been incorporated into the overall decorative theme. The pub boasts a fifty-foot bar with a brass foot rail and draws its beer through refrigerated lines from a cooler located directly below the bar. This is definitely the place to get the coldest draft in town! The several televisions around the pub guarantee that sports fans don't have to miss that all-important game just to enjoy a cold beer and a delicious meal.

This casual place is clearly enjoyed by locals and out-of-town visitors alike. Locals stroll right into the bar and procure themselves a seat and a pint of "the usual." Visitors like me wait to be seated by the friendly and informative wait staff. Unfortunately, Debbie was out hunting other historic buildings on the evening I visited. My server seated me at a pleasant wooden table, where I watched the food being delivered to other patrons in the hope that it might enable me to make up my mind.

All the menu choices were appealing. How to choose among Potato-Encrusted Rockfish, Crab Cakes, Crab Imperial, Bratwurst with Sauerkraut, the Barbecue Platter, St. Louis Ribs, and Mesquite-Roasted Chicken? The specials listed on the chalkboard were Steamed Mussels in Garlic Butter and Seasoned Pub Chips with Ranch Dressing. However, another guest at the hotel where I was staying had recommended the Crispy Seafood Potato Skins, which include shrimp, scallops, and crabmeat in a bubbling Rose Sauce. What a great choice! Other guests were clearly enjoying the Fish and Chips and a variety of fabulous pub sandwiches like the Sly Fox (turkey, Swiss cheese, Thousand Island Dressing, and Coleslaw on a grilled sourdough roll) and the Chesapeake Chicken (a toasted kaiser roll topped with grilled breast of chicken, cheddar, and piping-hot Crab Dip). Whatever your choice, you won't leave the table still hungry.

My server tried to persuade me to enjoy a

slice of the homemade Chocolate Godiva Cheesecake or Crème Brûlée Cheesecake. Both looked exceptional, as did the Caramel Apple Granny Pie and the Carrot Cake. Debbie and I will just have to visit on another day to sample more of what the Washington Street Pub has to offer.

CRAB DIP

3 8-ounce packages cream cheese, softened
¼ cup shredded cheddar cheese
2 tablespoons sherry
1½ teaspoons crab base
1½ teaspoons Old Bay seasoning
1 teaspoon basil
pinch of cayenne pepper
2 tablespoons horseradish
1 teaspoon bacon fat
¼ cup diced yellow onion
1 teaspoon chopped garlic
2 tablespoons diced tomato
1 pound crabmeat, picked
chips, crostinis, or pitas

In a large saucepan, place cream cheese, cheddar, sherry, crab base, Old Bay, basil, cayenne, and horseradish. Melt contents over very low heat, stirring constantly until smooth. Remove from heat. In a medium skillet, heat bacon fat and sauté onions and garlic until cooked. Add tomatoes and heat until warmed through. Remove from heat and drain. Add onion mixture to hot cheese mixture and stir to combine. Add crabmeat, stirring carefully to avoid breaking up lumps. Serve hot with chips, crostinis, or pitas. Yields 5 cups.

MARYLAND CRAB SOUP

1 tablespoon olive oil
3 stalks celery, diced
1 medium yellow onion, diced
6 cups chicken stock
6 cups beef stock
6 cups crab stock
1½ teaspoons thyme
1½ teaspoons pepper
1½ teaspoons Old Bay seasoning
2 bay leaves
24 ounces mixed vegetables
2 15-ounce cans diced tomatoes with juice
1½ cups V8 juice
1 pound crabmeat, picked

In a large stockpot, heat oil and sauté celery and onions until translucent. Add stocks, thyme, pepper, Old Bay, and bay leaves. Increase heat and bring to a boil. Add mixed vegetables, tomatoes, and V8. Simmer for 30 minutes. Add crabmeat and mix thoroughly, simmering until crab is heated through. Remove bay leaves before serving. Serves 16.

1800 Thames Street
Baltimore, MD 21231
www.johnstevenltd.com
410-327-5561

When you're walking around the Fells Point area of Baltimore and enjoying its many historic buildings, this unassuming structure may not attract your notice. However, once you realize that it's been voted one of Baltimore's best eateries in multiple years, John Steven's certainly deserves more than a glance. It was recommended to us by a chef at one of the most renowned restaurants in Baltimore as one of his favorites. So on our second trip to the area, we made it our first stop.

We parked along the waterfront just down the street from the Maritime Museum on a sunny day that was just a few degrees shy of being spring. Nevertheless, we enjoyed strolling the cobblestone streets before going in for an early lunch. Guests can enter through the bar area, which is situated in one of the two old row houses that comprise this restaurant. Parquet tables sit below a tin ceiling, and a simple bar runs the length of the room. From a side door, guests can access the two dining areas. The one on the patio is in use even in chilly weather. The

other is in the front room of the second row house. In its early days, this structure was utilized as a boardinghouse for sailors docking at the wharf across the street. We also received reports of a brothel operating on this spot. History has shown that the two are frequently linked, so we didn't find it hard to believe!

Today, the cozy dining room is decorated in shades of green, gold, and burgundy, with simple broadcloth checked curtains hanging at the windows. We took a table and perused the menu. Seafood is prominent here—Maryland Crab Soup, Fisherman's Wharf Clams, Fish and Chips, and of course Crab Cakes. We considered a variation on the theme and almost ordered the Clam Cakes. Then the Crab Bruschetta caught our attention—chunks of crab mixed with herbs, chopped tomatoes, and diced onions, then placed atop perfectly toasted bread that was not so crisp that the topping fell off and not so soft that the bread got soggy. Every delicious bite gave testimony to the statement on the menu claiming that the seafood here is so fresh that it "slept last night in the bay." If you're not a seafood lover, don't despair. New York Strips and Sirloins appear on the menu, as do pork and pasta dishes, burgers, and Muffalettas.

During your visit, don't miss the fascinating collection of fertility artifacts in the dining room's display case. The collection is the work of one of the restaurant's owners, Chuck Doerring. Interspersed with the icons is a terrific collection of old jazz magazines garnered from a junk pile somewhere. Chuck took over the business here in 1978 when he bought the longstanding Zeppi's Five Points Tavern. His son proudly suggested that Chuck name the eatery after his teddy bear.

So John Steven it was, and John Steven it remains today!

CRAB BRUSCHETTA

4 tablespoons diced plum tomatoes
4 teaspoons chopped fresh basil
1 teaspoon dried basil
1 teaspoon Old Bay seasoning
4 teaspoons grated Parmesan cheese
12 ounces lump crabmeat, picked
12 slices Italian bread
2 to 3 tablespoons olive oil

In a medium bowl, combine tomatoes, basil, Old Bay, and Parmesan. Add crabmeat and toss, being careful not to break up lumps. Toast bread slices and spread each with $1/12$ of the mixture. Place 3 slices bruschetta on each of 4 appetizer plates. Sprinkle with olive oil to finish. Serves 4.

BROILED SEA SCALLOPS

1 teaspoon olive oil
16 fresh sea scallops
½ cup white wine
½ cup lemon juice
1 teaspoon dill weed
1 tablespoon unsalted butter

In a medium sauté pan, heat oil and sauté scallops for 1 minute on each side. Add wine, lemon juice, and dill weed and bring to a boil. Reduce heat and simmer for about 5 minutes until liquid is reduced by half. Remove from heat and swirl in butter to thicken sauce. Serves 2.

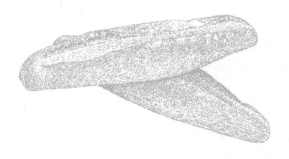

Griffins

Griffins City Dock Tavern
22-24 Market Space
Annapolis, MD 21401
www.griffins-citydock.com
410-268-2576

Upon entering the dusky blue building with slate blue trim, guests' eyes are immediately drawn to the bar area, which soars two and a half stories to the very eaves of the original structure. Shutters cover the tall, thin second-story windows, and a railing and landing from a previous staircase are still visible. The high exposed-brick walls are strewn with stuffed animals. These aren't of the amusement-park variety but real specimens, including an antelope and a ferocious-looking lion. Situated on a ledge near the entry, a bear cub looks out over regulars and tourists alike as they come to enjoy a pint or two at the bar.

The buildings that comprise Griffins were once multiple-family dwellings. Local historical accounts indicate that during the 1920s, the premises was used as a boardinghouse for the sailors and dockworkers at the port. Later, businesses such as a barbershop and a grocery occupied the site. During the 1950s, a clothing store utilized the space, selling not the latest fashions but practical apparel such as work clothes and boots.

For many of the years since that enterprise, the space has done duty as an eatery of some type. One bit of historical information we came across mentioned a luncheonette at this address. Our personal connotation of a luncheonette—staffed by waitresses in starched uniforms, serving regular customers a club sandwich or a BLT—seemed incongruous with the burly crowd that sidled in for meals when Annapolis was a workboat harbor. The previous enterprise, Captain Dan's Bar, and another, Dave's Oyster Bar—which featured shots, beer, and oysters—seemed more fitting. Those businesses gave way to the Dockside Restaurant, which, during its fifteen-year run at this location, garnered quite a reputation. Griffins City Dock Tavern has surpassed the Dockside's longevity, having been here for more than twenty years, providing seafood and American fare in a casual atmosphere that appeals to all.

I was seated at a tiny table for two tucked under the massive dark-wood staircase. I decided on just a bowl of soup so I'd have room for dessert. The delicious Maryland Cream of Crab had just the right hint of sherry and was bursting with large bits of crab. With a more voracious appetite, I might have chosen the Herb-Crusted Rockfish, the Soft-Shell Crab Sandwich, the Fish and Chips, or the Jamaican Jerk Sea Scallops. Instead, I devoted the remainder of my appetite to a piece of Boston Cream Pie Cheesecake, a unique dessert that was new to me. Karen, finished with her appointment, stopped in to help me polish off the last few bites. She agreed that the cheesecake variety of this traditional dessert was even better than its original counterpart.

TROPICAL FRUIT SALSA

1 cup diced fresh pineapple
1 mango, peeled and diced
1 papaya, peeled, seeded, and diced
1 large jalapeño pepper, seeded and chopped
   fine
3 tablespoons finely chopped red onion
1/3 cup finely chopped red bell pepper
1/3 teaspoon Caribbean jerk seasoning
2 tablespoons chopped cilantro

In a medium bowl, combine all ingredients except cilantro. Place in a sealed container and refrigerate for at least 1 hour. Just before serving, add cilantro, stirring well to combine. Yields about 3 cups.

TOMATO SAFFRON VINAIGRETTE

1½ tablespoons Dijon mustard
1½ teaspoons saffron threads
2 tablespoons minced shallots
½ cup champagne vinegar
½ cup diced tomatoes, drained
salt and pepper to taste
1½ teaspoons chopped tarragon
1 cup olive oil

Combine first 7 ingredients in a mixing bowl. Add oil in a steady stream, stirring constantly. Whisk until well blended. Yields about 2 cups.

HONEY-GLAZED BABY CARROTS

2 pounds baby carrots
1/3 cup unsalted butter
1/3 cup honey
2 tablespoons lemon juice
1/4 teaspoon ground ginger
1 tablespoon chopped fresh mint, if desired

Preheat oven to 350 degrees. Boil or steam carrots for 2 to 3 minutes. Shock carrots in cold water, drain, and set aside. In a separate pan, melt butter over medium heat. Add honey, lemon juice, ginger, and mint and bring to a boil. Reduce heat and allow mixture to simmer for 10 to 15 minutes. Remove from heat. Add carrots to pan. Toss carrots in glaze. Place carrots and glaze in a medium baking dish and bake for 20 minutes. Serves 8.

The Wharf Rat Camden Yards
206 West Pratt Street
Baltimore, MD 21201
www.thewharfrat.com
410-244-8900

Oyster, Lamb, and Guinness Stew and Fresh Corned Beef with Chopped Cabbage in Pickling Spice topped the menu here on St. Patrick's Day, the occasion of our first visit to The Wharf Rat. We thoroughly enjoyed the cheery atmosphere of this wonderful old building. The menu is a delightful mixture of American favorites and English specialties. The starters include Maryland Steamed Shrimp, Mrs. Rooney's Chili, Cheese Fries, and RAF Wings in Barbecue, Honey Barbecue, Spicy, and Jerk varieties. Among the many interesting salads, the Fried Chicken Salad with fresh mixed greens, bacon, Stilton cheese, and Balsamic Vinaigrette sounded particularly good. Karen was duly impressed by English choices such as Shepherd's Pie, Bangers and Mash, and even a Ploughman, which is a traditional English pub lunch of Stilton, Brie, and cheddar, served with whole-grain mustard, Chutney, a small salad, and multigrain rolls. The entrées run the gamut from Crab Cakes and Mussels Marinara to Henry VIII's Meat Loaf, Jameson Baby Back Ribs, and various steaks. The large selection of uniquely named sandwiches looked fabulous.

Karen, sticking with her heritage, opted for lightly fried Orange Roughy in Oliver Ale Batter, served with British-Style Fries. Debbie loved the Southern Seafood Gumbo, loaded with shrimp, crabmeat, fish, and andouille sausage. Our server encouraged us to try a Blackfriar Stout Float, which tasted like an old-fashioned malted milkshake—absolutely divine! Owner Bill Oliver was generous enough to give us the recipe for this delicious dessert. He even persuaded his master brewer to design a recipe to enable our readers to create the stout for themselves.

There is no doubt that this is one of the finest brewpubs we've visited. With more than a dozen in-house brews to choose from, patrons are spoiled. We were particularly impressed by the beer menu that also listed food suggestions. The Oliver Summer Light sounded wonderful, as did the Oliver Pagan Porter, a smooth brown ale with a hint of licorice. The Oliver Hot Monkey Love is said to make even the strongest among us pen love notes after a second glass!

When the port of Baltimore was still young, this building was one of many that contained shops purveying clothing, textiles, and shoes. Business was transacted on the ground floor, and the merchants were housed above. This block was home to Moses Shepard, the benefactor of the Shepard and Enoch Pratt Hospital. During the mid-1900s, the Pratt Furniture Company ran its business from here for more than forty years. Despite its age, the facade of this Civil War-era structure is still grand. The dark green and gold paintwork is attractively embellished by the pilasters and the window hoods constructed from cast iron. Inside, Tiffany lamps are suspended over wooden tables and bentwood chairs. Guests enjoy the several large collections of beer mugs, beer bottles, and British pub signs hanging on the original brick walls. We felt right at home here, and we know you will, too.

 BLACKFRIAR STOUT FLOAT

Chocolate Brownie (see below)
2 scoops French vanilla ice cream
1½ to 2 cups stout
¼ cup whipped cream

Place a Chocolate Brownie in a parfait glass. Add ice cream. Fill glass with stout. Add whipped cream. Serves 1. Note: The Wharf Rat Camden Yards uses Blackfriar Stout.

CHOCOLATE BROWNIES

1 cup Dutch process dark cocoa powder
1¼ cups butter or margarine
5 extra large eggs, room temperature
2 cups sugar
1 tablespoon Kahlua
1½ teaspoons vanilla
½ cup unbleached flour

Preheat oven to 350 degrees. Butter a 9½-by-14-inch pan and dust it with cocoa powder. Place cocoa powder and butter in a heat-proof container and warm on stove until butter melts, stirring occasionally. Combine eggs, sugar, and Kahlua in a mixing bowl and beat for 5 minutes. Add butter mixture, vanilla, and flour and beat on low until combined and of uniform color. Pour batter into pan and bake for 25 to 30 minutes. Let brownies cool in pan. Serves 10.

BLACKFRIAR STOUT

5 pounds British pale malt
1 pound roasted barley
¾ pound crystal malt
½ pound chocolate malt
½ pound smoked malt
1 pound flaked maize
1 teaspoon gypsum
1 ounce Fuggles hops
1 ounce Cascade hops
¼ teaspoon Irish moss
1 package Ringwood Ale yeast
2 ounces Golding hops

Crush the grains. Combine grains with gypsum and 2¼ gallons water heated to 165 degrees. The mash will stabilize at 155 degrees. Hold this temperature for 60 minutes. Sparge with 4½ gallons water at 175 degrees. Bring wort to a boil and add Fuggles hops. Continue boiling for 1 hour. During final 15 minutes, add Cascade hops and Irish moss. After boiling, remove spent hops and sparge. Cool wort. Transfer wort to a fermenting vessel and add yeast. When fermentation is completed after 3 to 5 days, transfer to a covered container. Add Golding hops in a cheesecloth bag for easy removal. Condition for 2 to 3 weeks. Remove bag of Golding hops and bottle or keg the stout. This deep black beer with a rich brown head is chocolaty and satisfying. Yields 5 gallons. Note: If you are unsure about what equipment to use, consult an experienced brewer before attempting recipe.

The Valley Inn

10501 Falls Road
Brooklandville, MD 21022
www.valleyinn1830.com
410-828-8080

According to the National Register of Historic Places, The Valley Inn began life in 1832, when it was known as the Brooklandville House. Visitors can still see its original stone construction today. Our research indicated that a good well on the property led to its use as a stagecoach stop, where wayfarers refreshed themselves before continuing to Baltimore via the Galls Turnpike. The building's history is closely tied to that of the Green Spring Valley branch of the Baltimore and Susquehanna Railroad. The front door of the structure is to the south, facing the tracks. This railroad line, one of the first in the United States, provided regular service by horse-drawn carriage for nearly twenty years prior to the widespread use of steam locomotives.

The building served not only as a tavern stop for travelers but also as the local post office beginning in 1870, when ownership was transferred to Dr. Henry S. Hunt. When the property was bought by James Mather for his wife in 1873, she took over the postmistress duties as well as ownership of the tavern. Through the years, the Mathers acquired adjacent properties, expanding their holdings around the tavern through 1894. Sometime during their tenure, the establishment became known as the Tagart Hotel and Store, and general merchandise was added to the list of offerings. The property was conveyed to the Mathers' daughter, Emilla, in 1893. It was during her time that the inn's affiliation with the horse industry began. It hosted the start of the 1897 Maryland Hunt Cup.

The name Valley Inn was first used in 1921, when Colonel John A. Hatfield took the helm. He had fought in France during World War I and later saw action in World War II. The link between the inn and horse lovers continued under Hatfield, as the first polo club in Maryland played on the grounds. Indeed, John Vernou Bouvier III, the father of Jackie Kennedy Onassis, played a chukker or two on these fields. Hunt scenes and racing pictures dominate the décor in today's dining rooms.

Old photos and other memorabilia line two large cases in the restaurant's vestibule. A small placard tells of the troupe of exiled Russian entertainers that performed here during the 1920s. Another mentions writers H. L. Mencken and F. Scott Fitzgerald, who are said to have visited once or twice. Listening to the comments of two women who were friends of the family, we deduced that many of the photos must be of the Hatfields. The women had obviously been frequenting the restaurant for quite some time because as they looked at the photos, they reminisced about many of the activities in which they'd taken part.

In town for a late lunch, we enjoyed a quick

plate of Fried Oysters and a slice of Chocolate Layer Cake before heading on our way. The menu is traditional, and guests are certain to find longtime favorites. The appetizers include Oysters on the Half Shell, Shrimp Cocktails, and French Onion Soup, while the entrée page lists Sirloin Steaks, Lamb Chops, Crab Cakes, Veal Marsala, and Seafood Newburg among its offerings. We urge you to step into The Valley Inn and step back to the past.

CRAB CAKES

1 egg
½ cup mayonnaise
1 teaspoon Old Bay seasoning
½ teaspoon chopped parsley
1 tablespoon dry mustard
1 teaspoon wet mustard
2 tablespoons Worcestershire sauce
3 slices white bread, crusts removed, diced
1 pound jumbo lump crabmeat, picked

Preheat oven to 425 degrees. In a medium bowl, combine egg, mayonnaise, Old Bay, parsley, mustards, Worcestershire, and bread. Fold in crabmeat, being careful not to break up lumps. Form mixture into 5 patties. Place on a baking sheet, bake for 8 minutes, then broil until golden brown. Serves 5.

STEWED TOMATOES

1 tablespoon oil
1 small onion, chopped
1 small bell pepper, chopped
2 stalks celery, chopped
48-ounce can whole tomatoes
½ cup sugar
1 bay leaf
2 tablespoons cornstarch
2 tablespoons water

Add oil to a medium stockpot and sauté onions, peppers, and celery until tender. Add tomatoes, sugar, and bay leaf. Bring to a boil. Reduce heat to a simmer. In a small bowl, combine cornstarch and water to make a slurry. Add slurry slowly to tomatoes, stirring well until desired thickness is reached. Cook for 15 minutes. Remove bay leaf before serving. Yields 6 cups.

Brewer's Alley Restaurant & Brewery

124 North Market Street
Frederick, MD 21701
www.brewers-alley.com
301-631-0089

Brewer's Alley is not only the name of this casual eatery on one of Frederick's main thoroughfares, it is also a part of Frederick's history. During Frederick's early years, Brewer's Alley was actually a street, located where South Court Street stands today. A long line of brew houses once occupied that area, the last of which was owned by John Kuhn, whose brewery on the bank of Carroll Creek was consumed by fire in 1901. In 1996, the Brewer's Alley of today revived the longstanding brewing tradition by becoming Frederick's first brewpub.

Not only is the name historic, but the location is significant as well. The first residents of Frederick held a lottery in 1765 to raise money for a town hall and market house on this location. Construction was completed in 1769. The structure served its original purpose for over a hundred years, surviving the onslaught of the city by General Jubal Early and his Confederate forces during the Civil War. In 1873, the growing town replaced the market house with offices, provid-

ing space for a farmers' market to the rear of the property. Upon becoming the seat of city government, the structure saw many events related to Frederick's political history. As an opera house and theater, it hosted many important social and entertainment activities. The memorial service for President William McKinley was held here in 1901; D. W. Griffith's film *Birth of a Nation* was shown here in 1926; and *Madame Butterfly* was performed by the Manhattan Opera Company that same year. Immediately after World War I, American Legion fund-raisers, quite popular with local residents, were hosted here.

The bar area and a dining room are located in the original structure, where the brick walls provide a backdrop for pleasant, casual meals. This eatery's popularity led to the construction of a newer dining room to the rear. The walls throughout are lined with an eclectic mix of stained-glass windows, posters, and black-and-white photos, interspersed with old golf clubs, lacrosse sticks, and oars.

The extensive menu includes appetizers such as Barbecued Shrimp, Jalapeño Cheese-Stuffed Pretzels, and Lump Crab and Poblano Chili Cheese Dip. Selections such as the Beer Cheese Soup and the Chili contain beer from the Brewer's Alley repertoire. We both started with the soup of the day, Orange-Carrot Soup with Tarragon, which was delicious. The Smoked Pulled Pork Barbecue Sandwich that Debbie chose came with Nut Brown Beer-B-Que Sauce. The po-boy special of the day and the burgers were popular throughout the dining room the day we visited, as was Karen's selection, Pan-Asian Grilled Chicken Salad with Oriental Sesame-Mango Dressing. Other entrée choices included Wood-

Fired Smokehouse Macaroni and Cheese, Sautéed Jumbo Gulf Shrimp and Crawfish Pasta, Baby Back Ribs, Cedar-Plank Salmon, and Grilled Porkchops. We were on the front end of a week-long tour, so we reluctantly declined desserts like Bananas Foster Bread Pudding, Apple Pie-Stuffed Soft Pretzel, and Christine's Nutella Cheesecake, a chocolate-hazelnut concoction. The restaurant was quite busy during our meal, proving that Frederick's local history continues to thrive at this establishment.

BANANA PECAN-CRUSTED SALMON

1 sweet potato, cut into ¼-inch medallions
2 teaspoons 5-spice powder
salt to taste
2 tablespoons olive oil, divided
2 8-ounce salmon fillets
pepper to taste
3 tablespoons Banana Nut Crunch cereal, ground to breadcrumb consistency
½ cup pineapple juice
4 tablespoons butter
½ cup chopped spinach

Preheat oven to 350 degrees. Toss sweet potato medallions with 5-spice powder, a little salt, and 1 tablespoon olive oil. Place in a single layer on a baking sheet and bake for 10 to 15 minutes until tender. Heat a medium sauté pan and add remaining tablespoon olive oil. Season fillets with salt and pepper and sear on both sides until golden brown. Remove fillets from pan and set in a shallow baking pan. Coat topside with cereal, then bake for 6 to 7 minutes. Deglaze pan with pineapple juice and continue to cook until reduced by ¼. Swirl in butter. Remove from heat.

Heat oil to 350 degrees in a deep fryer. Divide spinach into 2 portions and drop into oil; be very careful, as spinach will spit oil for about 10 seconds. Once spinach ceases bubbling, remove from fryer and drain on paper towels. Plate each fillet with a serving of spinach and half of sweet potato medallions. Pour Pineapple Sauce over fillets. Serves 2.

LUMP CRAB AND POBLANO CHILI CHEESE DIP

1 or 2 poblano peppers, roasted, skin and seeds removed
2 8-ounce packages cream cheese, softened
4 teaspoons horseradish sauce
2 teaspoons lime juice
salt and white pepper to taste
½ pound backfin crabmeat, picked
bread or tortilla chips

Preheat oven to 325 degrees. Purée peppers in a small blender. Place puréed peppers, cream cheese, horseradish sauce, and lime juice into a regular-sized blender and season to taste. Beat ingredients on low speed until combined. Adjust seasonings as necessary. Fold in crabmeat with a spatula, being careful not to break up lumps. Place in an ovenproof container and cover with foil. Bake for 10 to 15 minutes until dip bubbles slightly. Serve with bread or tortilla chips. Serves 2 to 4.

Summit Station Restaurant & Brewery

227 East Diamond Avenue
Gaithersburg, MD 20877
www.summit-station.com
301-519-9400

As I scanned the menu, the Brick-Fired White Pizza immediately caught my eye. The Nachos were every bit as appealing—traditional yellow corn tortillas topped with black beans, melted cheddar and Monterey Jack, Pico de Gallo, and Lime Sour Cream. But I'd seen several orders delivered to nearby tables and decided I just couldn't do Summit Station's Nachos justice. On another visit, with Debbie along, we'll get an order to share. Each item was as interesting as the next. I looked through the salads and was tempted by the Carne Asada Insalata. Grilled Chile Marinated Flank Steak together with Baby Greens, Charred Corn in a Creamy Blue Cheese Dressing is a flavor combination that appeals to me. Had Debbie been along, she may have stopped pondering once she got to the sandwich choices, specifically the Grilled Lime Marinated Red Snapper on Toasted Sourdough. I paused at the Fish and Chips selection, considering giving the nod to my English heritage. After looking at entrée selections such as Teriyaki Salmon,

Jambalaya Pasta, and Chicken Piccata, I returned to the sandwiches and opted for the Mesa Grilled Chicken and a cup of Tomato Basil Soup. Both were delicious! Although too full for dessert on that occasion, I know I'll be back to try one of the homemade Crème Brûlées or a Brewmaster's Draft Root Beer Float.

Summit Station is best known for its award-winning selection of beers. Connoisseurs can taste all kinds, from the Nut Brown and the North Pole Porter to the dark Diamond Stout. Patrons love the unusual Spiced Holiday Ale with its hints of nutmeg, allspice, orange zest, cinnamon, ginger, vanilla, honey, and cloves.

The establishment that serves up these delightful libations is housed in the J. A. Belt Building, the oldest commercial property in Gaithersburg. In July 1889, John A. Belt, a prominent Gaithersburg businessman, purchased the southwest corner of Diamond and Summit Avenues for a mere two hundred dollars. He subsequently constructed this building, which at the time was one of the largest in the county. Part of the Belt Building was used for a store and another portion for public functions. That section was known as Norman Hall. Since Mr. Belt was not just a successful businessman but also served as Gaithersburg's postmaster and town commissioner, Norman Hall saw use as the post office, the town hall, and the local polling place. Not surprisingly, because of its stage, Norman Hall quickly became the center for social and cultural events as well, hosting theater, lectures, recitals, and graduations. At one point, Norman Hall even served as the town's first library.

In September 1903, Mr. Belt was away on business when a fire began in a stock of brooms stored in the building. The flames quickly spread, engulfing the store's oil and flammables, then sweeping on to a large stock of ammunition. Employees were unable to salvage any company records or store stock as they fled the building. The loss was estimated at twelve thousand dollars, a blow from which Mr. Belt was never able to recover. Considering the type of merchandise that went up in flames, it's amazing that Summit Station is here for us to enjoy today.

 SANTA FE QUESADILLA ROLL

12-inch chipotle tortilla
1 tablespoon garlic butter
4-ounce chicken breast, cooked and diced
1 roasted red pepper, diced
1 cup shredded iceberg lettuce
¼ cup shredded cheddar Jack cheese
½ cup tomato adobe sauce
¼ cup corn relish
¼ cup sour cream

Place tortilla on a large cutting board. Spread tortilla with garlic butter up to ½ inch from edge. In a small bowl, gently toss chicken, red peppers, lettuce, cheese, and sauce. Place mixture on half of tortilla. Dollop corn relish and sour cream on top of chicken mixture. Roll tortilla tightly and secure with 2 toothpicks. Using a sharp serrated knife, cut tortilla in 2 diagonally. Serves 2.

CAJUN SAUSAGE SUPREME

12-inch pizza crust
¾ cup pizza sauce
½ roasted red pepper, diced
¼ cup shaved red onion
2 ounces andouille sausage, grilled
½ cup shredded mozzarella cheese
1 tablespoon Parmesan cheese
½ teaspoon crushed red pepper

Preheat oven to 450 degrees. Place crust on a lightly greased pizza tray. Spread sauce evenly on crust up to ½ inch from edge. Scatter roasted peppers, onions, and sausage evenly over sauce. Sprinkle cheeses over other ingredients. Scatter crushed red pepper over cheeses. Bake for 10 to 15 minutes until golden and bubbly. Yields 8 slices.

Murphey's Pub

11782 Somerset Avenue
Princess Anne, MD 21853
410-651-4155

The building that houses Murphey's Pub is believed to be the oldest frame structure in the state of Maryland, dating to 1744. Back then, the building was called the Washington Hotel, which maintained a reputation for good cheer and hospitality. We can attest that, after two hundred years, their reputation is still going strong.

As we sat in the back room, it was easy to tell that this is a popular place for locals. Everyone seemed to know everyone else, and they all agreed that the food here is good, served promptly and with a generous hand. The menu is stuffed full of old favorites, from burgers and traditional salads to sandwiches and pies. Debbie devoured the Grilled Cheese and Tomato Sandwich with a green salad on the side, while Karen sampled the Egg, Tuna, and Chicken Salads in the Trio Salad Special.

The old dining room has retained the original wooden latticework ceiling and the original brick fireplace at one end of the room. Brass sconces and a selection of antique china decorate the walls. We admired the candle-making equipment and the ancient rifle above the fireplace.

In this day and age, the practice in previous centuries of separating the sexes seems curious. When we inquired about the unique double staircases in the hotel lobby, we were told that one was for men and the other for ladies in hoop skirts. The men's stairs have handrails on both sides, so that gentlemen who had imbibed a little too much could still get themselves up the stairs to bed using both hands. On the "other hand," the ladies needed to hold their dresses with one hand to prevent themselves from tripping and so required only a single handrail on one side of the stairs!

With buildings of this age, the guest list is always intriguing. Judge Samuel Chase, a signer of the Declaration of Independence and a resident of Princess Anne, visited here once or twice. Basil Rathbone once had the room at the top of the stairs while in town performing in a play at the University of Maryland-Eastern Shore. Many others of note have dined and slept here during the long tenure of the Murphey family.

Over such a long history, owners have of course come and gone. But for almost seventy years now, the business has remained with one family. Leonard and Daisy V. Shrieves took over the operation of the hotel from the Wallop family in 1936. Three years later, they were able to purchase the business. Their daughter, Mary, and her husband, Robert Murphey, continued as innkeepers, raising their own family on the premises. In 1978, Mary's son, Robert, and his wife, Cheryl, bought the hotel. Known then as the Hotel Inn, it was a popular spot for travelers and locals alike. The fourth generation of the family has now moved into the business. Colleen Murphey and her parents operate the restaurant as Murphey's Pub, while Colleen's grandmother

Mary still oversees the hotel part of the business. It must be said that by serving delicious traditional meals in welcoming surroundings, the Murpheys appear to be creating quite a bit of history themselves!

 STEWED TOMATOES

2 16-ounce cans tomatoes
1 cup sugar
2 teaspoons nutmeg
2 teaspoons cinnamon
3 slices stale bread, cubed
1 tablespoon butter
1 tablespoon cornstarch

Drain tomatoes and place them in a medium saucepan. Reserve ¼ cup of liquid and add remaining liquid to saucepan. Mash tomatoes with a large fork. Add sugar, nutmeg, cinnamon, bread, and butter. Stir to combine over medium heat. Bring to a simmer and cook for about 15 minutes until flavors are well blended. In a small bowl, mix cornstarch into reserved tomato liquid. Stir until well combined. Add mixture a little at a time to stewed tomatoes until they are thickened as desired. Serves 6.

 POTATO SOUP

5 or 6 large baking potatoes, peeled and cubed
1 small onion, diced
3 slices bacon, chopped
10 cups chicken stock
1 tablespoon dried chives
3 tablespoons butter
2 tablespoons salt
½ teaspoon black pepper
1 cup diced ham
1 cup milk
3 eggs, beaten

Place potatoes, onions, and bacon in a large cooking pot. Add stock. Bring pot to a boil on stove. Reduce heat to medium and simmer about 12 minutes until potatoes are just done. Add remaining ingredients and stir well. Remove from heat and serve. Serves 12.

26 Market Space
Annapolis, MD 21401
www.riordans.com
410-263-5449

Riordan's started as a private residence, later becoming a boardinghouse when its second and third stories were used by officers from the nearby United States Naval Academy. At that time, the first floor also had ties to the water, since it functioned as a produce market supplying ships in the Severn-Annapolis Harbor. Over the years, the store evolved from a market into a drugstore. It eventually also sold hardware and finished its retail life as a clothing store. Today, this history is reflected in the large collection of antique signs and beer trays hung around the walls. Many products are represented, but cigars and whiskey are most often featured. Don't forget to check out the moose head toward the rear of the establishment and the various stuffed birds "flying" around the room.

Guests enjoy the friendly staff, the good food, and the comfortable surroundings here at Riordan's. Inside, the tables are adorned in green-and-white-checked tablecloths, and the Tiffany lampshades are all gorgeous. The wooden floors, bentwood chairs, and tiny black and white tiles on the floor in the bar area hint at the past. The polished wooden bar extends the whole length of the building and has a brass bar along the top

for resting your arms and another along the bottom for resting your feet in comfort. There are four televisions inside the saloon, so no one has to miss their favorite sporting event while sampling the local brews or snacking on a seafood appetizer. Outside, what was once a red-brick building is now painted green with cream trim around the windows. A large green awning gives a little shade to the summer visitors who prefer to eat in the sunshine and enjoy the marvelous view of the busy Annapolis waterfront.

There are many delicious items to choose from on the lunch menu. But for those who have difficulty making up their minds, the lunch specials are carefully delineated on a single piece of paper. On the day I visited, Rockfish, Mahi-Mahi, and Sea Scallops were featured side by side with Philly Cheese Steak, Riordan's Beef Stew, and Baked Pollo Sada, a popular Mexican dish with chicken, cheeses, and Salsa. Among the appetizers were Crab Vegetable Soup, Baked Vegetable Quesadilla, Baked Oysters Rockefeller, and Southwestern Chicken Rolls. I was told that Riordan's Hot Crab Dip is by far the most popular item with the locals, though. Tempted by the Fish and Chips and the Shrimp and Scallops Casino, I eventually chose the Grilled Salmon BLT, which featured crisp bacon and a superb Lemon Dill Mayonnaise. My side dish of scrumptious Potato Wedges was so good that Debbie, who popped in just for a moment, snatched a few to eat on the way to another establishment!

The atmosphere here is redolent of a traditional Irish pub, and not much has changed in the past twenty years. May customers continue to enjoy the friendly service and good food for twenty more!

MARYLAND BARBECUED SHRIMP

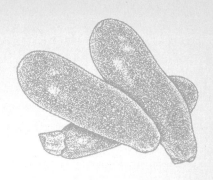

2 teaspoons butter
1 medium onion, chopped fine
1½ cups ketchup
1/3 cup water
4 tablespoons Worcestershire sauce
4 tablespoons brown sauce
1½ tablespoons vinegar
¾ teaspoon dry mustard
6 dashes of Tabasco sauce
2 teaspoons tomato paste
36 large shrimp
18 strips bacon

Preheat oven to 450 degrees. In a large skillet, melt butter over medium heat and sauté onions until translucent. Add remaining ingredients except shrimp and bacon and bring to a boil. Turn heat to low and simmer covered for 20 minutes to make sauce. Peel and devein shrimp. Wrap each shrimp in half a strip of bacon. Place wrapped shrimp in a single layer in a baking pan. Bake for 20 to 25 minutes until bacon is brown. Remove from oven and drain most of bacon drippings. Pour sauce over top of shrimp and return pan to oven for 3 to 5 minutes. Serves 6.

ZUCCHINI CASSEROLE

½ cup butter
½ cup chopped onions
2 cloves garlic, crushed
3 or 4 medium zucchini, sliced
salt and pepper to taste
1 teaspoon dill
1 pint cherry tomatoes
8 ounces cheddar cheese, cubed
1 cup Italian-seasoned breadcrumbs

Preheat oven to 350 degrees. In a large skillet, melt butter over medium heat. Sauté onions and garlic until translucent. Add zucchini, salt and pepper, and dill. Sauté for 5 minutes, then remove from heat. Drain liquid and set aside. Butter a 3-quart baking dish and layer zucchini with tomatoes and cheese. Combine breadcrumbs and about half of reserved liquid and sprinkle over top of casserole. Bake uncovered for 25 minutes. Serves 8.

CHAPTER 9

Getting Away from It All

The Imperial Hotel and Restaurant

After a good bit of hard work, most of us like to get away, to have a change of pace. Each of the establishments here has provided a destination for individuals to do just that. And they continue to provide a means of modern escape, whether it's for an overnight stay or a good meal. We've saved these restaurants for last because, after our diligence in completing this book, we're ready. . . . And we invite you to come along.

Atlantic Hotel

2 North Main Street
Berlin, MD 21811
www.atlantichotel.com
410-641-3589

Berlin's Main Street was once part of the path that connected the Assateague Indians with the neighboring Pocomoke tribe. During colonial times, the path became the main route up the Eastern Shore and was known as the Philadelphia Post Road. Along that thoroughfare, the town of Berlin grew around a three-hundred-acre land grant patented in 1677. Later, much of that acreage became known as the Burley Plantation. It is believed that the town's name was derived from the Burleigh Inn, once a tavern along the Philadelphia Post Road. In today's world of fast talking and lack of enunciation, the jump from *Burleigh Inn* to *Berlin* isn't too much of a stretch.

The Atlantic Hotel was built along the picturesque Main Street in 1895. It was one of many, because at the time Berlin boasted more hotels than nearby Ocean City. Well frequented by tourists, it was also popular with traveling salesmen, otherwise known as "drummers," since they were always trying to drum up sales. In order to attract their business, the hotel offered bus service from the rail station to the hotel, where, upon arrival, the salesmen were treated to popular fare such as country ham, fried chicken, crab dishes, and diamond-backed terrapin. In the mornings, the bus distributed the salesmen to the scattered country stores throughout the area, collecting them again before dinner. After the business of the day, a writing room was provided, where the men could have a desk or tabletop to write up their orders. Today, that writing room is known as Drummer's Café, which serves casual fare in an attractive Victorian atmosphere.

Original owners Horace and Virginia Harmonson built the hotel after a fire in 1894 destroyed the National Hotel, previously located on the site. Through the rough times of the mid-1900s, it passed through a series of hands. Charles and Violet Coats operated the hotel into the 1960s. For the next two decades, possession continued to bounce around, finally landing in the protection of the Atlantic Hotel Partnership, which, returning the hotel to its previous grandeur, earned a State Historic Trust Preservation Award along the way.

We were fortunate not only to dine at but also to stay at the Atlantic Hotel. After checking in, we were torn between relaxing in our room and peeking into some of the hotel's nooks and crannies. Ultimately, curiosity won out and we wandered, discovering some of this old dame's treasures.

The menu in the main dining room holds its own share of treasures, featuring starters such as Pecan-Barbecued Shrimp and Crab Crepes, as well as entrées like Beef Tournedos in Gouda Demi-Glace and Veal with Ricotta Gnocchi and Roasted Asparagus. We started with a delicious Brown Sugar-Topped Brie in a Vanilla Crepe.

Karen followed that with the Sushi Tuna entrée, while Debbie was adventurous and sampled the Antelope with Jalapeño and Dried Fruit Chutney. Dessert was not to be missed. We ended with the Blackberry and Peach Bread Pudding and the Lemon Cheesecake, topped with sour cherries. There was so much more we wanted to sample—which sounds like a good excuse for future visits.

SEAFOOD BISQUE

1 pound shrimp
1 teaspoon oil
1 teaspoon salt
4 cups water
7 tablespoons unsalted butter
1 cup sliced cleaned leeks, white part only
8 ounces mushrooms, sliced thin
1/3 cup chopped parsley
1/4 cup flour
1/4 pound scallops
1/4 pound cod or other flaky white fish
1 cup heavy cream
3/4 cup puréed plum tomatoes
1/3 cup dry sherry
salt and pepper to taste
fresh dill for garnish

Peel and devein shrimp, reserving shells. Heat oil in a medium sauté pan and cook shrimp shells until bright red. Add 1 teaspoon salt and water and simmer for 10 minutes. Strain liquid and remove shells, reserving liquid. In the same pan, melt butter with leeks, mushrooms, and parsley and gently sweat until vegetables are clear. Add flour, cooking lightly to make a roux. Pour in reserved liquid from shrimp shells, stir-

ring constantly. Add seafood and cook at low temperature for 6 to 8 minutes until seafood is done. Add cream, tomato purée, and sherry. Adjust salt and pepper. Garnish with dill. Serves 6.

BAILEYS IRISH CREAM CHEESECAKE

2 cups crushed Oreo cookies
1/4 cup butter, melted
2 tablespoons chocolate chips
4 8-ounce packages plus 1/2 package cream cheese
1 1/2 cups sugar
1 cup Baileys Irish Cream
6 eggs
1 tablespoon vanilla
1/4 cup semisweet chocolate

Preheat oven to 325 degrees. Combine cookie crumbs and butter and press into bottom and 1 inch up sides of a springform pan. Bake for 7 to 10 minutes. Sprinkle chocolate chips across bottom of pan. Set aside. Reduce oven to 250 degrees. Whip all remaining ingredients except chocolate until smooth, being careful not to overmix. Pour batter into crust and bake in a water bath for 90 minutes until set. Put in a cool place and let sit for 3 hours before releasing springform. Melt chocolate and drizzle over top of cheesecake to garnish. Serves 12 to 16.

IMPERIAL HOTEL

208 High Street
Chestertown, MD 21620
www.imperialchestertown.com
410-778-5000

Karen uses the term *high street* to refer to a town's main thoroughfare. It's one that reflects her English roots but is also a term that many American communities have put to use quite literally. Chestertown is no exception. Sitting proudly along High Street is The Imperial Hotel, constructed in 1903 by Wilbur Hubbard with the intention of having retail space on the first floor and rooms for boarders above. The original blueprints are framed and hang in the lobby today. When the structure was refurbished in 1985, the effort won the Restoration Project Award from the Maryland Trust for Historic Preservation, no small task in a state this historic!

Owners Jan Macdonald (also an English-woman) and her husband, Dick O'Neill, acquired the property in 1999 after retiring from the business world. The eleven guest rooms on the hotel's second and third floors are individually decorated with authentic period furnishings, creating a haven that allows guests to truly get away to another time.

The dining room's ambiance is one of quiet elegance, created by cream-colored walls with crisp white trim and white and hunter-green table linens. I was seated in a tufted Victorian parlor chair at a table for two. Across the room, a family was sharing Sunday dinner, the parents patiently teaching their young children the art of fine dining. The dinner menu is abbreviated, each choice as tempting as the next. Karen most certainly would have selected the Roasted Beet and Apple Salad, had she been along. The Mediterranean Salad was popular, and I watched many plates of Oysters Norfolk being delivered and enjoyed. The entrée menu varies but might be headed by Mushroom Phyllo with Caramelized Onions and Red Pepper Coulis or Tuna in Saffron and Sun-Dried Tomato Broth. Pecan- and Peanut-Encrusted Rack of Lamb was on the menu the day I dined, but I opted for the unusual Thai-Style Swordfish, served atop a bed of rice. It was garnished with a lovely Yellow Curry and Lemon Grass Sauce and thinly sliced Sautéed Zucchini. After entrées like that, it's difficult to even think about dessert, but dessert at The Imperial is not to be missed. The Almond Panna Cotta with Dried Apricot Compote, a regular feature on the dessert menu, looked as delicious as it sounds. The Ginger Spice Cake with Caramel Oranges and Ginger Ice Cream would be my choice every time it's on the menu.

After the meal, many of the guests retreated to one of the wide verandas, a perfect spot to relax, read a book, or overlook the charming downtown area. For those interested in more active pursuits, boating, kayaking, and cycling opportunities are available nearby. I happened to be in town during the annual Jazz Festival but had to be on my way before I had a chance to enjoy the music. Nonetheless, the town and The Imperial Hotel are reason enough to return.

 SEARED DUCK BREAST

2 tablespoons olive oil
4 duck breasts, trimmed of fat
1 medium onion, chopped
2 cloves garlic, minced
1-inch piece of peeled ginger, minced
1 cup dry sherry
3 tablespoons soy sauce
2 cups orange juice

Heat oil in a medium sauté pan. Add duck and cook on all sides to desired doneness. Set duck aside and allow to rest. Add onion to sauté pan and cook until translucent. Add garlic and ginger. Cook for 2 minutes. Add sherry and reduce by ⅓. Add soy sauce and orange juice. Simmer until sauce thickens. On a cutting board, slice duck against the grain into thin slices. Fan meat onto plates. Spoon sauce over meat. The Imperial Hotel serves this dish with basmati rice and grilled and sliced mango or peaches. Serves 4.

 PORK TENDERLOIN IN ROSEMARY SAUCE

1 tablespoon butter
1 tablespoon oil
2 12-ounce pork tenderloins
1 tablespoon chopped fresh rosemary leaves
1 teaspoon chopped fresh thyme leaves
½ teaspoon salt
¼ teaspoon freshly ground pepper
½ cup vermouth
1 cup light cream

In a skillet over high heat, heat butter and oil until very hot. Add pork and sear until well browned on all sides. Add rosemary, thyme, salt, pepper, and vermouth. Cover, reduce heat to medium-low, and simmer for about 10 minutes until juices run clear when tested with a fork. Do not overcook. Remove pork from skillet and keep warm. Over high heat, boil vermouth rapidly until reduced by half. Stir in cream and heat through. Slice pork into ½-inch slices and arrange on plates. Pour sauce over pork. Serves 4.

1844

30 Trevanion Road
Taneytown, MD 21787
www.antrim1844.com
410-756-6812

The dining experience begins with hors d'oeuvres served in the Drawing Room or the formal gardens. The menu changes daily, but what never alters is the fact that the evening offerings are exquisite. Appetizers such as Smoked Salmon Cheesecake, Two Melon Soup with Mint Cream, and Velouté of Butternut Squash are all divine. The prix fixe meal continues with a green salad, followed by an intermezzo of sorbet. The entrée choices may include the traditional Filet Mignon, perhaps with Bacon and Walnuts or Boursin and Shrimp. Salmon with Roast Garlic or with Tasso and Brie usually appears among the offerings. On one sample menu, we found the Porcupine Shrimp quite intriguing. On another, the Crab and Pine Nut Lasagna would definitely have been the choice. The selection of equally wonderful desserts is the perfect way to end your meal. Once you realize that Michael Gettier was the first Maryland chef to be invited to cook at the James Beard House in New York, you'll fully appreciate his sumptuous offerings here in the foothills of the Catoctin Mountains at Antrim 1844.

Dinner in Antrim's Smokehouse Restaurant is definitely a unique experience. The brick floors, whitewashed walls, heavy beams, and multiple fireplaces certainly create an eye-catching ambiance when juxtaposed with the traditional furniture and table linens. Intrigued by the beehive oven just to the left of the largest of the fireplaces, we tried to imagine just what had been crafted there through the years.

County Antrim in Ireland was the birthplace of Colonel Andrew Ege, who gave the name to this property before passing it on to his daughter as a wedding gift. Purchased by Chief Justice George Washington Clabaugh of the Washington, D.C., District Court, Antrim remained in his family for a century. The lovely brick structure with white trim sits in stately fashion atop a slight knoll. At its most successful, the estate was a thriving twenty-five-hundred-acre plantation. Today, fully restored, the mansion and estate function as a country-house hotel on twenty-four acres. Nine guest rooms are available within the mansion and eighteen additional rooms and suites in the dependencies. The Cottage offers a stay in the original plantation office. The Barn has two rooms, each with its own private deck overlooking the woods and babbling brook. The Carriage House features six well-appointed suites, while the Birnie House contains five rooms decorated with lavish Victoriana. We settled into the Smith House and thoroughly enjoyed our surroundings, which transported us back more than a century and a half.

If you're an overnight guest, the morning begins with a continental breakfast delivered to your room, followed by a delicious country breakfast served in the dining room at nine o'clock. Afternoon Tea gives guests the opportunity to enjoy the soaring ceilings and carved marble fireplaces of the Drawing Room. Legend states that General George Meade used Antrim as the Union army's headquarters prior to the Battle of Gettysburg, fought just fifteen miles away. In fact, Meade's entire Army of the Potomac used Taneytown as an encampment in hopes of luring General Robert E. Lee's army south to this area. The history of the region and the luxury of Antrim 1844 were enough to get us here, and more than enough to make us sorry to go.

TWO MELON SOUP

1 cantaloupe melon
1 honeydew melon
½ cup white wine, divided
⅛ teaspoon vanilla
pinch of salt
fresh mint leaves
2 tablespoons Midori liqueur
whipped cream

Carefully remove skin from melons, saving the fruit. Slice in half and remove seeds. Purée each melon separately in a food processor or blender; a blender will give a smoother soup. Add ¼ cup white wine, vanilla, and salt to cantaloupe. Add mint leaves to honeydew, then purée. Add remaining wine and liqueur to honeydew. Pour cantaloupe mixture and honeydew mixture separately into each serving bowl from either side of the bowl at the same time; for best results, serve in clear bowls or martini glasses. Garnish each bowl with additional mint leaves and whipped cream. Serves 6.

GRILLED LAMB FILLET WITH APPLE-ALMOND COMPOTE

4-pound lamb fillet, cleaned
1½ pounds sugar
2 pounds apples, peeled and sliced
10-ounce package slivered almonds
¾ cup plus 2 tablespoons vinegar
pinch of rosemary
1 cup plus 1 tablespoon butter

Grill lamb to desired doneness. While grilling, caramelize sugar by placing it in a sauté pan over medium heat until it turns a golden brown. Add apples and almonds. Cook for 1 minute, then add vinegar and cook for an additional minute. Add rosemary and butter just before serving. To serve, spoon compote onto a serving plate and place lamb on top. Serves 6.

 TAPANADE

½ cup pitted black olives
¼ cup pitted green olives
1¼ ounces anchovies
¼ cup olive oil
1½ teaspoons mustard
1 teaspoon cognac
crostinis

Purée all ingredients together in a food processor. Leave coarse. Serve with crostinis. Serves 6 as an appetizer.

The Westlawn Inn
North Beach, MD

9200 Chesapeake Avenue
North Beach, MD 20714
www.mdlocations.com
410-257-0001

In the days before the Chesapeake Bay Bridge was built, connecting the western portion of Maryland with the Eastern Shore, the western portion's twin beach towns of Chesapeake Beach and North Beach were a bustling resort area. Trains from Washington, D.C., pulled into the depot just down the road, bringing loads of revelers looking for summer sunshine and fun. Steamships from Baltimore arrived regularly, bringing tourists anxious to enjoy the thrills of the boardwalk and the amusement park. A large hotel now stands on that site, but pictorial memories have been preserved for display on its walls.

Obviously, visitors from that earlier era needed somewhere to stay while they were here. In the days before well-recognized hotel chains, they turned to boardinghouses instead. Such was the original function of The Westlawn Inn. On its second floor, rows and rows of small bedrooms once housed vacationers. During the tenure of Dr. and Mrs. West, for whom the inn is named, guests were carefully screened to make sure that no room was let to a couple who were not married. On a recent house tour for a women's group, one of the tour members told

owner Lee Travers that she'd spent her honeymoon here at the boardinghouse in 1943. Love must have been in the air, because on the evening of our visit, a young man had just proposed and been accepted. The cheers at the bar for the young couple rivaled those at any hotly contested sporting event.

Lee is not only in the restaurant business but the construction business as well, specializing in custom-built homes. He's certainly utilized his expertise at The Westlawn, fashioning the bar from old guest-room doors, reconfiguring the original carnival glass light fixtures, and using as many of the old windows and window frames as possible. The lobby of the restaurant is decorated with a Victorian sofa and parlor chairs, in keeping with the building's original era. The main dining room is at the front of the house, in the area once occupied by a screened-in porch. A beautiful wood floor and clean colors of gray and white provide an understated atmosphere that lets the fabulous food speak for itself.

The menu offers a variety of selections, from appetizers to slightly larger portions called "Small Plates" to traditional entrée-sized servings. We originally declared our interest in the Small Plate choice of Truffle Lobster Risotto. However, after our server came and discussed the menu and the evening's specials, we decided to further scrutinize the selections. It's difficult to choose when the chef is offering things such as Jumbo Shrimp Piccata over Dried Tomato Risotto, Coffee-Crusted Duck, Prosciutto-Wrapped Monkfish, and Rockfish with Butternut Squash Relish. Wanting to sample it all, we ultimately decided on the Veal Scaloppine with Chive Spaetzle and Butternut Squash Purée and the Masa-Crusted

Rockfish with Mascarpone Whipped Potatoes and Honey-Glazed Fall Vegetables. When we'd spoken with Lee Travers prior to our meal, he'd sung the praises of his chef. After savoring the chef's concoctions, we told Lee the compliments he'd given didn't begin to describe the masterpieces we'd been served.

SHRIMP AND GRITS

6 cups milk
½ cup butter
salt and white pepper to taste
1 cup quick grits
¾ cups grated cheddar cheese
20 16-20 count shrimp, cooked, peeled, and deveined
Tasso Cream (see below)
Southern Greens (see next column)

Heat milk to scalding but not boiling. Add butter and salt and white pepper. Slowly add grits. Reduce heat and cook for about 20 minutes until liquid is absorbed, being careful not to scorch. Stir in cheese. Plate grits and top with shrimp. Serve with Tasso Cream and Southern Greens. Serves 4.

TASSO CREAM

3 tablespoons chopped tasso ham
2 tablespoons oil
2 teaspoons chopped garlic
½ small onion, diced
1 tablespoon Cajun seasoning
½ cup white wine
2 tablespoons rice wine vinegar
½ cup chicken stock
3 cups heavy cream

In a medium sauté pan, sauté ham in oil. Add garlic and onions and continue to cook until soft but not browned. Add Cajun seasoning and sauté for 1 minute. Deglaze with wine, vinegar, and chicken stock. Reduce by half. Add cream. Reduce until cream coats the back of a spoon. Yields 2 cups.

SOUTHERN GREENS

2 bunches young mustard, turnip, or collard greens
4-ounce slab country bacon
1 cup diced onions
2 cloves garlic, minced
¼ teaspoon red pepper flakes
1 cup chicken stock
1 cup water
salt and pepper to taste
sugar to taste
cider vinegar to taste

Clean greens and remove stems. In a large sauté pan, cook bacon until fat is rendered and bacon is crisp. Add onions, garlic, and red pepper flakes. Cook until onions and garlic are translucent. Add greens in batches, stirring until slightly wilted. Continue to add greens until all are incorporated. Use equal amounts of chicken stock and water to cover greens. Bring to a simmer. Cook greens at least 40 minutes until tender but resilient. Drain greens and season to taste with salt and pepper, sugar, and vinegar. Serves 4.

Cornish Manor
Restaurant & Lounge

830 Memorial Drive
Oakland, MD 21550
301-334-6499

A real-estate brochure once read, "If ever you had a thought to buy a country home, it would be wise to see this." The brochure advertised an eighteen-room house on twenty acres built upon "the most beautiful tract in Garrett County." Additional selling points included spring water piped from town, electric lights, and a Bell telephone. The structure was built in 1868 as a summer house for a Washington, D.C., judge, and the advertised sale was being conducted by the residence's second owner, forced to sell because of poor health. At the time, the estate was known as Ethelhurst, named for the owner's daughter. Later owners renamed it Cornish Manor, after their own last name. That name has been kept through the years and through various owners, including the Markwood family, who took ownership in 2004 and subsequently restored this gem of a house.

The crisp white exterior is trimmed in hues of burgundy and deep hunter green. An extensive porch adds to the inviting aura. Inside, the main hall is trimmed in dark wood, and the doorways open to attractive dining rooms on either side. We were seated at the juncture of what was once a parlor and the enclosed sun porch, which provided a cheery, sunny ambiance. An interesting period chandelier combining brass and lead crystal hung above, adding to the luster of the dining room. Further Victorian flair was added by an ornate mirror on the rear wall and myriad Tiffany lamps hanging throughout the room. The dining room to the right of the entry hall is more subdued but equally lovely. Anchored by a corner fireplace, it features an enormous pocket door.

The restaurant is operated under the auspices of Jacques Hourtal, with whom we were able to chat after the busy lunch crowd gradually subsided. Before visiting with him, we'd pondered our choices of Cornish Manor Chicken Salad, Mussels Mariner, a Turkey Melt, and a Brazilian-Style Salad concocted of shrimp, black beans, corn, and heart of palm. Ultimately, we chose the quiche of the day, which was a delicious Spinach and Feta, and the Melted Brie Sandwich, which was an upscale version of a BLT on sourdough. We splurged and had dessert, opting for the Raspberry Swirl Cheesecake and the Vermont Apple Cake with Maple Frosting, both providing a nice end to an enjoyable midday meal.

For dinner, both the French Onion Soup and the Old Cornish-Style Carrot Soup with ginger and nutmeg sound appealing. Appetizers such as Escargots Burgundy and Frog Legs Provençal hint at a French touch. We also found the combination of Fried Onion Rings and Artichokes quite interesting. The selection of entrées is ample, featuring pastas, steaks, poultry, and seafood. The Floridian Grilled Tuna with Citrus Salsa and the Fresh Orange Roughy baked in fresh herbs, walnuts, and hazelnut liqueur sound tasty and unique. Even the Oven-Roasted Chicken is prepared creatively, with options for three different finishes. Whether you plan to enjoy Cornish Manor with friends or business associates or for a special occasion, it has a menu, ambiance, and style for everyone.

SAUTÉED JACK DANIEL'S TROUT

½ cup butter
4 8-ounce trout, deboned
¼ cup crushed pecans
½ cup lemon juice
¾ cup Jack Daniel's

Melt butter in a large sauté pan. Over low heat, pan-fry trout about 2 minutes on each side. Remove trout from pan. Combine pecans, lemon juice, and Jack Daniel's. Pour into pan to deglaze. Reduce sauce by half. Pour over trout and serve. Serves 4.

MUSSELS MARINER

16 fresh mussels
1 tablespoon chopped shallots
2 teaspoons chopped garlic
1 tablespoon finely chopped parsley
½ cup white wine
1 bay leaf
½ cup heavy cream

Rinse mussels in cold running water while scrubbing with a vegetable brush. Discard any broken shells. In a medium pot, steam mussels with shallots, garlic, parsley, wine, and bay leaf. Continue cooking about 5 minutes until mussels open. Remove mussels from broth. Add cream and reduce slightly. Remove bay leaf. Place mussels in 2 bowls. Spoon broth over top. Serves 2.

The General Braddock Inn

4830 Schley Avenue
Braddock Heights, MD 21714
301-371-0411

The menu at The General Braddock Inn has two sets of appetizers. The one labeled "The Classics" contains entries like Stuffed Mushrooms, Fried Calamari, and Marinated Beef Tips. The second set, falling under the heading "With a Twist," features combinations like Spicy Shrimp Canapés, Shiitake and Blue Cheese Bruschetta, and Spicy Scallops over Wilted Spinach. My daughter and I would have been happy to sample each and every one. Actually, the entire menu is organized in this manner, which really helps diners focus on what sort of cuisine interests them. The main-course selections list toppings and sauces available to accompany Filet Mignon, New York Strip Steak, and Pan-Seared Salmon; the choices include Au Poivre, Mushroom Duxelle, and Crab Imperial, a veritable roll call of classic cuisine. Crab Cakes, Stuffed Shrimp, Fettuccine Alfredo, and Pan-Seared Chicken are other classic selections. We were thoroughly delighted by the Grilled Vegetable Napoleon and the Toasted Almond-Encrusted Chicken with Honey-Wasabi Glaze. My daughter particularly liked the pineapple-infused rice that accompanied

the latter dish and thought that Karen's daughter would have liked it, too.

Originally, the Braddock Heights area was a resort community for wealthy Frederick County citizens. It offered many exclusive boardinghouses for both men and women coming to enjoy popular attractions such as a slide, a carousel, and an observatory. Bachelors and young ladies would rendezvous at the dance pavilion, then stroll down the proverbial lovers' lane, which runs along the western side of the building and can still be seen from the dining room. Their destination was the romantic freshwater springs at the foot of the hill.

One summer, a group of businessmen, deciding that the festivities along Maryland Avenue were an invasion of their privacy, pitched a tent in the woods down the street. They subsequently purchased several acres at the end of Schley Avenue and built the Camp Schley Inn, for men only. They named it after a Frederick-born war hero who had found fame in the battle at Santiago Bay, Cuba, in the Spanish-American War. During Prohibition in the 1920s, the inn operated as a speakeasy.

In 1941, the inn was purchased by a young couple, who added rooms, cottages, and a row of apartments. Ten years later, deciding that the elevation was perfect for skiing, they renamed the property the Braddock Heights Skiway and gave birth to the state's first ski resort. Although the featured activity had changed, wealthy and influential residents still flocked to the area to relax and have fun. Once, on her way to Camp David, Ethel Kennedy spied the inn and brought her clan for a day on the slopes.

The ski resort is no longer operational, and

the carousel is long gone. Today, the fun is in the creations of chef Regina Bradley, niece of owner Patrick Weed. The restaurant delivers not only on food but on atmosphere as well. The restful maize walls and white trim of the main dining room allow visitors to get away from it all once again.

SPICY SHRIMP CANAPÉS

4 tablespoons butter, softened
1 teaspoon cayenne pepper
1 tablespoon dried parsley
1 teaspoon crushed red pepper
1 tablespoon plus 1 teaspoon minced shallots, divided
salt and pepper to taste
juice of ½ lime
8 jumbo shrimp, peeled and deveined
3 cloves garlic
2 slices wheat toast
¼ cup goat cheese
2 to 4 lime wedges

Combine butter, cayenne, parsley, red pepper, 1 tablespoon shallots, salt and pepper, and lime juice to make Chili Butter. Refrigerate to solidify. After Chili Butter has solidified, use half of it in a medium sauté pan to sauté shrimp with garlic, remaining shallots, and additional salt and pepper. Crush garlic with the heel of a knife while cooking; do not mince or use a press. Melt remaining Chili Butter separately and reserve. Cut each toast slice into 4 triangles. Lightly brush each piece with reserved Chili Butter. Divide

cheese evenly into 8 small pieces and place a piece in center of each buttered triangle. Press 1 shrimp onto each piece of bread, using cheese to hold it in place. Place 4 canapés on each of 2 plates. Garnish with lime wedges. Serves 2.

TOASTED ALMOND-ENCRUSTED CHICKEN WITH HONEY-WASABI GLAZE

2 eggs
1 cup water, divided
2 5-ounce chicken breasts
1 cup flour
1½ cups sliced almonds
3 tablespoons olive oil, divided
2 tablespoons minced shallots
1 teaspoon minced garlic
3 tablespoons wasabi powder
¼ cup white wine
½ cup honey

Whip eggs with ½ cup water. Dredge chicken in flour, dip in egg mixture, then coat with almonds. Heat 2 tablespoons olive oil in a nonstick skillet over medium heat. Brown chicken. Reduce heat and cook chicken just until done, adding olive oil if needed. Meanwhile, heat a small sauté pan over medium-high heat. Add 1 teaspoon olive oil. Sauté shallots and garlic until translucent. Whisk in wasabi powder. Add wine and stir to form a paste. Whisk in remaining water. Reduce mixture slightly. Add honey and heat just until bubbly. Remove from heat. Serve over chicken. Serves 2.

THE DEER PARK INN

65 Hotel Road
Deer Park, MD 21550
www.deerparkinn.com
301-334-2308

What is now The Deer Park Inn was once part of the grand Deer Park Hotel Resort, which served well-to-do families from 1872 to 1929. The hotel is, unfortunately, long gone, but this "summer cottage" remains to remind us of the luxury experienced by prominent families of yesteryear. The house was built around 1890, designed by Baltimore architect Josiah Pennington. Details of the construction such as the high-ceilinged entry and the lovely staircase in the foyer let guests know that this was no ordinary cottage.

The landing of the staircase has a charming angular window seat beneath expansive windows swathed in lace. The upstairs fireplaces, surrounded by ceramic tiles in hues of loden green and mulberry, are a treasure. The original tub, commode, and sink still appoint the third guest room. Like the bathroom fixtures, most of the antiques found throughout the house are original, including a bed that came from one of the first Sears and Roebuck mail-order catalogs. The museum-like quality of these pieces is due to the circumstances under which the house

changed hands. The first owners lost everything they had in the stock-market crash of 1929. They never even returned to the home to try to sell off their belongings to raise much-needed cash. The house was sold as it had been the last time they were there. Subsequent owners have obviously taken great care of the treasures they've come to own.

Today's proprietors had no intention of buying the Pennington Cottage when they first visited. However, they quickly fell in love with all it had to offer, including the opportunity for owner-chef Pascal Fontaine to step away from the administrative duties of an executive chef and get back to the real reason he became a chef— the transformation of fresh ingredients into a masterpiece. In other words, cooking.

Meals are served in two dining rooms located just off the foyer. Rich wallpaper and crystal chandeliers create the appropriate ambiance for the offerings of Pascal's kitchen. Creations such as Shrimp Provençal, Vegetarian Spanakopita, Orange Horseradish-Crusted Salmon, and Curried Chicken with Coconut Sauce grace the menu. These delectable entrées are preceded by starters such as Pumpkin and Butternut Squash Soup, Honey-Roasted Pear Salad with Goat Cheese, and Yellow and Red Beet Salad. Among the desserts, the Chocolate Pâté is exquisite. So, start to finish, a meal here is truly an experience, made even more palatable by the realization that this creativity and freshness are available at a cost competitive with the popular chain establishments. What a find!

Pascal and his wife, Sandy, told us they really like to use local ingredients, including local wines, produce, and, of course, Deer Park water, which those of us from other areas have sipped in the bottled variety. Since it comes from local springs, guests at the inn not only use it for drinking but shower in it as well!

PAIN PERDU
WITH BANANAS AND RUM

½ cup milk
¼ cup heavy cream
2 eggs
1 teaspoon vanilla
1 tablespoon granulated sugar
pinch of salt
4 ¾-inch-thick slices day-old French bread
¾ cup butter, divided
4 bananas, cut into ½-inch-thick slices
2 tablespoons brown sugar
2 tablespoons dark rum

Preheat oven to 400 degrees. In a shallow dish, combine milk, cream, eggs, vanilla, granulated sugar, and salt. Soak bread slices, turning once. In a medium sauté pan, heat 1 tablespoon butter over high heat and cook bread about 2 minutes until golden brown. Reserve bread in oven while preparing banana topping. Heat remaining butter in a skillet over medium heat and cook banana slices until soft. Sprinkle with brown sugar. Caramelize on high heat, then flambé with rum. Top reserved bread (pain perdu) with banana mixture and serve. Serves 4.

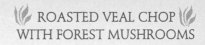

ROASTED VEAL CHOP
WITH FOREST MUSHROOMS

¾ cup butter, divided
2 shallots, minced
2 cloves garlic, chopped
1 pound forest mushrooms (yellow-foot chanterelles, shiitake, oyster), cleaned
1 teaspoon salt
½ teaspoon freshly ground pepper
2 tablespoons olive oil
8 veal chops
½ cup dry white wine
1 cup chicken stock
1 cup heavy cream
1 tablespoon chopped tarragon

Preheat oven to 400 degrees. In a medium skillet, heat 2 tablespoons butter and sauté shallots and garlic. Add mushrooms and sauté for about 4 minutes until most of the water in mushrooms has evaporated. Season with salt and pepper. Reserve. Heat olive oil in a large frying pan. Season veal chops, then brown on both sides. Remove from frying pan and place in a large roasting pan. Finish cooking in oven for about 12 minutes. Pour wine into frying pan and reduce slightly. Add chicken stock and reduce by half. Add cream and reduce by half again. Finish with tarragon and remaining butter. Plate veal chops, top with mushrooms, and spoon Tarragon Cream Sauce over top. Serves 4.

George's
ON MT. VERNON SQUARE

Peabody Court Hotel
612 Cathedral Street
Baltimore, MD 21201
www.peabodycourthotel.com
410-727-1314

What were once luxury apartments built in 1928 have now been converted into a luxury hotel. Nestled in the charming and elegant Mt. Vernon Square district of downtown Baltimore, which embodies more than a century of elegance and refinement, the Peabody Court Hotel is conveniently located within easy reach of the city's cultural district and perennial favorites like Camden Yards and the Inner Harbor. As a matter of fact, the Enoch Pratt Free Library and Antique Row are within walking distance, and The Walters Art Museum is right across the street. This proximity is reflected in the hotel's restaurant, George's on Mt. Vernon Square, where the menu items are works of art in themselves. The Lalique Salmon is comprised of Atlantic salmon poached in white wine and lemon juice. The Delacroix Chicken features oven-roasted breast of chicken baked with crabmeat and topped with Imperial Crab Sauce. The Briosco consists of beef slices seasoned with Teriyaki, then tossed with snow peas and carrots and served over penne

pasta and garnished with sesame seeds and Chinese noodles.

The lunch menu pays tribute to significant individuals. The George Washington Sandwich includes turkey on focaccia bread, topped with sage cheddar and Cranberry Mayonnaise; George Peabody is linked to the traditional club sandwich; and George Herman Ruth's name adorns a sandwich of thinly sliced prime rib with melted Swiss on French bread.

In fact, this trio of Georges was the inspiration for the naming of the restaurant. This area of Baltimore was chosen as the site of the first monument to George Washington and was subsequently named for the president's Virginia estate. George Peabody was a Massachusetts-born philanthropist who became a longtime resident of Baltimore. During his lifetime, Peabody gave approximately $8 million in support of educational endeavors. Pictures lining the walls of the restaurant depict his generosity toward such endeavors as the Peabody Orchestra, the Peabody Department of Dance Art, and other worthwhile undertakings. The third member of this set, George Herman "Babe" Ruth, was one of Baltimore's native sons. The walls boast pictures of him as well.

Everything about the Peabody Court Hotel reflects the opulence of the era in which it was built. The building, constructed in the Renaissance Revival style, is oriented to face the monument and its picturesque square. A six-foot Baccarat chandelier and Mr. Peabody's richly paneled library grace the lobby area, allowing guests to feel as if they're being welcomed into someone's richly appointed home. A curving staircase leads to the second-story restaurant, which has richly painted burgundy walls topped with intricate dentil molding. Adding to the stately décor are a comfortable leather sofa and wingback chairs. It was a wonderful atmosphere in which we enjoyed a traditional breakfast before our sojourn led us away. However, the gracious amenities and the unobtrusive, attentive service are sure to draw us back again.

 GEORGE WASHINGTON SANDWICH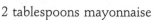

2 tablespoons mayonnaise
2 tablespoons chopped cranberries
1 teaspoon cranberry juice
1 focaccia roll
2 slices turkey breast
1 slice sage cheddar cheese

In a small bowl, stir together mayonnaise, cranberries, and cranberry juice until well combined. Slice roll in half. Spread both cut sides of roll with Cranberry Mayonnaise. Layer turkey and sage cheddar on bottom half of roll. Replace top of roll. Serves 1.

 URBAN TIMBALE

2 zucchini
2 yellow squash
2 small eggplants, peeled
2 large portabello mushrooms
1 roasted red pepper, seeded
1 cup balsamic vinaigrette
1 to 1½ cups cooked basmati rice
2 rosemary spikes

Cut zucchini, yellow squash, eggplants, mushrooms, and pepper into 1-inch pieces and place in a shallow dish. Pour vinaigrette over top and marinate for at least 15 minutes, stirring every 5 minutes. Grill vegetables for 3 to 5 minutes on each side until cooked through. Using a circular timbale mold, assemble 2 timbales with rice at bottom and vegetables layered on top. Spike with rosemary. Serves 2.

ROASTED VIDALIA ONION SOUP

2 tablespoons cornstarch
2 tablespoons water
1 large Vidalia onion, sliced thin
2 tablespoons butter
4 medium potatoes, diced
4 cups heavy cream
¼ cup chicken base
1 bay leaf
¼ teaspoon black pepper
1 tablespoon white wine

In a small bowl, combine cornstarch and water to form a slurry. In a large sauté pan, sauté onions in butter for about 5 minutes until translucent. Set aside. Fill a large stockpot ¾ full of water and bring to a boil. Blanch potatoes for 2 minutes. Drain and set aside. In a separate pot, heat cream, chicken base, bay leaf, pepper, and wine. Bring to a simmer. Add slurry a little at a time, stirring well to incorporate, until desired thickness is reached. Add onions and potatoes and mix well. Cook a further 5 minutes. Remove bay leaf and serve. Serves 6.

Treaty of Paris Restaurant

58 State Circle
Annapolis, MD 21401
www.annapolisinns.com
410-263-2641

In 1694, when the capital was moved from the more southern St. Mary's City to Annapolis, this wedge-shaped lot was laid out for use by the town drummer. Annapolis used the drummer as an alternative to a town crier. His main responsibility was to convey public information through a variety of intricate drumbeats. Another of his duties was to call the Maryland General Assembly to session.

Drummer's Lot, as lot 49 became known, was owned by many important names in the state's history—Bordley, Chew, Dulaney, Dorsey, and Pica, among numerous others. In 1772, respected businessman and civic leader Thomas Hyde was granted a long-term lease on the property. He constructed the front portion of what is now the Maryland Inn on the lot. Ten years later, when advertised for sale, the structure was described as "an elegant brick house in a dry and healthy part of the city."

In 1784, Sarah Bell opened a tavern at the house. The inn remained popular throughout the nineteenth century, having been acquired by the Maryland Hotel Company in 1868. During that period, it was the most prominent hotel in Annapolis and a popular meeting spot for important national, state, and military figures. This military connection created an interesting twist when in 1898 Spanish admirals were quartered here as prisoners of war. Today, the Maryland Inn is one of the three buildings that comprise the Historic Inns of Annapolis, which have been carefully restored and grandly decorated with period antiques and reproductions and together offer more than 120 lovely guest rooms.

The Treaty of Paris Restaurant is located on the ground floor of the Maryland Inn. The restaurant is named in honor of the treaty that ended the Revolutionary War. Although the privileges of American independence were hard-won, they were not necessarily welcomed by all. A tunnel running from the adjoining King of France Tavern to the statehouse was a means of undetected getaway for signers of the controversial treaty. Other political figures simply used the tunnel as a method of getting from work to meals in inclement weather. Today, it is disguised within the tavern's wine cellar.

In the restaurant, dark beams and uneven brick walls tell of the building's early years. We were seated at a table next to a shuttered window near what was once the cooking fireplace. Layers of soot declared the many meals that were prepared in that space, while implements on display gave a glimpse of what those cooking chores may have been like. We enjoyed a traditional breakfast before setting out on a day of research. Had we been there for lunch, we may have ordered the Chesapeake Salad, which includes shrimp, scallops, and lump crab, or the Spinach Salad, tossed with pine nuts and Mandarin Orange Dressing. Appetizers on the dinner menu lean toward a wide range of seafood options. Beef

Wellington, Prime Rib, Rack of Lamb, Stuffed Rockfish, and Crab Cakes are among the entrée selections. Meals are served with Cornbread Sticks or the restaurant's renowned Popovers. All are tasty reasons to go back in time!

 VEAL OSCAR

12 ounces veal scaloppine
salt and pepper to taste
¼ cup flour
2 tablespoons butter
4 ounces backfin crabmeat, picked
8 spears white asparagus
4 tablespoons Béarnaise sauce

Pound veal between sheets of wax paper or roll with a marble rolling pin until very thin. Salt and pepper both sides and lightly dredge in flour. Melt butter in a skillet and sauté veal until pure white. Put veal on 2 plates and top each portion with half of crabmeat, 4 spears asparagus, and dollops of Béarnaise. Broil until lightly browned. Serves 2.

 ANNAPOLITAN SALAD

1 bunch romaine lettuce
1 head red leaf lettuce
4 artichoke hearts
24 small to medium shrimp, cooked
Green Goddess Dressing (see below)

Arrange lettuce on 4 salad plates. Quarter artichoke hearts and place 4 quarters and 6 shrimp on each plate. Cover with dollops of dressing. Serves 4.

GREEN GODDESS DRESSING

2 cups mayonnaise
½ bunch scallions, diced
1 tablespoon chopped chives
1 tablespoon chopped parsley
1 tablespoon chopped tarragon
3 anchovies, mashed

Combine ingredients thoroughly with a whisk. Yields 2 cups.

Restaurant Index

Abacrombie Fine Food & Accommodations, 124

Annapolis: Chart House Restaurant, 36; Griffins City Dock Tavern, 166; McGarvey's Saloon & Oyster Bar, 42; Middleton Tavern, 52; Rams Head Tavern, 106; Reynolds Tavern and Tea Room, 8; Riordan's Saloon, 178; Treaty of Paris Restaurant, 198

Antrim 1844, 186

Atlantic Hotel, 182

Aunt Fairie's Tea, 24

Baldwin's Station, 80

Baltimore: Abacrombie Fine Food & Accommodations, 124; The Brass Elephant, 138; Gardel's Supper Club, 88; George's on Mt. Vernon Square, 196; John Steven, Ltd., 164; Lisa Anne's Decadent Gifts & Tea Room, 20; The Owl Bar, 62; Petticoat Tea Room, 16; Sabatino's Italian Restaurant, 66; Thir-Tea-First Street Café! & Tea Room, 26; True at The Admiral Fell Inn, 96; The Wharf Rat Camden Yards, 168; The Wharf Rat Fells Point, 112

Bayard House Restaurant, The, 34

Berlin: Atlantic Hotel, 182; Globe Theater & Bistro, 64

Bistro St. Michaels, 136

Blair Mansion Inn, 142

Boonsboro: Old South Mountain Inn, 156

Braddock Heights: The General Braddock Inn, 192; John Hagan's Tavern, 158

Brass Elephant, The, 138

Brewer's Alley Restaurant & Brewery, 172

Brick Ridge, 76

Brome-Howard Inn, The, 38

Brooklandville: The Valley Inn, 170

Buckeystown: The Inn at Buckeystown, 128; Quills at the Catoctin, 118

Carriage House Inn, 58

Casselman Inn, The, 146

Chart House Restaurant, 36

Chesapeake City: The Bayard House Restaurant, 34

Chestertown: The Imperial Hotel and Restaurant, 184; Kettledrum Restaurant & Tea Room, 12; White Swan Tavern, 4

Columbia: Historic Oakland, 18; The Kings Contrivance, 140

Comus Inn at Sugarloaf Mountain, The, 132

Cornish Manor Restaurant, 190

Cumberland: JB's Steakhouse, 152

Deer Park: The Deer Park Inn, 194

Deer Park Inn, The, 194

Dickerson: The Comus Inn at Sugarloaf Mountain, 132

Easton: The Inn at Easton, 134; Kendall's Steak & Seafood, 78; Restaurant Columbia, 122;

Washington Street Pub, 162
Elkridge: The Elkridge Furnace Inn, 40
Elkridge Furnace Inn, The, 40
Ellicott City: Tersiguel's, 120; Tiber River
    Tavern, 114
Emmitsburg: Carriage House Inn, 58

Fair Hill: Fair Hill Inn, 60
Fair Hill Inn, 60
Firestone's Restaurant, 82
Frederick: Brewer's Alley Restaurant & Brewery,
    172; Firestone's Restaurant, 82; Isabella's
    Taverna & Tapas Bar, 92; Venuti's Ristorante,
    110
Frostburg: Tombstone Café, 150

Gabriel's Inn, 98
Gaithersburg: Summit Station Restaurant &
    Brewery, 174
Gardel's Supper Club, 88
General Braddock Inn, The, 192
George's on Mt. Vernon Square, 196
Georgetown: The Kitty Knight House, 108
Globe Theater & Bistro, 64
Grantsville: The Casselman Inn, 146; Penn Alps
    Restaurant, 148
Griffins City Dock Tavern, 166
Gypsy's Tearoom, 6

Hagerstown: The Plum, 86
Harrison's Chesapeake House, 68
Havre de Grace: The Vandiver Inn, 126
Historic Cozy Restaurant, 70
Historic Oakland, 18

Ijamsville: Gabriel's Inn, 98
Imperial Hotel and Restaurant, The, 184

Inn at Buckeystown, The, 128
Inn at Easton, The, 134
Inn of Silent Music, 48
Isabella's Taverna & Tapas Bar, 92

JB's Steakhouse, 152
Johanssons Dining House, 84
John Hagan's Tavern, 158
John Steven, Ltd., 164

Kendall's Steak & Seafood, 78
Kent Manor Inn & Restaurant, 104
Kettledrum Restaurant & Tea Room, 12
Kings Contrivance, The, 140
Kitty Knight House, The, 108

Laurel: The Little Teapot at Montpelier Man-
    sion, 10
Lisa Anne's Decadent Gifts & Tea Room, 20
Little Orleans: Town Hill Hotel Bed and Break-
    fast, 154
Little Teapot at Montpelier Mansion, The, 10

Maggie's, 90
McGarvey's Saloon & Oyster Bar, 42
Middleton Tavern, 52
Middletown: Aunt Fairie's Tea, 24
Milton Inn, The, 56
Mount Airy: Brick Ridge, 76
Mrs. K's Toll House Restaurant, 74
Murphey's Pub, 176

North Beach: The Westlawn Inn, 188
North Bethesda: Strathmore Tea Room, 14
North East: The Victorian Tea Cup, 22

Oakland: Cornish Manor Restaurant, 190

Old Angler's Inn, 54
Old Field Inn, 102
Old South Mountain Inn, 156
Owl Bar, The, 62
Oxford: Robert Morris Inn, 30

Penn Alps Restaurant, 148
Petticoat Tea Room, 16
Plum, The, 86
Port Deposit: The Union Hotel, 44
Potomac: Old Angler's Inn, 54
Prince Frederick: Old Field Inn, 102
Princess Anne: Murphey's Pub, 176

Quills at the Catoctin, 118

Rams Head Tavern, 106
Rams Head Tavern at Savage Mill, 100
Restaurant Columbia, 122
Reynolds Tavern and Tea Room, 8
Riordan's Saloon, 178
Robert Morris Inn, 30

Sabatino's Italian Restaurant, 66
Savage: Rams Head Tavern at Savage Mill, 100
Sherwood's Landing at The Inn at Perry Cabin, 32
Silver Spring: Blair Mansion Inn, 142; Mrs. K's Toll House Restaurant, 74
Sparks: The Milton Inn, 56
St. Mary's City: The Brome-Howard Inn, 38
St. Michaels: Bistro St. Michaels, 136; Sherwood's Landing at The Inn at Perry Cabin, 32; St. Michaels Crab & Steak House, 46; 208 Talbot, 130

St. Michaels Crab & Steak House, 46
Stevensville: Kent Manor Inn & Restaurant, 104
Strathmore Tea Room, 14
Summit Station Restaurant & Brewery, 174
Sykesville: Baldwin's Station, 80

Taneytown: Antrim 1844, 186
Tersiguel's, 120
Thir-Tea-First Street Café1 & Tea Room, 26
Thurmont: Historic Cozy Restaurant, 70
Tiber River Tavern, 114
Tilghman Island: Harrison's Chesapeake House, 68
Tombstone Café, 150
Town Hill Hotel Bed and Breakfast, 154
Treaty of Paris Restaurant, 198
True at The Admiral Fell Inn, 96
208 Talbot, 130
Tylertown: Inn of Silent Music, 48

Union Hotel, The, 44

Valley Inn, The, 170
Vandiver Inn, The, 126
Venuti's Ristorante, 110
Victorian Tea Cup, The, 22

Washington Street Pub, 162
Westlawn Inn, The, 188
Westminster: Gypsy's Tearoom, 6; Johanssons Dining House, 84; Maggie's, 90
Wharf Rat Camden Yards, The, 168
Wharf Rat Fells Point, The, 112
White Swan Tavern, 4

Recipe Index

Appetizers

Chicken Liver Pâté, 93
Clams Annie, 47
Crab and Artichoke Dip, 113
Crab Bruschetta, 165
Crab Dip, 91, 163
Crab with Olives, 137
Crostini All'aglio Arrosto, 111
Curried Chicken Apple Puffs, 19
Hot Crab Dip, 99
Lump Crab and Poblano Chili Cheese Dip, 173
Mushroom and Brie Tartlets, 41
Mushroom Empanadillas, 93
Potato Chips with Blue Cheese Fondue and
    Chives, 63
Spicy Shrimp Canapés, 193
Tapanade, 187

Apples

Applesauce Nut Bread, 147
Curried Chicken Apple Puffs, 19
German Apple Puff Pancakes, 49
Grilled Lamb Fillet with Apple-Almond Com-
    pote, 187
Lettuceless Salad, 87

Artichokes

Crab and Artichoke Dip, 113

Beans

Baked Beans, 147

Black Beans, 43
Melini Veal Chop with White Bean Ragout, 57

Beef

Burgundy Beef, 43
English Shepherd's Pie, 21
The Woodley, 87

Beer

Beer Batter, 101
Blackfriar Stout, 169
Blackfriar Stout Float, 169

Bread Pudding

Bread Pudding, 75
Easy As Pie Bread Pudding, 17
New Orleans Bread Pudding, 71
Nut Brown Pudding, 149
Pecan Raisin Bread Pudding, 159
Pain Perdu with Bananas adn Rum, 195

Breads

See also Scones
Applesauce Nut Bread, 147
Caramel Cream French Toast, 155
Crostini All'aglio Arrosto, 111
Pineapple Fritters, 143
Thick Focaccia Bread, 111
Yeast Rolls, 69

Cabbage

Chinese Vegetable Slaw, 33
Coriander Cabbage, 125
Potted Red Cabbage, 11

Cakes

Lemon Poppy Seed Cake, 5
Miniature Almond and Cherry Cakes, 19

Carrots

Chinese Vegetable Slaw, 33
Honey-Glazed Baby Carrots, 167
Szechuan Vegetables, 53

Cheese

Broccoli Soup with Brie and Almonds, 159
Mushroom and Brie Tartlets, 41
Potato Chips with Blue Cheese Fondue and
    Chives, 63
Potato Gratin, 119
Roasted Red Pepper and Brie Salad, 81
Seared Sea Scallops with Parmesan Custard, 133

Cheesecake

Amaretto Cheesecake, 81
Baileys Irish Cream Cheesecake, 183

Cherries

Miniature Almond and Cherry Cakes, 19
Seneca Red Jacket Duck in Bing Cherry Sauce,
    119

Chicken

Breast of Chicken di Saronno, 61
Buffalo-Style Pizza, 153
Chicken Champagne, 91
Chicken Chesapeake, 75

Chicken Miranda, 85
Curried Chicken Apple Puffs, 19
Curried Chicken Salad with Dried Apricots, 15
Jamaican Fricasseed Chicken, 129
Mango Chicken Salad, 23
Santa Fe Quesadilla Roll, 175
Toasted Almond-Encrusted Chicken with
    Honey-Wasabi Glaze, 193
Twin Cities Chicken, 77
Warm Chicken Salad, 151

Chocolate

Chocolate Brownies, 169
Chocolate Mousse, 91, 123
Chocolate-Cranberry Scones, 39
Chocolate-Dipped Strawberries, 21

Clams

Cioppino, 83
Clams Annie, 47

Condiments

Black-Eyed Pea Salsa, 115
Corn Relish, 33
Devonshire Cream, 23
Mango-Lime Butter, 53
Tomatillo Salsa, 89
Tropical Fruit Salsa, 167

Cookies

Lemon Bars, 9
Lemon Butter Cookies, 7
Raspberry Almond Bars, 5
Shrewsbury Cakes, 11

Corn

Corn Pudding with Crab, 137

Corn Relish, 33
Kitty's Corn Salad, 17
Puff Pastry-Wrapped Maryland Rockfish with
   Corn-Crab Sauce, 125
Turkey Corn Soup, 71

Crab

Backfin Crab Cakes, 69
Chicken Chesapeake, 75
Corn Pudding with Crab, 137
Crab and Artichoke Dip, 113
Crab and Shrimp White Pizza, 59
Crab Bruschetta, 165
Crab Cakes, 83, 153, 171
Crab Dip, 91, 163
Crab Imperial, 143
Crab Louis, 141
Crab Salad with Fried Green Tomatoes, 65
Crab with Olives, 137
Cream of Crab Soup, 37
Hot Crab Dip, 99
Lump Crab and Poblano Chili Cheese Dip, 173
Maryland Crab Cakes, 79
Maryland Crab Soup, 163
Oysters Imperial, 47
Peekytoe Crab Salad on Red Endive, 15
Rockfish Chesapeake, 157
Seafood Gazpacho, 139
Seafood Imperial, 57
Seafood Pot Pie, 35
Spicy Crab and Shrimp Soup, 31
Veal Oscar, 103, 199

Cranberries

Chocolate-Cranberry Scones, 39
Orange-Cranberry Scones, 7

Desserts

See also Bread Pudding, Cakes, Cheesecake,
   Chocolate, Cookies, Pies
Blackfriar Stout Float, 169
Egg Custard, 149
English Trifle, 141
Fresh Fruit Romanoff, 41
Grilled Pineapple with Vanilla Rum Sauce, 89
Pain Perdu with Bananas and Rum, 195
Rose Poached Pears, 25
Sticky Fig and Ginger Pudding, 135

Duck

Seared Duck Breast, 185
Seneca Red Jacket Duck in Bing Cherry Sauce,
   119
Smoked Duck and Mushrooms, 127

Eggs

Egg Custard, 149
Rolled Cilantro Omelet, 49
Smoked Pepper Flan, 125

Fish

See also Rockfish, Salmon, Trout
Broiled Striped Bass, 69
Macadamia Nut-Crusted Grouper, 53
Seafood Bisque, 183
Southwest Cornbread Catfish, 85

Fruit

See also Apples, Cherries, Cranberries, Mango,
   Pears, Pineapple, Raspberries, Strawberries
Curried Chicken Salad with Dried Apricots, 15
Fresh Fruit Romanoff, 41
Pain Perdu with Bananas and Rum, 195
Peach Sauce, 81

Sticky Fig and Ginger Pudding, 135
Two Melon Soup, 187

Grits
Shrimp and Grits, 189

Ham
Black Beans, 43
Rockfish Chesapeake, 157
Tasso Cream, 189

Ice Cream
See Sorbets and Ice Cream

Lamb
Grilled Lamb Fillet with Apple-Almond Compote, 187
Roasted Rack of Lamb with Pistachio and Raspberry Sauce, 123

Lemon
Lemon Bars, 9
Lemon Butter Cookies, 7
Lemon Poppy Seed Cake, 5
Lemon Sabayon, 133

Liver
Chicken Liver Pâté, 93

Lobster
Atlantic Lobster and Salmon Sausage, 97
Green Tomato Lobster Bisque, 65
Seafood Imperial, 57

Mango
Mango-Lime Butter, 53
Tropical Fruit Salsa, 167

Mushrooms
Mushroom and Brie Tartlets, 41
Mushroom Empanadillas, 93
Portabello Mushroom Sandwich, 105
Pot Pie of Wild Mushrooms, 55
Roasted Veal Chop with Forest Mushrooms, 195
Smoked Duck and Mushrooms, 127
Urban Timbale, 197
The Woodley, 87

Mussels
Cioppino, 83
Mussel Soup with Curry, 61
Mussels Mariner, 191
Seafood Imperial, 57

Nuts
Applesauce Nut Bread, 147
Bakewell Tart, 9
Broccoli Soup with Brie and Almonds, 159
Grilled Lamb Fillet with Apple-Almond Compote, 187
Macadamia Nut-Crusted Grouper, 53
Pecan Raisin Bread Pudding, 159
Pecan-Crusted Rockfish, 59
Pecan-Encrusted Salmon, 77
Raspberry Almond Bars, 5
Roasted Rack of Lamb with Pistachio and Raspberry Sauce, 123
Toasted Almond-Encrusted Chicken with Honey-Wasabi Glaze, 193

Oysters
Oyster Casserole, 31
Oysters Imperial, 47
Oysters with Champagne Sauce, 131

Seafood Pot Pie, 35
Skipjack Oyster Bisque, 13

Pancakes
German Apple Puff Pancakes, 49

Pasta
Rigatoni with Veal Sauce, 67

Pears
Rose Poached Pears, 25

Peppers
Green Chili Stew, 115
Lump Crab and Poblano Chili Cheese Dip, 173
Roasted Red Pepper and Brie Salad, 81
Smoked Pepper Flan, 125

Pies
Alabama Tomato Pie, 155
Bakewell Tart, 9
Pot Pie of Wild Mushrooms, 55
Seafood Pot Pie, 35
Shoo-Fly Pie, 147

Pineapple
Grilled Pineapple with Vanilla Rum Sauce, 89
Pineapple Fritters, 143
Tropical Fruit Salsa, 167

Pizza
Buffalo-Style Pizza, 153
Cajun Sausage Supreme, 175
Crab and Shrimp White Pizza, 59

Pork
Marinated Skewered Pork Tenderloin, 33
Pork Tenderloin à l'Orange, 39

Pork Tenderloin in Rosemary Sauce, 185

Potatoes
English Shepherd's Pie, 21
Potato Chips with Blue Cheese Fondue and
   Chives, 63
Potato Gratin, 119
Potato Soup, 177
Roasted Red Potato Soup, 27

Quail
Roast Quail, 105

Rabbit
Braised Rabbit, 45

Raspberries
Raspberry Almond Bars, 5
Roasted Rack of Lamb with Pistachio and
   Raspberry Sauce, 123

Rice
Urban Timbale, 197
White Truffle Risotto, 97

Rockfish
Cornmeal-Crusted Rockfish, 35
Maryland Rockfish Salad, 107
Pecan-Crusted Rockfish, 59
Puff Pastry-Wrapped Rockfish with Corn-Crab
   Sauce, 125
Rockfish Chesapeake, 157

Salad Dressings
Buttermilk Dressing, 87
Champagne Vinaigrette Dressing, 129
Dijon Vinaigrette, 45
Green Goddess Dressing, 199

Louis Dressing, 141
Tomato Saffron Vinaigrette, 167

Salads

Annapolitan Salad, 199
Chinese Vegetable Slaw, 33
Crab Louis, 141
Crab Salad with Fried Green Tomatoes, 65
Curried Chicken Salad with Dried Apricots, 15
Kitty's Corn Salad, 17
Lettuccless Salad, 87
Mango Chicken Salad, 23
Peekytoe Crab Salad on Red Endive, 15
Roasted Red Pepper and Brie Salad, 81
Savory Shrimp Salad, 113
Shrimp Salad, 101
Strawberry Salad, 25
Warm Chicken Salad, 151
Watercress Salad, 45

Salmon

Atlantic Lobster and Salmon Sausage, 97
Banana Pecan-Crusted Salmon, 173
Cedar Plank Salmon with Tomato Coulis, 109
Horseradish-Encrusted Salmon, 157
Pecan-Encrusted Salmon, 77
Salmon with Orange Horseradish Crust, 55
Vegetable Bowl with Grilled Salmon, 37

Sandwiches

George Washington Sandwich, 197
Portabello Mushroom Sandwich, 105
Santa Fe Quesadilla Roll, 175
Turkey Triangles, 27
The Woodley, 87

Sauces

Butterscotch Sauce, 135
Lemon Sabayon, 133
Peach Sauce, 81
Ponzu Sauce, 107
Tasso Cream, 189

Sausage

Cajun Sausage Supreme, 175

Scallops

Broiled Sea Scallops, 165
Coquilles Saint Jacques Provençal, 99
Low Country Shrimp and Scallops, 109
Pan-Roasted Scallops with Ginger and Lemon
    Grass Jus, 121
Seafood Bisque, 183
Seafood Imperial, 57
Seafood Pot Pie, 35
Seared Sea Scallops with Parmesan Custard, 133

Scones

Chocolate-Cranberry Scones, 39
Orange-Cranberry Scones, 7
Shortbread Scones, 41

Seafood

See also Clams, Crab, Lobster, Mussels, Oysters,
    Scallops, Shrimp
Cioppino, 83
Seafood Bisque, 183
Seafood Gazpacho, 139
Seafood Imperial, 57
Seafood Pot Pie, 35

Shrimp

Cioppino, 83
Crab and Shrimp White Pizza, 59

Fire Island Shrimp, 103
Low Country Shrimp and Scallops, 109
Maryland Barbecued Shrimp, 179
Maryland Old Bay Steamed Shrimp, 63
Savory Shrimp Salad, 113
Seafood Bisque, 183
Seafood Pot Pie, 35
Shrimp and Grits, 189
Shrimp Salad, 101
Spicy Crab and Shrimp Soup, 31
Spicy Shrimp Canapés, 193

Sorbets and Ice Cream
Coffee-Butterfinger Crunch Ice Cream, 131
Hibiscus Tea Sorbet, 13

Soup
American Bounty Vegetable Soup, 151
Broccoli Soup with Brie and Almonds, 159
Cream of Crab Soup, 37
Curried Butternut Squash Soup, 79
Green Chili Stew, 115
Green Tomato Lobster Bisque, 65
Maryland Crab Soup, 163
Mussel Soup with Curry, 61
Potato Soup, 177
Roasted Red Potato Soup, 27
Roasted Tomato and Garlic Bisque, 127
Roasted Vidalia Onion Soup, 197
Seafood Bisque, 183
Seafood Gazpacho, 139
Skipjack Oyster Bisque, 13
Spicy Crab and Shrimp Soup, 31
Turkey Corn Soup, 71
Two Melon Soup, 187

Squash
Curried Butternut Squash Soup, 79
Szechuan Vegetables, 53
Urban Timbale, 197
Zucchini Casserole, 179

Strawberries
Chocolate-Dipped Strawberries, 21
Strawberry Salad, 25

Tomatoes
Alabama Tomato Pie, 155
Cedar Plank Salmon with Tomato Coulis, 109
Crab Salad with Fried Green Tomatoes, 65
Green Tomato Lobster Bisque, 65
Roasted Tomato and Garlic Bisque, 127
Stewed Tomatoes, 171, 177
Tomatillo Salsa, 89
Tomato Saffron Vinaigrette, 167

Trout
Ruby Trout with Black Butter, 121
Sautéed Jack Daniel's Trout, 191

Turkey
George Washington Sandwich, 197
Turkey Corn Soup, 71
Turkey Triangles, 27

Veal
Melini Veal Chop with White Bean Ragout, 57
Rigatoni with Veal Sauce, 67
Roasted Veal Chop with Forest Mushrooms, 195
Veal Oscar, 103, 199
Veal Saltimbocca, 67

Vegetables
See also Artichokes, Beans, Cabbage, Carrots,
    Corn, Mushrooms, Peppers, Potatoes,
    Squash, Tomatoes
American Bounty Vegetable Soup, 151
Broccoli Soup with Brie and Almonds, 159
Corn Pudding with Crab, 137

Eggplant Manicotti, 139
Lettuceless Salad, 87
Roasted Vidalia Onion Soup, 197
Southern Greens, 189
Szechuan Vegetables, 53
Urban Timbale, 197
Vegetable Bowl with Grilled Salmon, 37